Lab Manual for
Network+ Guide to Networks,
Third Edition

Michael Grice

COURSE
TECHNOLOGY
—✳—
™
THOMSON LEARNING

Australia • Canada • Mexico • Singapore • Spain • United Kingdom • United States

**COURSE
TECHNOLOGY**
™
THOMSON LEARNING

Lab Manual for Network+ Guide to Networks, Third Edition
is published by Course Technology

Managing Editor
William Pitkin III

Product Manager
Amy M. Lyon

Developmental Editor
Ann Shaffer

Production Editor
Brooke Booth, Trillium Project
Management

Technical Editor
Serge Palladino

Quality Assurance Testing
Marianne Snow, Chris Scriver

Senior Manufacturing Coordinator
Trevor Kallop

Associate Product Manager
David Rivera

Editorial Assistant
Amanda Piantedosi

Cover Design
Joel Sadagursky

Text Design
GEX Publishing Services

Compositor
GEX Publishing Services

BRIEF CONTENTS

TABLE OF CONTENTS

INTRODUCTION

Hands-on learning is the best way to master the networking skills necessary for both CompTIA's Network+ exam and a networking career. This book contains dozens of hands-on exercises that apply fundamental networking concepts as they would be applied in the real world. In addition, each chapter offers multiple review questions to reinforce your mastery of networking topics. The organization of this book follows the same organization as Course Technology's *Network+ Guide to Networks, Third Edition*, and using the two together will provide an effective learning experience. This book is suitable for use in a beginning or intermediate networking course. As a prerequisite, students should have at least six months of computer experience and should be familiar with some basic networking components, such as NICs and patch cables. Passing CompTIA's A+ certification exam would suffice in lieu of this experience.

FEATURES

In order to ensure a successful experience for instructors and students alike, this book includes the following features:

- **Network+ Certification Objectives** — Each chapter lists the relevant objectives from the CompTIA Network+ Exam.

- **Lab Objectives** — Every lab has a brief description and list of learning objectives.

- **Materials Required** — Every lab includes information on network access privileges, hardware, software, and other materials you will need to complete the lab.

- **Completion Times** — Every lab has an estimated completion time, so that you can plan your activities more accurately.

- **Step-by-Step Instructions** — Logical and precise step-by-step instructions guide you through the hands-on activities in each lab.

- **Review Questions** — Questions help reinforce concepts presented in the lab.

Note for instructors: Answers to review questions are available on the Course Technology Web site at *www.course.com/irc/*. Search on this book's ISBN, which is found on the back cover.

HARDWARE REQUIREMENTS

The following is a list of hardware required to complete all the labs in the book. The hardware requirements for many of the individual labs are less than what is listed here.

Note that none of the labs require more than three computers at any one time, so all of the labs could be performed with only three computers. You may choose to install multiple network operating systems on each computer, as this will allow you to boot into a particular operating system when necessary for a lab and reduce the number of computers needed. Disk space requirements will increase on computers with multiple operating systems.

- One computer with the following features:
  - At least one PII or AMD K7 processor (two PIII, PIV, or Xeon 733 Mhz processors or better recommended)
  - At least 512 MB of RAM
  - At least 200 MB disk space available for a DOS partition
  - At least 2 GB of unpartitioned disk space (4 GB recommended)
  - A CD-ROM drive
- Two computers with Pentium 133 MHz CPU or higher processors (733 MHz or better recommended) with the following features:
  - 128 MB of RAM minimum (256 MB recommended)
  - At least 2.0 GB of available storage
  - A CD-ROM drive
  - Hardware compatible with Windows Server 2003 Enterprise Edition (see *www.microsoft.com/whdc/hcl/search.mspx*)
- At least two computers compatible with Red Hat Enterprise Linux ES 3.x (see *http://hardware.redhat.com/hcl/*); any computer that meets the minimum requirements for Windows Server 2003 should also meet the minimum requirements for Red Hat Enterprise Linux EX 3.x
- Two computers with Pentium 233 MHz CPU or higher processors (300 MHz or better recommended) with the following features:
  - 64 MB of RAM minimum (128 MB recommended)
  - At least 2.0 GB of available storage
  - A CD-ROM drive
  - Hardware compatible with Windows XP Professional (see *www.microsoft.com/whdc/hcl/search.mspx*)
- At least one extra hard drive
- A telephone line or another type of connection to the Internet (cable, DSL, or faster preferred)
- Two modems

- A dial-up Internet account

- Internet access (this does not need to be through the dial-up account)

- At least five PCI Ethernet network interface cards with RJ-45 connectors

- CAT 5 UTP cabling to make cables

- At least six straight-through CAT 5 (or better) UTP patch cables

- At least three crossover CAT 5 (or better) UTP patch cables

- RJ-45 connectors

- A computer professional's toolkit that includes a Phillips-head screwdriver, a ground strap, and a ground mat

- A networking professional's kit that includes a cable tester, crimper, wire stripper, and a wire cutting tool

- Four 10/100 Ethernet hubs

- Access to two analog outside phone lines (or two digital lines and two digital-to-analog converters)

SOFTWARE/SETUP REQUIREMENTS

The following is a list of software required to complete all the labs in the book. Note that you can download an evaluation copy of Windows Server 2003 Enterprise Edition from the Microsoft Web site (*www.microsoft.com/windowsserver2003/evaluation/trial/evalkit.mspx*) and Novell NetWare 6.5 from the Novell Web site (*www.novell.com/products/netware/eval.html*).

- At least two copies of Windows Server 2003 Enterprise Edition

- At least two copies of Windows XP Professional

- One copy of Novell NetWare 6.5

- At least two copies of Linux Red Hat Enterprise Linux ES 3.x

- Novell Client for Windows NT/2000/XP 4.90

- Norton Antivirus 2004

- Cygwin software downloaded from *www.cygwin.com*, with the OpenSSH and XFree86 packages installed

- Microsoft Project 2003

- The Win32 version of the Ethereal Network Protocol Analyzer, downloaded from *www.ethereal.com*; version 0.9.16 was used to write this text, but newer versions will probably work as well

NOTES ON THE LABS

- Unless otherwise stated, at the beginning of each lab it is assumed that the student has turned on each computer but has not yet logged on

- On Windows XP computers, the Control Panel should set to Category View, which is the default; the default Start Menu should also be used

- On Windows Server 2003 computers, the default Start Menu should be used

- Windows XP figures in this book were created using the Classic theme

ACKNOWLEDGMENTS

I'd like to thank Amy Lyon, Ann Shaffer, and Brooke Booth for their dedication and hard work, and for bearing with me. I'd also like to thank the reviewers, who greatly helped to improve this edition:

Anu Desu   International Institute of the Americas, Phoenix Campus

Ryan Schultz   Old Dominion U's Information Technology Program (IT Pro)

Essie Bakhtiar   Clayton College and State University

Special thanks to Sydney Shewchuck, Heald College, for his many helpful comments. Thanks also to the Quality Assurance testers at Course Technology: Marianne Snow, Chris Scriver, Serge Palladino, and Christian Kunciw. Finally, I'd like to thank my lovely wife, Nancy.

AN INTRODUCTION TO NETWORKING

Labs included in this chapter

➤ Lab 1.1 Understanding Elements of a Network

➤ Lab 1.2 Building a Simple Peer-to-Peer Network

➤ Lab 1.3 Building a Simple Client/Server Network

➤ Lab 1.4 Sharing a Network Printer

Net+ Exam Objectives	
Objective	**Lab**
Identify the purpose, features, and functions of the following network components: hubs, switches, bridges, routers, gateways, CSU/DSU, Network Interface Cards/ISDN adapters/system area network cards, wireless access points, modems	1.1
Recognize the following logical or physical network topologies given a schematic diagram or description: star, bus, mesh, ring, wireless	1.1
Recognize the following media connectors and/or describe their uses: RJ-11, RJ-45, AUI, BNC, ST, SC	1.1
Identify the basic capabilities (i.e., client support, interoperability, authentication, file and print services, application support, and security) of the following server operating systems: UNIX/Linux, NetWare, Windows, Macintosh	1.2, 1.3, 1.4

LAB 1.1 UNDERSTANDING ELEMENTS OF A NETWORK

Objectives

When first learning about network components, it is often helpful to observe a live network and talk with experienced networking professionals. The concept of segments, connectivity devices, or structured wiring techniques, for example, can be more easily demonstrated on a real network than in a textbook. The goal of this lab is to explore some real-life examples of basic networking concepts. To complete this lab, you will be required to tour your school's computer laboratory or network and identify various networking components at that site. Alternately, your instructor might arrange to allow your class to tour a business network, guided by a willing network professional.

After completing this lab, you will be able to:

➤ Identify and sketch the organization's network topology

➤ Identify the nodes on a real-life network

➤ Identify a network's client software and network operating system

➤ Identify protocols used by a network

Materials Required

This lab will require the following:

➤ A network professional or instructor willing to give you a tour of your school's computer laboratory or data center or a network professional willing to give you a tour of a network at a business, or other site

➤ Pencil and paper

➤ Clipboard and straightedge

Estimated completion time: **1-3 hours**

LAB ACTIVITY

ACTIVITY

1. If you cannot tour your school's computer laboratory or data center, contact a business, school, or other organization and ask to interview the person in charge of their network. Explain that your purpose is purely educational and that you desire to learn more about networking. Also, explain that you will need to take notes.

2. Make the visit and, with the guidance of the network administrator, observe the organization's network. Remember to ask for details about the network's transmission media, physical topology, hardware, operating system, and protocols.

3. On a separate piece of paper, draw the site's network topology, using boxes to represent the components such as computers and printers. Draw lines to connect the components. You might also use network-diagramming software such as Microsoft Visio in order to diagram the network.

4. On your diagram, label servers with the letter "S," workstations with the letter "W," and printers with the letter "P." Label devices used to connect other devices together (such as a hub) with a "C." If you are unsure about a network component, label the box with the letter "O" for "other."

5. Ask the networking professional or instructor for specifics about the network operating system (NOS) types and versions and the client types and versions used within this network. Record this information.

6. Record the make and model of any network interface cards (NICs). Note how many different types of NICs this network uses. If the number of different types is high (for example, over six), ask the network administrator if this variability affects network maintenance and troubleshooting.

7. Record the protocols used in the network.

8. Ask the networking professional or instructor if any wireless LANs are used on this network. Record this information.

9. Ask the networking professional or instructor what sorts of measures they take in order to make the network secure. Ask them about the possible effects of an intrusion or the loss of data. Record this information.

10. If you toured an outside organization's network, thank the person you interviewed. Follow up later with a letter of thanks.

Certification Objectives

Objectives for the Network+ Exam:

➤ Identify the purpose, features, and functions of the following network components: hubs, switches, bridges, routers, gateways, CSU/DSU, Network Interface Cards/ ISDN adapters/system area network cards, wireless access points, modems

➤ Recognize the following logical or physical network topologies given a schematic diagram or description: star, bus, mesh, ring, wireless

➤ Recognize the following media connectors and/or describe their uses: RJ-11, RJ-45, AUI, BNC, ST, SC

Review Questions

1. Which of the following best describes a network's physical topology?
   a. the method by which multiple nodes transmit signals over a shared communications channel
   b. the physical layout of a network
   c. the distance spanned by a network's cable and wireless infrastructure
   d. the software used to ensure reliable connections between nodes on a network

2. Which of the following is the most popular type of modern network architecture for business?
   a. client/server
   b. terminal/mainframe
   c. peer-to-peer
   d. mainframe/dial-up

3. Which of the following elements is not required for a client to connect to a server on a client/server LAN?
   a. protocols
   b. media
   c. e-mail account
   d. client software

4. Which of the following are examples of client/server network operating systems? (Choose all that apply.)
   a. Windows XP
   b. Windows Server 2003
   c. UNIX
   d. NetWare

5. Network protocols are used to do which of the following? (Choose all that apply.)
   a. to ensure reliable delivery of data
   b. to determine the nearest printer for a print job
   c. to interpret keyboard commands
   d. to indicate the source and destination addresses for data packets

6. True or False? On a client/server network, clients may have only one protocol installed at any time.

7. A significant difference between the peer-to-peer and client/server network types is that a peer-to-peer network:

    a. is more difficult to set up

    b. does not allow for resource sharing between workstations

    c. does not usually provide centralized management for shared resources

    d. is more secure

8. Why is it necessary for each client on a client/server network to have a unique address?

9. Suppose an intruder has broken onto the network you visited. Which of the following are potential results? (Choose all that apply.)

    a. loss of data

    b. altered data (such as grades or billing information)

    c. The network might need to be recabled.

    d. The intruder might use this network's resource to abuse other networks.

LAB 1.2 BUILDING A SIMPLE PEER-TO-PEER NETWORK

Objectives

Peer-to-peer networks are commonly found in offices where only a handful of users have access to networked computers, as they do not scale well and do not provide good security. However, peer-to-peer networks are an excellent choice in a few situations because they are simple and inexpensive to configure. A home office with three to five computers and only a couple of users, for example, would make a good candidate for peer-to-peer networking. Even in client-server networks, users may find it convenient to allow other uses to access files on their computers. This is often a security risk, however, as a user may share files without sufficient or even without any security.

The goal of this lab is to become familiar with the methods for establishing a simple peer-to-peer network. During this lab you will be introduced to the hardware and software required to connect two workstations so that they can share each other's resources, such as files and CD-ROM drives.

After completing this lab, you will be able to:

➤ Build a simple peer-to-peer network

Materials Required

This lab will require the following:

➤ Two computers running Windows XP Professional, with Ethernet NICs with RJ-45 connectors, powered on for five minutes prior to the beginning of the lab; neither computer should be configured as a member of a domain

➤ A CD-ROM drive for one of the computers

➤ Access to both computers with the Administrator account (with different passwords)

➤ Client for Microsoft Networks and File and Printer Sharing for Microsoft Networks installed on both computers

➤ A crossover Category 5 (or better) UTP cable with RJ-45 connectors at either end, or two straight-through Category 5 (or better) UTP cables with RJ-45 connectors and a hub compatible with the NICs on both computers

➤ A CD with data files on it

Estimated completion time: **45 minutes**

LAB ACTIVITY

ACTIVITY

1. If you are using a crossover cable, plug one end of the crossover cable into the NIC in one machine and the other end into the NIC in the other machine. If you are using straight-through cables and a hub, plug one end of one of the cables into the NIC in one machine and the other end into the hub. Repeat with the second cable and the second computer. A link light on both NICs illuminates, indicating that each NIC has successfully connected.

2. On each machine, press **Ctrl+Alt+Del**. The Log On to Windows dialog box appears.

3. Log onto both machines as the Administrator. The Windows XP desktop appears.

4. Insert the CD-ROM in the CD-ROM drive. If both machines have a CD-ROM drive, select one at random. The machine with the CD-ROM in its CD-ROM drive will be *COMPUTER1*, and the other will be *COMPUTER2*.

5. On COMPUTER1, click **Start**, then click **Control Panel**.

6. Click the **Network and Internet Connections** icon. The Network and Internet Connections window opens.

7. Click **Set up or change your home or small office network**. The Network Setup Wizard opens.

8. Click **Next**. The next wizard window asks you to connect the network.

9. Click **Next**. The next wizard window asks you to select a connection method.

10. Click the **Other** option button. Click **Next**.

11. Select the **This computer belongs to a network that does not have an Internet connection** option button and then click **Next**. The next wizard window asks you to name your computer.

12. Type **Net+ Lab** in the Computer description text box. Type **COMPUTER1** in the Computer name text box. Click **Next**. The next wizard window asks you to name your network.

13. Type **NETPLUS** in the Workgroup name text box. Click **Next**. A dialog box appears summarizing the settings you have chosen.

14. Click **Next**. A dialog box appears briefly asking you to wait. The next wizard window indicates that you are almost finished.

15. Click the **Just finish the wizard; I don't need to run the wizard on other computers** option button, and then click **Next**. The Completing the Network Setup Wizard dialog box appears.

16. Click **Finish**. The Network Setup Wizard closes, and the System Settings Change dialog box appears.

17. Click **Yes** to restart the computer.

18. On *COMPUTER1*, press **Ctrl+Alt+Del**. The Log On to Windows dialog box appears. Log onto *COMPUTER1* again as the Administrator. The Windows XP desktop appears.

19. Click **Start**, then click **My Computer**. The My Computer window opens.

20. Right-click the icon for the CD-ROM drive, and select **Sharing and Security** from the pop-up menu. The Properties window opens, with the Sharing tab displayed.

21. Click **If you understand the risk but still want to share the root of the drive, click here**. (Because the CD-ROM is read-only, this action does not present a security risk.)

22. Click the **Share this folder on the network** check box. A check mark appears in the box. Replace the existing entry in the Share name text box with CD-ROM. Figure 1-1 shows the Properties window as you share the CD-ROM on a computer.

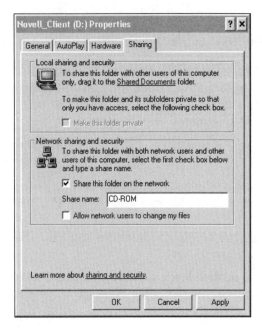

Figure 1-1 Sharing a CD-ROM drive

23. Click the **Allow network users to change my files** check box to remove the check mark.

24. Click **OK**. The Properties window closes.

25. Repeat Steps 5 through 17 on *COMPUTER2*, using **COMPUTER2** as the name of the computer in Step 12.

26. On *COMPUTER2*, click **Start**, then click **MyNetwork Places**. The My Network Places window opens.

27. Right-click the icon for the CD-ROM drive on *COMPUTER1* and click **Explore** in the pop-up menu. The Connect to computer1 dialog box appears.

28. Type **Administrator** in the User name text box, and type the password for *COMPUTER1* in the Password text box. Click **OK**. A folder containing the files on the CD-ROM on *COMPUTER1* appears.

29. Log off both computers.

Certification Objectives

Objectives for the Network+ Exam:

➤ Identify the basic capabilities (i.e., client support, interoperability, authentication, file and print services, application support, and security) of the following server operating systems: UNIX/Linux, NetWare, Windows, Macintosh

Review Questions

1. What physical topology did you use to create your peer-to-peer network?

    a. bus

    b. tree

    c. star

    d. cube

2. Which two of the following issues make peer-to-peer networks less scalable than client/server networks?

    a. Each time a new user is added, the peer-to-peer network cabling must be reinstalled between nodes.

    b. Adding nodes to a peer-to-peer network results in diminished overall network performance.

    c. Adding nodes to a peer-to-peer network increases the risk that an intruder can compromise a shared data folder.

    d. Adding new resource sharing locations and ensuring that all authorized users have access to new resources becomes less manageable as the peer-to-peer network grows.

3. Which of the following operating systems will allow you to create a peer-to-peer network from a group of workstations? (Choose all that apply.)

    a. MS-DOS

    b. Windows XP Professional

    c. Windows Server 2003

    d. NetWare 6.5

4. Which of the following components are *not* necessary in order to create a peer-to-peer network from a group of workstations? (Choose all that apply.)

    a. client software

    b. NIC

    c. network media

    d. Web browser

    e. network operating system

5. What is the primary difference between peer-to-peer and client/server architectures?

6. True or False? On a peer-to-peer network consisting of four Windows XP workstations, each user can individually control which of her local data files she wants to share with other users.

LAB 1.3 BUILDING A SIMPLE CLIENT/SERVER NETWORK

Objectives

Client/server networks are found in all but the smallest organizations. While client/server networks are more difficult to configure than a peer-to-peer network, they are more scalable and can grow larger than peer-to-peer networks can. With more than a handful of computers, a peer-to-peer network quickly becomes unwieldy. In a client/server network, however, you can manage user accounts and network resources such as printers from a single machine. For instance, in order to change the printer used by all users on a peer-to-peer network, you would need to go to each machine and configure the new printer. Imagine having to do this on 500 machines! In a client/server network, however, you can typically change this setting on the server for all users.

The goal of this lab is to become familiar with the methods for establishing a simple client-server network. During this lab you will be introduced to the hardware and software required to connect one or more workstations to a server. As part of the setup for this lab, both the server and the workstation need to be configured with an IP address. Computers and other network devices use the IP address to find other computers. You will learn about addressing beginning with Chapter 2.

After completing this lab, you will be able to:

➤ Build a simple client/server network

➤ Add a Windows XP client computer to a Windows Server 2003 domain

Materials Required

This lab will require the following:

➤ One computer named *WORKSTATION1* running Windows XP Professional with an Ethernet NIC, powered on for five minutes prior to the beginning of the lab and configured with an IP address of 192.168.54.2; this computer should not be configured as a member of a domain

➤ Access to the Windows XP computer as a regular user

➤ One computer named *SERVER1* running Windows Server 2003 Enterprise Edition with an Ethernet NIC, powered on for five minutes prior to the beginning of the lab and configured with an IP address of 192.168.54.1

➤ *SERVER1* configured as the domain controller for the *netpluslab.net* domain

➤ *WORKSTATION1* configured to use 192.168.54.1 as its DNS server

➤ Access to the Windows Server 2003 computer and the *netpluslab.net* domain as the Administrator

➤ On the Windows Server 2003 computer, a CD-ROM drive with a CD-ROM in it

➤ A user account named netplus in the Users group in the *netpluslab.net* domain on the Windows Server 2003 computer

➤ An Ethernet or Fast Ethernet hub compatible with both NICs

➤ Two straight-through Category 5 (or better) UTP cables with RJ-45 connectors at either end

---

Estimated completion time: **60 minutes**

LAB ACTIVITY

ACTIVITY

1. Plug one end of one of the cables into the hub. Plug the other end of the cable into one of the computers. The link light on both the hub and on the NIC in the back of the computer should illuminate.

2. Repeat Step 1 to connect the other computer to the hub.

3. On the Windows Server 2003 computer, press **Ctrl+Alt+Del**. The Log On to Windows dialog box appears.

4. If you do not see the Log on to drop-down menu beneath the Password text box, click **Options**, type **Administrator** in the User name text box, and type the password for this account in the Password textbox. Click the **Log on to** list button and then click **NETPLUSLAB**. Click **OK**. The Windows Server 2003 desktop appears.

5. Click **Start**, then click **My Computer**.

6. Right-click the icon for the CD-ROM drive and then click **Sharing and Security** in the pop-up menu.

7. Click the **Share this folder** option button. Record the name in the Share name text box. This is the name by which the shared CD-ROM drive will be identified on the other computer. Click **OK**.

8. On the Windows XP computer, press **Ctrl+Alt+Del** to display the Log On to Windows dialog box. Log on as the Administrator. The Windows XP desktop appears.

9. Click **Start**, then click **Control Panel**. The Control Panel opens. Click the **Performance and Maintenance** icon.

10. Click the **System** icon. The System Properties window opens.

11. Click the **Computer Name** tab.

12. Click **Network ID**. The Network Identification Wizard opens. Click **Next**.

13. Click the **This computer is part of a business network, and I use it to connect to other computers at work** option button. Click **Next**.

14. Click the **My company uses a network with a domain** option button. Click **Next**.

15. Click **Next**.

16. Enter **netplus** in the User name text box. Enter the password for the net-plus account in the Password text box. Enter *NETPLUSLAB.NET* in the Domain text box. Click **Next**. Figure 1-2 shows the Network Identification Wizard.

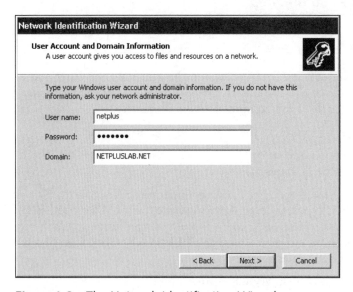

Figure 1-2   The Network Identification Wizard

17. Now you will enter information about the Windows XP computer itself. In the Computer name text box, enter *WORKSTATION1*. In the Computer domain text box, enter **NETPLUSLAB.NET**. Click **Next**. The Domain User Name and Password dialog box appears.

18. In the User name text box, enter **Administrator**. Enter the password for this account in the Password text box. Enter **NETPLUSLAB.NET** in the Domain text box. Click **OK**.

19. The wizard asks you to add a user account to this computer. The wizard should have already selected the **Add the following user** option button, displayed **netplus** in the User name text box, and displayed **NETPLUSLAB.NET** in the User domain text box. If not, complete these settings now. Click **Next**.

20. The wizard asks you what sort of access the netplus user should have to this computer. Make sure the **Standard user** option button is selected, and click **Next**.

21. Click **Finish**. The Computer Name Changes dialog box appears, informing you that you must restart the computer for the changes to take effect.

22. Click **OK**. The Computer Name Changes dialog box closes.

23. Click **OK** again. The System Properties dialog box closes.

24. The System Settings Change dialog box opens, asking if you want to restart your computer now. Click **Yes** to reboot the computer.

25. When the computer has rebooted, press **Ctrl+Alt+Del** to display the Log On to Windows dialog box. If the Log on to drop-down menus is not visible, click **Options**. In the User name text box, enter **netplus**. In the Password text box, enter the password for this account. Select **NETPLUSLAB** from the Log on to drop-down menu. Click **OK**.

26. Click **Start**, then click **My Computer**. The My Computer window opens.

27. Click **My Network Places** in the left pane.

28. Click **Entire Network** in the left pane.

29. Double-click the **Microsoft Windows Network** icon.

30. Double-click the **Netpluslab** icon.

31. Double-click the *SERVER1* icon. A list of all the folders shared on *SERVER1* appears.

32. Right-click the folder name you recorded in Step 7. Click **Explore** in the pop-up menu. You see a list of the contents of the CD-ROM.

33. Log off both computers.

Certification Objectives

Objectives for the Network+ Exam:

➤ Identify the basic capabilities (i.e., client support, interoperability, authentication, file and print services, application support, and security) of the following server operating systems: UNIX/Linux, NetWare, Windows, Macintosh

Review Questions

1. Which of the following are or could be shared as resources across a network? (Choose all that apply.)

    a. Microsoft Word and other office software

    b. printers

    c. documents

    d. network interface cards

2. True or False? Even in a client/server network, it is possible to share documents between individual users' computers as you can in a peer-to-peer network.

3. You are the network administrator for a small company. When users take vacations, they would like to allow other users to update the files stored on their computers. Additionally, several users have complained that they have accidentally deleted important files on their local computer, and would like some way to recover them. How would you recommend that they store their files?

   a. make multiple copies on their local hard drive

   b. store the files on the server, which is backed up nightly

   c. make copies of the file on a floppy disk

   d. burn the files onto a CD-ROM

4. A very large organization might have thousands of servers. Do the benefits of client/server networks still apply to such an organization?

   a. no, because managing so many servers is difficult

   b. no, because the organization can rely on a large peer-to-peer network to share files instead

   c. yes, because it is easier to manage thousands of servers than it is to manage the hundreds of thousands of workstations that such an organization might have

   d. yes, because managing thousands of servers is no more difficult than managing a few servers

5. In this lab, what kind of network service did you configure on your client/server network?

   a. management service

   b. mail service

   c. Internet service

   d. file service

LAB 1.4 SHARING A NETWORK PRINTER

Objectives

The ability to share network resources among all the users in an organization is an important reason why networks are so widely used. To print a document without a network, a user would need a printer directly attached to her computer, or she would need to copy the document onto a floppy and find a computer with an attached printer. In an organization with even a few employees, this can be both expensive and time-consuming. In an organization with thousands of employees, this can waste an enormous amount of time, and cost the organization a great deal of money.

In this lab you will share a network printer so that users can access it. In the process, you will become familiar with the methods used to share network resources. Depending on the make and model of the printer, the steps required to install printer drivers may vary from the steps provided here.

After completing this lab, you will be able to:

➤ Build a simple client/server network

➤ Share a networked printer on a Windows Server 2003 client/server network

Materials Required

This lab will require the following:

➤ The network and computers required for Lab 1.3

➤ A printer that is compatible with Windows Server 2003 Enterprise Edition

➤ Drivers for the printer that are compatible with Windows Server 2003; these drivers should be available either among the default drivers installed with Windows Server 2003 or in a known location on a disk or CD-ROM

➤ Drivers for the printer that are compatible with Windows XP, and knowledge of their location; these drivers should be available either among the default drivers installed with Windows XP or in a known location on a disk or CD-ROM

➤ A printer cable that you can use to attach the printer to the Windows Server 2003 computer

➤ A printer port, such as LPT1, available on the Windows Server 2003 computer

➤ Paper in the appropriate printer tray

Estimated completion time: **30 minutes**

LAB ACTIVITY

ACTIVITY

1. Attach one end of the printer cable to the printer. Attach the other end of the printer cable to the Windows Server 2003 computer.

2. Power on the printer.

3. Press **Ctrl+Alt+Del** to display the Log On to Windows dialog box. Log onto the Windows Server 2003 computer as the Administrator. The Windows Server 2003 desktop appears.

4. Click **Start**, then click **Printers and Faxes**. The Printers and Faxes window opens.

5. Double-click the **Add Printer** icon. The Add Printer Wizard opens.

6. Click **Next**.

7. Make sure that the **Local printer attached to this computer** option button is selected. Note that many network printers have their own network cards and do not need to be attached to a computer at all. Deselect the **Automatically detect and install my Plug and Play printer** check box. Click **Next**.

8. Select the **Use the following port** option button. Select the appropriate printer port (such as LPT1) from the drop-down menu next to the Use the following port option button. Click **Next**.

9. Now you must select a printer driver. If the printer drivers are known to be among the default drivers installed with Windows Server 2003, select the manufacturer for the printer in the Manufacturer window, select the printer model in the Printers window, click **Next**, and then skip ahead to Step 11. If the drivers for the printer are on a CD-ROM or floppy disk, insert the CD-ROM or floppy disk into the appropriate drive and click **Have Disk**. The Install From Disk dialog box opens. Figure 1-3 shows the Add Printer Wizard as you select a printer driver.

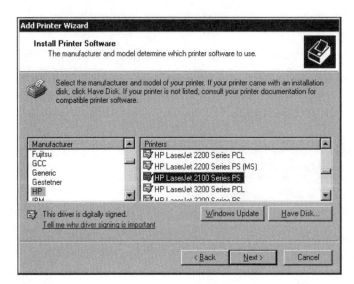

Figure 1-3   Selecting a printer driver

10. Click **Browse**, select the location of the printer drivers, highlight the name of the printer driver, and click **Open**. Click **OK**, and then click **Next**.

1

11. The wizard asks you to enter a name for the printer. Type **NetplusPrinter** in the Printer name text box. Click **Next**.

12. Verify that the **Share name** option button is selected. Enter **NetplusPrinter** in the Share name text box. Click **Next**. The Add Printer Wizard dialog box appears, indicating that the share name that you entered may not be accessible from some MS-DOS workstations.

13. Click **Yes**.

14. Now you are ready to enter the location of the printer. Enter **Netplus Lab** in the Location text box, and click **Next**.

15. The wizard gives you the opportunity to print a test page. Make sure the **Yes** option button is selected, and click **Next**.

16. Click **Finish**. The Add Printer Wizard closes.

17. The NetplusPrinter dialog box opens, indicating that the test page is being printed. The test page prints. Click **OK**.

18. On WORKSTATION1, press **Ctrl+Alt+Del** to display the Windows XP logon screen. Enter **netplus** in the User name text box and the password for this account in the Password text box. Make sure that **NETPLUSLAB** is selected from the drop-down menu next to Log on to. Click **OK**. The Windows XP desktop appears.

19. Click **Start**, and then click **Printers and Faxes**. The Printers and Faxes window opens.

20. Below the Printer Tasks heading, click **Add a printer**. The Add Printer Wizard opens.

21. Click **Next**.

22. Make sure that the **A network printer, or a printer attached to another computer** option button is selected. Click **Next**.

23. Now you must select a printer. Make sure that the **Find a printer in the directory** option button is selected, and click **Next**. The Find Printers dialog box opens.

24. Enter **NetplusPrinter** in the Name text box. Verify that **Entire Directory** is selected in the In drop-down menu. Click **Find Now**. The printer you just added to the Windows Server 2003 computer appears in the window at the bottom of the Find Printers dialog box. Figure 1-4 shows the Find Printers dialog box.

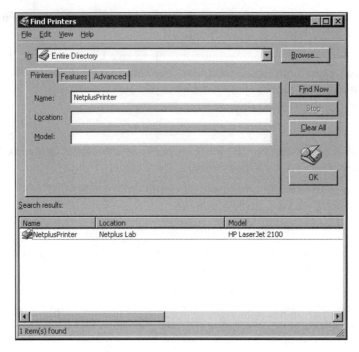

Figure 1-4   Finding a printer

25. Click **NetplusPrinter** to highlight it and click **OK**.

26. Click **Finish**. The Add Printer Wizard closes, and the "Netplus Printer on server1" icon appears in the Printers and Faxes window.

27. Right-click the **NetplusPrinter on server1** icon and select **Properties** from the pop-up menu.

28. Click **Print Test Page**. The Netplus Printer on server1 dialog box opens, indicating that you have printed a test page. The test page prints.

29. Click **OK**.

30. Click **OK** again. You have successfully accessed a printer shared on a Windows Server 2003 computer from a client workstation.

31. Log off both computers.

Certification Objectives

Objectives for the Network+ Exam:

➤ Identify the basic capabilities (i.e., client support, interoperability, authentication, file and print services, application support, and security) of the following server operating systems: UNIX/Linux, NetWare, Windows, Macintosh

Review Questions

1. Many printers come with network cards so that they do not need to be attached to a computer. How would the process of sharing such a printer differ from sharing a printer attached to a computer? (Choose all that apply.)

   a. You would need to configure the printer with an address so that other computers can find it.

   b. The process would not differ.

   c. You would have to add the printer to the Windows Server 2003 domain, just as you did the Windows XP computer in Lab 1.3.

   d. You would not need to connect the printer to another computer via a cable.

2. Users may share printers in a peer-to-peer network. What are the potential disadvantages of this? (Choose all that apply.)

   a. A user could easily misconfigure or turn off his workstation, preventing all other users from accessing the attached printer.

   b. No one will be able to use the printer if the network is down.

   c. The printer will not be backed up.

   d. The printer will not be under centralized control.

3. In this lab, what kind of network service did you configure on your client/server network?

   a. management service

   b. mail service

   c. print service

   d. file service

4. Suppose that you configured software on a Windows Server 2003 computer, which checked printers on the network to make sure that they were operating correctly. What sort of network service would this software be providing?

   a. file service

   b. print service

   c. management service

   d. mail service

5. How can you tell if a printer is shared or not?

   a. The word "shared" is written on the printer icon.

   b. There is no way to tell.

   c. There is a small hand at the bottom of the printer icon.

   d. Each shared printer appears in the Shared Printers folder.

NETWORKING STANDARDS AND THE OSI MODEL

Labs included in this chapter

➤ Lab 2.1 IP Address Assignments

➤ Lab 2.2 Configuring TCP/IP for a Windows XP Computer

➤ Lab 2.3 Finding the MAC Address of Another Computer

➤ Lab 2.4 Looking at Network Connections on a Windows XP Computer

➤ Lab 2.5 Viewing Ethernet Frames

Net+ Exam Objectives	
Objective	**Lab**
Specify the main features of 802.2 (LLC), 802.3 (Ethernet), 802.5 (token ring), 802.11b (wireless), and FDDI networking technologies, including: speed, access, method, topology, media	2.5
Identify the seven layers of the OSI model and their functions	2.2, 2.4, 2.5
Given an example, identify a MAC address	2.3
Given output from a diagnostic utility (e.g., Tracert, Ping, Ipconfig, etc.), identify the utility and interpret the output	2.2, 2.3, 2.4
Given a network configuration, select the appropriate NIC and network configuration settings (DHCP, DNS, WINS, protocols, NetBIOS/host name, etc.)	2.2

LAB 2.1 IP ADDRESS ASSIGNMENTS

Objectives

A Regional Internet Registry (RIR) is an organization that assigns IP addresses to public and private organizations. At the time of this writing there are four RIRs: the American Registry for Internet Numbers (ARIN), the Asia Pacific Network Information Centre (APNIC), the Latin American and Caribbean Internet Addresses Registry (LACNIC), and Réseaux IP Européens (RIPE). Each RIR assigns IP addresses in a different area. ARIN, for instance, assigns IP addresses for North America, part of the Caribbean, and part of Africa.

As a network administrator, you may sometimes find that you need to track down the owner of a particular IP address. For instance, you may discover that a host at an IP address outside of your network is generating excessive amounts of traffic to your Web server, sending your mail server unsolicited commercial e-mail, or otherwise abusing your network. In order to ask whoever owns this host to stop, you must be able to contact the owner. You can use the Web site of an RIR in order to find this. All of the RIRs maintain a Web site and a WHOIS database, which tracks IP assignments. You can find the Web sites for each organization at *www.arin.net*, *www.apnic.net*, *www.lacnic.net*, and *www.ripe.net*. Often IP address assignments are divided further. An ISP, for instance, will usually delegate some of its IP addresses to its customers.

In this lab you will use the `nslookup` command to find the IP address of a site. Then you will look up that IP address on the ARIN site.

Note that the steps in this lab were correct at the time this book was published. If ARIN changes its Web site significantly, the steps may not work exactly as written. However, you should still be able to go to *www.arin.net* and follow the links for WHOIS.

After completing this lab, you will be able to:

➤ Describe the function of an RIR

➤ Track down the organization owning an IP address

Materials Required

This lab will require the following:

➤ A computer running Windows XP Professional with a connection to the Internet (and instructions on how to access it, if necessary)

➤ Internet Explorer configured as needed to access Web sites on the Internet

➤ A Web site address (such as *www.cisco.com*) whose IP address was assigned by ARIN; your instructor should tell you which Web site to use

Estimated completion time: **20-25 minutes**

LAB ACTIVITY

ACTIVITY

1. Press **Ctrl+Alt+Del** to display the Log On to Windows dialog box. Log onto the Windows XP computer. The Windows XP desktop appears. If necessary, perform whatever steps are necessary to access the Internet.

2. Click **Start**, point to **All Programs**, point to **Accessories**, and then click **Command Prompt**. A command prompt window opens.

3. In the command prompt window, type **nslookup** followed by a space and then the name of the Web site assigned to you by your instructor. (For instance, if you were assigned *www.cisco.com*, you would type nslookup www.cisco.com.) Press **Enter**. The output of this command should look similar to Figure 2-1.

Figure 2-1 Typical output from the nslookup command

4. You should see the IP address of the Web site directly under the name of the Web site. In Figure 2-1, for instance, the IP address of *www.cisco.com* is 198.133.219.25. Below, record the IP address you found. Some Web sites may have multiple IP addresses. If this is the case, record the last IP address found.

5. Click **Start**, and then click **Internet Explorer**. Internet Explorer opens.

6. In the Address bar, type **http://www.arin.net/whois** and then press **Enter**. The ARIN WHOIS Database Search page opens.

7. In the Search for text box, type the IP address you recorded in Step 4. Click **Submit Query**. The query results appear.

8. Record the name of the organization to which the IP address belongs. In some cases, more than one organization may be listed. For instance, an organization and its ISP may be listed.

9. Log off the computer.

Certification Objectives

Objectives for the Network+ Exam:

➤ This lab does not directly map to an objective on the exam; however, it does teach a skill that is valuable to networking professionals

Review Questions

1. A host has been overwhelming your Web server. You look up the IP address on *www.arin.net* to determine its owner, but ARIN's Web site tells you that LACNIC owns the IP address. What should you do?

   a. Complain to the owner of the www.lacnic.net Web site.

   b. Look up LACNIC in the Regional Internet Registry.

   c. Look up the owner of the IP address on the LACNIC Web site.

   d. Look up the owner of the IP address on the APNIC Web site.

2. What might happen if no organization were responsible for IP addressing on the Internet? (Choose all that apply.)

   a. Organizations might try to use the same ranges of IP addresses.

   b. Addressing on the Internet would be physically impossible.

   c. nothing

   d. The Internet would use another protocol besides IP.

3. You look up an IP address on *www.arin.net* and two organizations are listed. What does this mean?

   a. The two organizations share the IP address assignment.

   b. One organization sold the IP address to the second.

   c. The RIR made a mistake.

   d. One organization delegated the IP address to the second.

4. What is a Regional Internet Registry responsible for?

   a. maintaining Internet connectivity

   b. registering Internets

   c. assigning IP addresses

   d. signing up users with ISP accounts

5. Which of the following are situations where contacting the owner of an IP address would be useful? (Choose all that apply.)

    a. A host outside your network has been attempting to log onto your servers without your permission.

    b. A host inside your network has been attempting to log onto your servers without your permission.

    c. A host outside your network has been attempting to send large amounts of unsolicited commercial e-mail, or spam.

    d. A host outside your network has been accessing your Web site once an hour.

LAB 2.2 CONFIGURING TCP/IP FOR A WINDOWS XP COMPUTER

Objectives

While addressing at the Data Link layer usually does not require configuration, addressing at the Network layer usually does. Without properly configured network addresses, two hosts can't communicate with each other over the network using Network layer protocols. The network address is a logical address, and does not correspond to any physical attribute of the computer.

On a TCP/IP network, the Network layer address is the IP address. It consists of four numbers with values between 0 and 255 separated by dots. For instance, 10.172.255.93 is a valid IP address. When written in binary, each number in an IP address is eight bits long, and these numbers are often called octets. The subnet mask is also important. The subnet mask also consists of four octets separated by dots. However, only certain values are allowed. A host with an improperly configured subnet mask may not be able to communicate with some or any hosts. In this lab, you will use the Ipconfig utility to display a computer's IP configuration.

In this lab, you will configure an IP address and subnet mask on a host so that it can communicate with other hosts on a network. You will then use the ping (Packet Internetwork Groper) command to verify that two hosts can communicate with each other at the Network layer in a TCP/IP network. The ping command sends one or more packets using the Internet Control Message Protocol (ICMP) to a remote computer. If the remote computer receives these packets, it sends a reply. If the sender receives the replies, then the ping command was successful.

After completing this lab, you will be able to:

➤ Configure an IP address on a Windows XP computer

Materials Required

This lab will require the following:A hub A computer running Windows Server 2003 Enterprise Edition or Windows XP Professional, configured with an IP address of 192.168.54.1 and with a NIC connected to the hub with a straight-through Category 5 (or better) cableA computer running Windows XP Professional configured as a member of the NETPLUS workgroup with a NIC connected to the hub with a straight-through Category 5 (or better) UTP cable but with no IP address configuredAccess to the Windows XP computer as the Administrator

Estimated completion time: **20 minutes**

LAB ACTIVITY

ACTIVITY

1. On the Windows XP computer, press **Ctrl+Alt+Del**. The Log On to Windows dialog box appears.

2. Log onto Windows XP as the Administrator. The Windows XP Desktop appears.

3. Click **Start**, then click **My Network Places**. The My Network Places window opens.

4. Click **View network connections** in the left pane. The Network Connections window opens.

5. Right-click the **Local Area Connection** icon, then click **Properties** in the pop-up menu.

6. Double-click **Internet Protocol (TCP/IP)**. The Internet Protocol (TCP/IP) Properties dialog box opens.

7. Click the **Use the following IP address** option button.

8. Enter **192.168.54.2** in the IP Address text box.

9. Enter **255.255.255.0** in the Subnet Mask text box.

10. Enter **192.168.54.1** in the Default gateway text box.

11. Click the **Use the following DNS server addresses** option button.

12. In the Preferred DNS server text box, enter **192.168.54.1**.

13. Click **OK** to close the Internet Protocol (TCP/IP) Properties window.

14. Click **OK** to close the Local Area Connection Properties window.

2

15. Now you will verify that you have successfully configured an IP address for the Windows XP computer. Click **Start**, then click **Run**. The Run dialog box opens.

16. Type **cmd** in the Open text box and press **Enter**. A command prompt window opens.

17. Type **ping 192.168.54.1** and press **Enter**. The Windows XP computer sends four ICMP packets to 192.168.54.1, and indicates that it has received four replies from the remote computer.

18. Type **ipconfig** and press **Enter**. The computer prints its IP address, subnet mask, and default gateway. Does this match the information you entered in the Internet Protocol (TCP/IP) Properties dialog box in Steps 8, 9, and 10?

19. Log off.

Certification Objectives

Objectives for the Network+ Exam:

➤ Identify the seven layers of the OSI model and their functions

➤ Given output from a diagnostic utility (e.g., Tracert, Ping, Ipconfig, etc.), identify the utility and interpret the output

➤ Given a network configuration, select the appropriate NIC and network configuration settings (DHCP, DNS, WINS, protocols, NetBIOS/host name, etc.)

Review Questions

1. Which of the following information is included in the results of the ping command? (Choose all that apply.)

   a. the operating system used by the remote computer

   b. the IP address or name of the remote computer

   c. the number of packets that were lost

   d. the time it took for the reply to be received

2. Which of the following commands can you use to print information about a computer's Network layer configuration?

   a. netstat

   b. ipconfig

   c. arp

   d. ping

3. How can you verify that two hosts are connected and communicating properly?

   a. From one host, run the `ping` command to the other host.

   b. From a third host, run the `ping` command to both hosts.

   c. Run the `arp` command on both hosts.

   d. Run the `ipconfig` command on both hosts.

4. What type of protocol does the `ping` command use?

   a. TCP/IP

   b. UDP

   c. ICMP

   d. ARP

5. A Dynamic Host Control Protocol (DHCP) server can be used to assign IP addresses automatically. Why might this be useful to a network administrator?

6. On many networks, DHCP is used to assign workstations their IP addresses. However, DHCP is rarely used to assign addresses for servers. Why?

   a. DHCP is too expensive.

   b. DHCP is not scalable enough.

   c. Servers are frequently moved around, while workstations are not.

   d. Workstations are frequently moved around, while servers are not.

LAB 2.3 FINDING THE MAC ADDRESS OF ANOTHER COMPUTER

Objectives

The MAC address operates at the Media Access Control sublayer of the Data Link layer. It is a unique address assigned by the manufacturer when the NIC is built. In TCP/IP networks, the Address Resolution Protocol (ARP) allows a computer to associate another computer's MAC address at the Data Link layer with its IP address at the Network layer. A computer keeps track of these associations in its ARP cache. If a computer does not see packets from one of the computers whose MAC address is in its ARP cache for a certain period of time, then the computer removes that MAC address from its ARP cache. This is called the ARP cache timeout.

A MAC address consists of two parts. The first consists of six characters assigned to the vendor by the IEEE known as the Block ID. The second part consists of six characters assigned by the vendor known as the Device ID. Each MAC address should be unique. Each character in a MAC address is a hexadecimal number, consisting of numbers from 0 through 9 and letters from a through f. A MAC address is often represented with colons or dashes between every pair of characters, such as 00:60:97:7F:41:A1 or 00-60-97-7F-41-A1.

2

You can use the `arp` command to look at the entries in a computer's ARP cache and to find the MAC addresses of other computers it has communicated with on its local network segment. Incorrect ARP entries can prevent two computers from communicating. For instance, on very rare occasions two computers will be found on the same network with identical MAC addresses (generally due to manufacturer error). These computers will have difficulty communicating with other computers on that network. More commonly, replacing a computer's NIC may prevent that computer from communicating with other computers on the network until their ARP cache entries time out.

In this lab you will use the `arp` command to find the MAC address of another computer.

After completing this lab, you will be able to:

➤ Use the `arp` command to find and set the MAC address of another computer

Materials Required

This lab will require the following:

➤ The network required in Lab 1.4, consisting of a computer running Windows Server 2003 Enterprise Edition with an IP address of 192.168.54.1, a computer running Windows XP with an IP address of 192.168.54.2, a hub, and two straight-through Category 5 (or better) UTP cables connecting the NICs on the computers to the hubs

➤ Access to the Windows Server 2003 computer as the Administrator

➤ Access to the Windows XP computer as an ordinary user

Estimated completion time: **20-30 minutes**

LAB ACTIVITY

ACTIVITY

1. Press **Ctrl+Alt+Del** on the Windows XP computer. Log on to the computer as the ordinary user. The Windows XP desktop appears.

2. Click **Start**, then click **Run**. The Run dialog box opens.

3. Type **cmd** in the Open text box and press **Enter**. A command prompt window opens.

4. You will now test network connectivity between the Windows XP computer and the Windows Server 2003 computer. Type **ping 192.168.54.1** in the command prompt window and press **Enter**. The Windows XP computer indicates that it has received four replies from 192.168.54.1. See Figure 2-2 for an example of the output produced. This indicates that the two computers can communicate with each other over the network. If they could not, the ping command would display an error message such as "Request timed out."

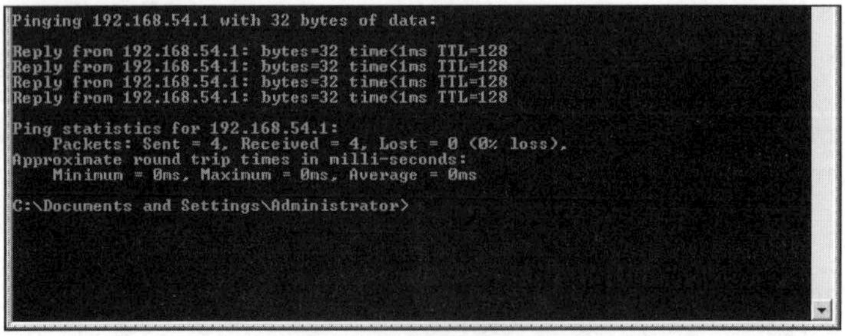

```
Pinging 192.168.54.1 with 32 bytes of data:

Reply from 192.168.54.1: bytes=32 time<1ms TTL=128
Reply from 192.168.54.1: bytes=32 time<1ms TTL=128
Reply from 192.168.54.1: bytes=32 time<1ms TTL=128
Reply from 192.168.54.1: bytes=32 time<1ms TTL=128

Ping statistics for 192.168.54.1:
    Packets: Sent = 4, Received = 4, Lost = 0 (0% loss),
Approximate round trip times in milli-seconds:
    Minimum = 0ms, Maximum = 0ms, Average = 0ms

C:\Documents and Settings\Administrator>
```

Figure 2-2   Typical output from the ping command

5. Repeat Steps 1 through 4 on the Windows Server 2003 computer, logging on as the Administrator. Use the IP address **192.168.54.2** in Step 4.

6. On the Windows Server 2003 computer, type **arp -a** in the command prompt window and press **Enter**. The computer prints a list of IP addresses and the physical addresses, or MAC addresses, associated with each. Record the MAC address for 192.168.54.2, the Windows XP computer.

7. Now you will replace the actual MAC address of the Windows XP computer with a bogus MAC address and see how it affects the ability of the two machines to communicate with each other.

8. In the command prompt window, type **arp -s 192.168.54.2 00-11-22-33-44-55** and press **Enter**. The Windows Server 2003 computer changes the MAC address it knows for the Windows XP computer.

9. Type **arp -a** and press **Enter**. What is the MAC address for the Windows XP computer now?

10. On the Windows XP computer, repeat Step 4. Are you able to ping the Windows Server 2003 computer successfully?

11. In the command prompt window, type **ipconfig /all**. The computer prints detailed information about its network configuration, including its MAC address. Does this MAC address match the one for the Windows XP computer that you found in Step 6?

12. Now you will delete the ARP entry you created for the Windows XP computer. On the Windows Server 2003 computer, type **arp -d** and press **Enter**. All ARP entries are deleted. For your reference, Table 2-1 lists some options for the arp command in Windows.

Table 2-1   Options for the arp command in Windows

Command	Action
arp -a	Displays all the addresses in the ARP cache
arp -s	Adds a static, or permanent, entry to the ARP cache
arp -d	Deletes all entries from the arp cache

13. On the Windows XP computer, repeat Step 4. Are you able to communicate with the Windows Server 2003 computer successfully now?

14. Log off both computers.

Certification Objectives

Objectives for the Network+ Exam:

➤ Given an example, identify a MAC address

➤ Given output from a diagnostic utility (e.g., Tracert, Ping, Ipconfig, etc.), identify the utility and interpret the output

Review Questions

1. What is the MAC address you found for the computer at 192.168.54.2?

2. Which of the following is a valid MAC address?
   a. 01–ba–cd–dh–83–21
   b. 01–ba–cd–de–83–21–42
   c. 01–ba–cd–de–83–21–42–a0
   d. 01–ba–cd–de–83–21

3. Which of the following commands can you use to find a Windows XP computer's MAC address from a command prompt window on that computer?
   a. ipconfig
   b. ipconfig /all
   c. arp -a
   d. netstat

4. Which of the following commands can you use to find the MAC address of another computer on the same network?
   a. ipconfig
   b. ipconfig /all
   c. arp -a
   d. netstat

5. Under what circumstances is it possible for a computer to have more than one MAC address?

   a. never

   b. if a computer has more than one NIC

   c. if a computer has more than one NIC, but only if it is acting as a router

   d. if a computer is a router

6. You have just replaced the NIC on a server, making no other changes. It can communicate with all the computers on its network but one. What is the most likely explanation for this?

   a. The new NIC is not working properly.

   b. Both computers have the same MAC address.

   c. The remote computer has the old MAC address entry in its ARP cache.

   d. The remote computer has a bad NIC.

7. Which of the following is a function of the Data Link layer?

   a. arranging data in proper sequence at their destination

   b. encrypting data prior to transmission

   c. dividing data into distinct frames

   d. issuing electrical signals onto a wire

8. What part of a data frame checks to make sure that the data arrived exactly as it was sent?

   a. CRC

   b. start delimiter

   c. payload

   d. padding

LAB 2.4 LOOKING AT NETWORK CONNECTIONS ON A WINDOWS XP COMPUTER

Objectives

The Transport layer ensures that data travels from the source host to the destination host. Transport layer protocols may check for errors. They may also ensure that data arrives in the proper order. In the TCP/IP stack, TCP is the protocol operating at the Transport layer. Because TCP is a connection-oriented protocol, the computers on both ends of a TCP connection must keep track of the status of the connection.

You can use the `netstat` command on Windows, UNIX, and other operating systems to look at active connections. This command can show detailed information about active

2

network connections, including their status, the number of bytes sent over the network, and other information. UDP, on the other hand, is a connectionless protocol and does not keep track of the connection. As a result, the `netstat` command provides much less information about UDP connections.

After completing this lab, you will be able to:

➤ Use the `netstat` command to view information about the Transport layer

Materials Required

This lab will require the following:

➤ The network required in Lab 1.4, consisting of a computer running Windows Server 2003 Enterprise Edition with an IP address of 192.168.54.1, a computer running Windows XP with an IP address of 192.168.54.2, a hub, and two straight-through Category 5 (or better) UTP cables connecting the NICs on the computers to the hubs

➤ Terminal Services running on the Windows Server 2003 computer, and the computer configured to allow users to log on remotely

➤ Access to both computers as the Administrator

Estimated completion time: **20 minutes**

LAB ACTIVITY

ACTIVITY

1. On the Windows XP computer, press **Ctrl+Alt+Del**. The Log On to Windows dialog box appears.

2. Select **Workstation1 (this computer)** from the Log on to drop-down menu. Then, log onto Windows XP as the Administrator. The Windows XP desktop appears.

3. Click **Start**, then click **Run**. The Run dialog box opens.

4. Type **cmd** and press **Enter**. A command prompt window opens.

5. Type **netstat** and press **Enter**. The computer displays information about all open connections on the computer, or returns to the prompt if there are none.

6. Now you will open a new TCP connection by using the Remote Desktop Connection. This program is used to log onto Windows machines remotely. In this lab, you will just use it to create a TCP connection. Click **Start**, point to **All Programs**, point to **Accessories**, point to **Communications**, and then click **Remote Desktop Connection**. The Remote Desktop Connection window opens.

7. Type **192.168.54.1** in the Computer text box. Click **Connect**. The Log on to Windows dialog box for the Windows Server 2003 computer appears in the Remote Desktop Connection window.

8. On the Windows Server 2003 computer, press **Ctrl+Alt+Del** to display the Log On to Windows dialog box. Log on as the Administrator. The Windows Server 2003 desktop appears.

9. Repeat Steps 3 and 4 to open a command prompt window.

10. In the command prompt window, type **netstat** again and press **Enter**. The computer displays information about the connection, indicating the protocol used, the status of the connection, the local address, the destination address, and the ports used by each side of the connection. The status of the connection should be established. What is the protocol used by the Remote Desktop Connection? Figure 2-3 shows the output of the netstat command.

Figure 2-3 Output from the netstat command

11. Type **netstat -e** and press **Enter**. The computer prints information about the number of bytes sent and received, and about the number of packets sent and received. Table 2-2 shows options for the netstat command.

Table 2-2 Options for the netstat command

Command	Action
netstat -a	Displays all connections and listening ports
netstat -e	Displays Ethernet statistics
netstat -s	Displays statistics per protocol
netstat -r	Displays the routing table
netstat -n	Displays numbers instead of names (usually used with the –a or –r options)

12. Type **ping 192.168.54.2** and press **Enter**. The computer indicates that it has received four replies from 192.168.54.2.

13. Type **netstat -e** again and press **Enter**. Has the number of packets sent and received increased?

14. Type **netstat -s** and press **Enter**. The computer prints information about individual protocols used.

15. Close the Remote Desktop Connection and log off both computers.

Certification Objectives

Objectives for the Network+ Exam:Identify the seven layers of the OSI model and their functions Given output from a diagnostic utility (e.g., Tracert, Ping, Ipconfig, etc.), identify the utility and interpret the output

Review Questions

1. What protocol is used by the Remote Desktop Connection?
   a. ICMP
   b. TCP
   c. UDP
   d. IP

2. About which protocols does the netstat -s command print information? (Choose all that apply.)
   a. ARP
   b. ICMP
   c. TCP
   d. UDP

3. At what layer of the OSI model does TCP work?
   a. Physical layer
   b. Data Link layer
   c. Network layer
   d. Transport layer

4. At what layer of the OSI model does IP work?
   a. Physical layer
   b. Data Link layer
   c. Network layer
   d. Transport layer

5. A user is having difficulty connecting to a remote Web site. After the user attempts to connect, the netstat command tells you that the connection state is established. Where in the OSI model is the problem probably located?

   a. at the Data Link layer

   b. at the Network layer

   c. at the Transport layer

   d. somewhere above the Transport layer

6. Why doesn't the netstat command display any information about ICMP connections?

   a. ICMP does not function at the Transport layer.

   b. ICMP is not a true protocol.

   c. ICMP is a connectionless protocol.

   d. ICMP is considered unimportant.

Lab 2.5 Viewing Ethernet Frames

Objectives

A network protocol analyzer is a software program or hardware device that reads packets or frames directly from a computer's NIC and allows you to view them or to save them for later viewing. This process is called capturing the frames. A network protocol analyzer also decodes the frames captured so that you can look at the individual parts of the frame. Even though a network protocol analyzer captures frames, the packets are typically of the most interest to a network administrator.

Microsoft Network Monitor is a network protocol analyzer available on Windows Server 2003, as well as on other versions of Windows. You can use a network protocol analyzer to examine the traffic on a network one frame at a time, or one part of a frame at a time. As you gain experience at looking at network traffic, you can also use Network Monitor to look for potential problems. For instance, you can look at Transport layer information in a series of packets to determine if the computer on the other end is sending data too quickly. With a little experience, Network Monitor or other network protocol analyzers can be invaluable troubleshooting tools.

It is important to keep in mind that a network protocol analyzer such as Network Monitor can be used to violate a user's privacy. As such, it should not be used carelessly or lightly.

After completing this lab, you will be able to:

➤ Use Network Monitor to look at captured frames

Materials Required

This lab will require the following:

➤ The network required in Lab 1.4, consisting of a computer running Windows Server 2003 Enterprise Edition with an IP address of 192.168.54.1, a computer running Windows XP with an IP address of 192.168.54.2, a hub, and two straight-through Category 5 (or better) UTP cables connecting the NICs on the computers to the hubs

➤ Network Monitor installed on the Windows Server 2003 computer

➤ Access to the Windows Server 2003 computer as the Administrator

➤ Access to the Windows XP computer as any ordinary user

Estimated completion time: **60 minutes**

LAB ACTIVITY

ACTIVITY

1. On the Windows XP computer, press **Ctrl+Alt+Del**. The Log On to Windows dialog box appears.

2. Log on to Windows XP as an ordinary user. The Windows XP desktop appears.

3. Click **Start**, then click **Run**. The Run dialog box opens.

4. In the Open text box, type **cmd** and click **OK**. A command prompt window opens.

5. Type **ping -t 192.168.54.1** and press **Enter**. This sends ICMP packets continuously to the Windows Server 2003 computer, and ensures that packets are available when you open Network Monitor.

6. On the Windows Server 2003 computer, press **Ctrl+Alt+Del**. The Log On to Windows dialog box appears.

7. Log on as the Administrator. The Windows Server 2003 desktop appears.

8. Click **Start**, point to **All Programs**, point to **Administrative Tools**, and then click **Network Monitor**. The Microsoft Network Monitor window opens, and the Microsoft Network Monitor dialog box asks you to specify the network on which you want to capture data.

9. Click **OK**. The Select a network dialog box opens.

10. In the tree in the left pane, click the **plus sign (+)** next to Local Computer to expand the tree. Click **Local Area Connection** to highlight it, then click **OK**.

11. Click **Capture** on the menu bar, then click **Start**. Network Monitor begins to capture packets. Figure 2-4 shows Network Monitor in the process of capturing packets. The upper-right pane shows information about the number of packets captured by Network Monitor.

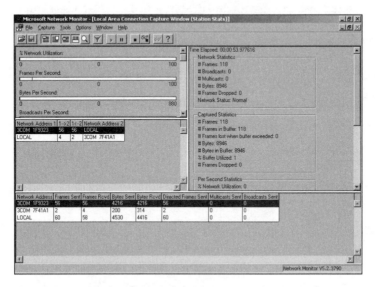

Figure 2-4   Microsoft Network Monitor

12. When the number of frames captured (# Frames under the "Captured Statistics" heading) is above 100, click **Capture** on the menu bar, and then click **Stop and View**. The Capture Summary window opens, similar to Figure 2-5. Each line summarizes information about a captured frame.

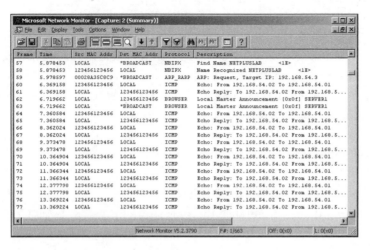

Figure 2-5   A network capture

13. Locate a frame with "ICMP" in the Protocol field and double-click that row. The list of frames remains in the top pane of the window, while a detailed description of each part of the selected frame appears in the middle pane and a representation of the frame in hexadecimal appears in the bottom pane. See Figure 2-6 for an example of a captured frame.

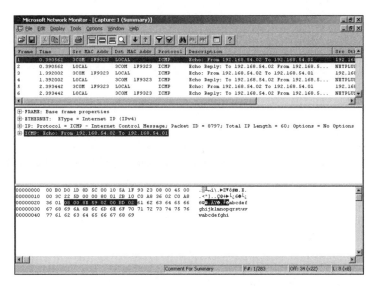

Figure 2-6 Individual frame in a network capture

14. By clicking the plus signs (+) in the middle pane, you can display detailed information about each part of the packet. Click the **plus sign (+)** next to FRAME. Network Monitor shows detailed information about the frame itself. What is the total frame length for the frame you've chosen?

15. Click the **plus sign (+)** next to ETHERNET. Network Monitor shows detailed information about the Ethernet portion of the frame. What is the source address of the packet? What is the destination address of the packet? What is the Ethernet Type?

16. Click the **plus sign (+)** next to IP. Network Monitor shows detailed information about the IP portion of the packet. What is the source address of the packet? What is the destination address of the packet? Is there a checksum in the IP portion of the packet?

17. Click the **plus sign (+)** next to ICMP. Network Monitor shows detailed information about the ICMP portion of the packet. Is there another checksum for this portion of the packet?

18. Close Network Monitor. Click **No** when asked if you want to save the capture. On the Windows XP computer, press **Ctrl+C** to stop the ping command.

19. Log off both computers.

Certification Objectives

Objectives for the Network+ Exam:

➤ Identify the seven layers of the OSI model and their functions

➤ Specify the main features of 802.2 (LLC), 802.3 (Ethernet), 802.5 (token ring), 802.11b (wireless), and FDDI networking technologies, including: speed, access, method, topology, media

Review Questions

1. At what layer in the OSI model were the source and destination addresses for the packet in Step 15 located?

2. In the frame you examined in Steps 13 through 17, which portions of the packet calculated a CRC checksum? What layers of the OSI model do they correspond to?

3. A user is unable to reach your company's Web site. From the user's workstation, you can ping the remote Web server. How might you use Network Monitor or another network protocol analyzer in order to troubleshoot the problem? (Choose all that apply.)

    a. by checking to see if the workstation is sending packets to the Web server

    b. by checking to see if the server is sending packets to the workstation

    c. by checking the workstation's IP configuration

    d. by checking the workstation's ARP configuration

4. Which protocols can be seen using Network Monitor? (Choose all that apply.)

    a. ICMP

    b. ARP

    c. TCP

    d. UDP

5. About which OSI layer does Network Monitor *not* provide information?

    a. Physical layer

    b. Data Link layer

    c. Network layer

    d. Transport layer

DATA TRANSMISSION AND NETWORKING MEDIA

Labs included in this chapter

➤ Lab 3.1 Learning Media Characteristics

➤ Lab 3.2 Creating a 10BaseT Crossover Cable to Connect Two Computers

➤ Lab 3.3 Comparing Throughput

➤ Lab 3.4 Understanding How a Category 5 Cable Fails

➤ Lab 3.5 Adding a Host to a Wireless Network

Net+ Exam Objectives	
Objective	**Lab**
Recognize the following media connectors and/or describe their uses: RJ-11, RJ-45, AUI, BNC, ST, SC	3.1, 3.2, 3.3, 3.4
Choose the appropriate media type and connectors to add a client to an existing network	3.1, 3.2, 3.3
Given a wiring task, select the appropriate tool (e.g., wire crimper, media tester/certifier, punch down tool, tone generator, optical tester, etc.)	3.2, 3.4
Given a network scenario, interpret visual indicators (i.e., link lights, collision lights, etc.) to determine the nature of the problem	3.2, 3.4
Specify the characteristics (e.g., speed, length, topology, cable type, etc.) of the following: 802.3 Ethernet standards, 10BaseT, 100BaseTX, 10Base2, 10Base5, 100BaseFX, Gigabit Ethernet	3.2, 3.3, 3.4
Specify the main features of 802.2 (LLC), 802.3 (Ethernet), 802.5 (Token Ring), 802.11b (wireless), and FDDI networking technologies, including speed, access, method, topology, and media	3.3, 3.5
Given a network troubleshooting scenario involving a wiring/infrastructure problem, identify the cause of the problem (i.e., bad media, interference, network hardware)	3.4
Identify the purpose, features, and functions of the following network components: hubs, switches, bridges, routers, gateways, CSU/DSU, network interface cards/ISDN adapters/system area network cards, wireless access points, modems	3.5

LAB 3.1 LEARNING MEDIA CHARACTERISTICS

Objectives

In this lab, you will learn about the costs and characteristics of network media and networking and computer equipment. This will give you experience in comparing costs of network components and network media. It will also give you an idea of the equipment needed to set up a network, and of the total costs involved in doing so.

Bear in mind that the cost of a certain medium includes not only the cost of the cable, but also the installation cost, maintenance costs, and the cost of replacing the medium if it becomes obsolete in the future. Additionally, the cost of networking and computer equipment and software will vary widely, depending on the vendor, the equipment chosen, and the licensing terms.

After completing this lab, you will be able to:

➤ Identify the costs and characteristics of Category 3 and Category 5 cable

Materials Required

This lab will require the following:

➤ Access to a retail store that sells computer networking equipment, or access to the Internet

➤ Pencil and paper

Estimated completion time: **30-180 minutes**

ACTIVITY

1. Visit a retail computer store (such as Best Buy or CompUSA) that sells Ethernet Category 5 cable, computers, software, and networking supplies. Alternately, visit a Web site (such as *www.cdw.com*) of a company that specializes in computers, software, and networking supplies. Record the Web address or the name of the store.

2. Record the cost of Category 5 cable sold by the foot. If the store does not sell cable by the foot, divide the price of the longest Category 5 cable you can find by its length in feet.

3. Record the cost of Category 3, Category 6, or Category 7 cable as you did in the previous step.

4. Record the cost and model information for an Ethernet, 100-Mbps, four-port hub with an RJ-45 connection for a workstation.

5. Record the cost and model information for an Ethernet, 100-Mbps, 16-port hub with an RJ-45 connection.

6. Record the cost and model information for a wireless access point.

7. Record the cost and model information for a typical desktop computer. If you have difficulty deciding on a model, choose one that is intermediate in price.

8. Record the cost and model information for a typical laptop computer. If you have difficulty deciding on a model, choose one that is intermediate in price.

9. Record the cost of an Ethernet 100-Mbps NIC with an RJ-45 connection.

10. Record the cost and model information for a 100-Mbps PCMCIA NIC with an RJ-45 connection for a laptop.

11. Record the cost and model information for a wireless network card for a laptop.

12. Record the cost of the full version of Microsoft Windows XP Professional.

13. Assume that you need to connect 50 workstations and 20 laptops to a network. Calculate and record the cost of these computers.

14. Assume that each workstation and each laptop requires 50 feet of cable. Calculate and record the cost of the total amount of Category 5 cable needed for each computer. For comparison, calculate and record the cost of the total amount of the Category 3, Category 6, or Category 7 cable you found in Step 3.

15. Assume that each workstation will use a NIC, and that each laptop will use both a network card and a wireless network card. Calculate and record the total cost.

16. Assume that one wireless access point will be required. (Additional wireless access points may be required depending on the physical layout of the building and other factors.) How many hubs are required to connect all the workstations and all the laptops to the network at the same time? Calculate and record the total cost for hubs and the wireless access point.

3

17. Assume that each computer requires a copy of Windows XP Professional. (While they may buy computers with an operating system already installed, many companies re-install the operating system. The terms of their licensing agreement with Microsoft may require them to purchase it a second time.) Calculate and record the cost of Windows XP Professional for each workstation and laptop.

18. Calculate and record the total cost of the network using Category 5 cable by adding up the totals you calculated in Steps 13 through 17. Do not include in the total the cost of the Category 3, Category 6, or Category 7 cabling you calculated in Step 14.

19. For comparison, calculate and record the total cost of the network using Category 3, Category 6, or Category 7 cable. Do this by summing the totals you calculated in Steps 13 through 17. Do not include the total the cost of the Category 5 cabling.

Certification Objectives

Objectives for the Network+ Exam:

➤ Recognize the following media connectors and/or describe their uses: RJ-11, RJ-45, AUI, BNC, ST, SC

➤ Choose the appropriate media type and connectors to add a client to an existing network

Review Questions

1. What type of connector does a 100BaseT network require?

   a. RJ-11

   b. BNC

   c. AUI

   d. RJ-45

2. What type of cable does a Thinnet network require?
   a. RG-58 A/U
   b. RG-62 A/U
   c. RG-59/U
   d. RG-8

3. What is the purpose of using terminators on a 10Base2 network?
   a. to eliminate noise
   b. to eliminate signal bounce
   c. to eliminate EMI
   d. to eliminate crosstalk

4. What is the maximum throughput of a 10Base5 network?
   a. 5 Mbps
   b. 10 Mbps
   c. 50 Mbps
   d. 100 Mbps

5. On a 10BaseT network, attenuation is addressed through the use of which of the following?
   a. amplifiers
   b. multiplexers
   c. repeaters
   d. RF generators

6. What is the maximum allowable segment length on a 10BaseT network?
   a. 85 feet
   b. 85 meters
   c. 185 feet
   d. 100 meters

7. Why is the maximum segment length on a 10Base2 network longer than that of a 10BaseT network?
   a. 10Base2 allows fewer nodes to connect to a shared channel, thus reducing attenuation.
   b. 10Base2 uses a bus topology, which is less susceptible to attenuation.
   c. 10Base2 uses terminators, which eliminate attenuation.
   d. 10Base2 uses coaxial cable, which is better shielded from noise than UTP.

LAB 3.2 CREATING A 10BaseT CROSSOVER CABLE TO CONNECT TWO COMPUTERS

3

Objectives

You may find it necessary to make cables from time to time. The phrase "making cables" actually refers to the process of properly attaching connectors to the ends of a length of cable. Many companies make their own cables to save money. Additionally, knowing how to make cables makes it easier to troubleshoot cabling problems.

Normal patch cables, also known as straight-through cables, are cables whose wire terminations on either end are identical. Another kind of cable is a crossover cable. In this type of cable, the transmit and receive pins in one of the cable's plugs must be reversed. A crossover cable allows two workstations to connect directly to each other (without a connectivity device in-between).

After completing this lab, you will be able to:

➤ Make a crossover Category 5 cable

➤ Directly connect two computers with an RJ-45 crossover cable by plugging one end of the cable into the NIC of one computer and the other end of the cable into the NIC of the second computer

➤ Use a cable tester to ensure cable integrity

Materials Required

This lab will require the following:

➤ At least 10 feet of Category 5 (or better) UTP cable without connectors

➤ Two RJ-45 connectors

➤ Two computers running Windows XP Professional configured to be in a workgroup named NETPLUS, with Ethernet NICs with RJ-45 connectors

➤ Access as the Administrator for both computers

➤ A network crimper

➤ A wire stripper

➤ A cable tester

➤ A wire cutting tool

Estimated completion time: **60 minutes**

LAB ACTIVITY

ACTIVITY

1. Use the wire cutter to make a clean cut at both ends of the UTP cable.

2. Use the wire stripper to remove one inch (or less) of the sheath from one end of the UTP cable. Do not strip the insulation from the individual wires inside the UTP cable, and take care not to damage the insulation on the twisted pairs inside.

3. Slightly separate the four wire pairs, but keep the pairs twisted around each other.

4. Hold the RJ-45 connector so that the opening faces you and the plastic flap is on the bottom. Push the wires into the RJ-45 connector so that each wire is in its own slot in the connector, in the order shown in Table 3-1. Use a crimping tool to punch down the cable. You have now completed one end of the cable.

Table 3-1   Pin numbers and color codes for creating a straight-through cable end

Pin number	Pair number	Use	Color
1	2	Transmit	White with green stripe
2	2	Receive	Green
3	3	Transmit	White with orange stripe
4	1	Receive	Blue
5	1	Transmit	White with blue stripe
6	3	Receive	Orange
7	4	Transmit	White with brown stripe
8	4	Receive	Brown

5. Repeat Steps 2 and 3 for the other end of the twisted-pair cable.

6. Hold the RJ-45 connector so that the opening faces you and the plastic flap is on the bottom, just as you did in Step 4. If you flip the RJ-45 connector over, the cable will not work. Push the wires into the RJ-45 connector so that each wire is in its own slot in the order shown in Table 3-2. Use a crimping tool to punch down the cable. This crosses the transmit and receive wires (both positive and negative), which allows the computers to communicate when connected. After completing this step, your crossover cable will be ready to use. Figure 3-1 shows an example of a crossover cable.

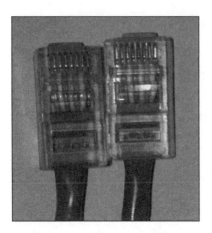

Figure 3-1   Crossover cable

Table 3-2   Pin numbers and color codes for creating a crossover cable end

Pin number	Pair number	Use	Color
1	3	Transmit	White with orange stripe
2	3	Receive	Orange
3	2	Transmit	White with green stripe
4	1	Receive	Blue
5	1	Transmit	White with blue stripe
6	2	Receive	Green
7	4	Transmit	White with brown stripe
8	4	Receive	Brown

7. Plug each end of the cable into the cable tester. If the lights on the tester turn on, proceed to the next step. If not, remove the ends of the cable with a wire cutter and repeat the first six steps of this lab. Making a cable properly on the first try is difficult.

8. Remove the cable ends from the cable tester.

9. Connect one end of the cable to the NIC of one computer.

10. Connect the other end of the same cable to the NIC of the second computer. The lights on each NIC turn on.

11. On one computer, press **Ctrl+Alt+Del**. The Log On to Windows dialog box appears. Log on as the Administrator. The Windows XP desktop appears.

12. Click **Start**, point to **All Programs**, point to **Accessories**, point to **Communications**, then click **Network Connections**.

13. Right-click the **Local Area Connection** icon. Select **Properties** from the pop-up menu that appears. The Local Area Connection Properties window opens.

14. Double-click **Internet Protocol (TCP/IP)**. The Internet Protocol (TCP/IP) Properties dialog box opens.

15. Click the **Use the following IP address** option button. In the IP address text box, enter **172.16.30.1**. In the Subnet mask text box, enter **255.255.255.0**. Click the **OK** button twice.

16. Repeat Steps 11 through 15 on the second computer, using an IP address of 172.16.30.2.

17. On the second computer, click **Start**, then click **Run**. The Run dialog box opens.

18. Type **cmd** and press **Enter**. A command prompt window opens.

19. Type **ping 172.16.30.1** and press **Enter**. The computer indicates that it has received four replies, demonstrating that the two computers can communicate with each other over the new cable.

20. Log off both computers.

Certification Objectives

Objectives for the Network+ Exam:

➤ Recognize the following media connectors and/or describe their uses: RJ-11, RJ-45, AUI, BNC, ST, SC

➤ Choose the appropriate media type and connectors to add a client to an existing network

➤ Given a wiring task, select the appropriate tool (e.g., wire crimper, media tester/certifier, punch down tool, tone generator, optical tester, etc.)

➤ Given a network scenerio, interpret visual indicators (i.e., link lights, collision lights, etc.) to determine the nature of the problem

➤ Specify the characteristics (e.g., speed, length, topology, cable type, etc.) of the following: 802.3 Ethernet standards, 10BaseT, 100BaseTX, 10Base2, 10Base5, 100BaseFX, Gigabit Ethernet

Review Questions

1. What is one use for a crossover cable?

    a. to connect a hub and a workstation

    b. to connect a workstation to a wall jack

    c. to connect two workstations directly

    d. to connect a workstation to a modem

2. Which of the following tools would be useful in creating a patch cable for a 100BaseT network?

    a. screwdriver

    b. crimper

    c. soldering iron

    d. pliers

3. In twisted-pair wire, how does the twist ratio affect transmission? (Choose all that apply.)

    a. The more twists per inch, the less crosstalk transmission will suffer.

    b. The more twists per inch, the slower the transmission.

    c. The more twists per inch, the more attenuation transmission will suffer.

    d. The more twists per inch, the faster the transmission.

4. What is the maximum speed at which Category 3 UTP can transmit data?

    a. 1 Mbps

    b. 10 Mbps

    c. 100 Mbps

    d. 1 Gbps

5. What type of cable would connect a workstation to the wall jack in the work area of a 10BaseT network?

    a. straight-through cable

    b. crossover cable

    c. coaxial cable

    d. punch-down cable

6. What type of cable is required for 100BaseFX?

    a. coaxial cable

    b. UTP

    c. STP

    d. fiber-optic cable

7. Which of the following are characteristics of a Thicknet network? (Choose all that apply.)

   a. vampire taps

   b. transceiver cable

   c. BNC connectors

   d. RJ-45 connectors

8. Which of the following would be the best medium for an environment that is subject to heavy EMI?

   a. fiber-optic cable

   b. RF

   c. infrared

   d. UTP

Lab 3.3 Comparing Throughput

Objectives

As a network administrator, you will often have to choose between different types of media, even within the same network. Throughput is often an important consideration in choosing between different network media. For instance, servers typically require faster media than most workstations, and some workstations will require faster media than others. Additionally, the types of applications in use on the network will also play a role in the types of media used. Some applications, such as streaming video, require more bandwidth than others, such as terminal access to a mainframe.

When comparing media types, it is often helpful to look at the actual transmission rates under realistic conditions. First, the actual transmission rates will often be different from the theoretical transmission rates. Many factors will prevent a computer from transmitting or receiving data at the theoretical rate. These include the quality of the cabling, noise, and the ability of the computer on either end to send to or receive data. Additionally, the bandwidth used by other computers on the network can limit the available bandwidth. Second, you will often need to verify that many applications work as expected with the intended media. With applications such as streaming video or IP telephony, factors such as latency and transmission rate make a big difference in whether or not users can successfully use the application. Testing new applications under realistic conditions can help you make the best decision possible about the type of network media you will use in your network.

After completing this lab, you will be able to:

➤ Measure the throughput on an Ethernet network

➤ Compare throughput on networks using different media

➤ Recognize that actual throughput may not reach the maximum throughput specified for a network

Materials Required

This lab will require the following:

➤ A Windows Server 2003 Enterprise Edition computer configured as a domain controller for the netpluslab.net domain with an IP address of 192.168.54.1 and a subnet mask of 255.255.255.0

➤ A Windows XP Professional computer in the netpluslab.net domain configured with an IP address of 192.168.54.2 and a subnet mask of 255.255.255.0

➤ Access as the Administrator to the Windows Server 2003 computer

➤ A 10-Mbps hub, and a 100-Mbps hub or a 10/100 hub

➤ 10/100 Ethernet NICs in each computer

➤ Two straight-through Category 5 (or better) UTP cables that can be used to connect the computers to a hub

➤ On the Windows Server 2003 computer, a shared folder named NETPLUS that can be accessed by the netplus user in the netpluslab.net domain; this folder should contain the file driver.cab copied from C:\WINDOWS\Driver Cache\i386

Estimated completion time: **25-30 minutes**

ACTIVITY

1. Connect the computers to the 10-Mbps hub.

2. On the Windows Server 2003 computer, press **Ctrl+Alt+Del**. The Log On to Windows dialog box opens. Log on as the Administrator. The Windows Server 2003 desktop appears.

3. Click **Start**, point to **All Programs**, point to **Administrative Tools**, then click **Performance**.

4. If the **System Monitor** icon in the left pane is not already selected, click it to highlight it.

5. Right-click the graph in the right pane. Select **Add Counters** from the pop-up menu. The Add Counters dialog box opens, as shown in Figure 3-2.

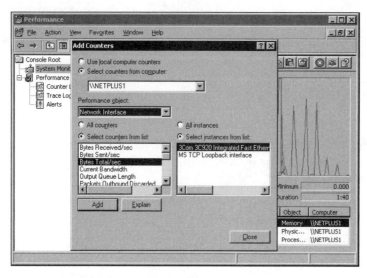

Figure 3-2   Add Counters dialog box

6. Select **Network Interface** from the Performance object drop-down menu. Make sure that the computer's NIC is selected. (The MS TCP Loopback interface is a software-only interface and should *not* be selected.)

7. Make sure that the **Select counters from list** option button is selected. Select **Bytes Total/sec** from the drop-down menu underneath the Select counters from list option button. Click **Add**. The computer adds the Bytes Total/sec counter to the list of metrics it will monitor.

8. Click **Close**. The Add Counters window closes.

9. If the Performance window shows any counters besides Bytes Total/sec at the bottom of the right pane of the Performance window, click these counters to highlight them. Press **Del** to delete them. You now see the NIC's current bandwidth.

10. On the Windows XP computer, press **Ctrl+Alt+Del**. The Log On to Windows dialog box appears. Log on to the computer as the Administrator. The Windows XP desktop appears.

11. Click **Start**, and then click **My Computer**. The My Computer window opens.

12. Click **Tools**, and then click **Map Network Drive**. The Map Network Drive window opens.

13. Choose driver letter **Z:** from the drop-down menu next to the Drive list box. Type **\\192.168.54.1\netplus** in the Folder text box and then click **Finish**.

14. A dialog box opens indicating that you are attempting to connect to \\192.168.54.1\netplus. The Connect to server1.netpluslab.net window

opens. (The dialog box may not appear if the password is the same on both computers. If so, go to Step 16.)

15. In the User name text box, enter **netplus@netpluslab.net**. In the Password text box, enter the password for the netplus account. Click **OK**.

16. Click **Start**, and then click **Run**. The Run dialog box opens.

17. Type **cmd** and press **Enter**. A command prompt window opens.

18. Type **mkdir C:\temp** and press **Enter**. The computer creates a new directory.

19. Type **notepad test.bat** and press **Enter**. A dialog box appears asking if you'd like to create the file.

20. Click **Yes**. The Notepad window opens.

21. In Notepad, type the following three lines:

    ```
    :Copy
    copy Z:\driver.cab C:\temp
    goto COPY
    ```

22. Close Notepad. A dialog box opens, asking if you want to save your changes. Click **Yes**.

23. At the command prompt, type **test** and press **Enter**. The batch file continuously copies the file onto the Windows XP computer from the shared folder on the Windows Server 2003 computer.

24. Look at the graph on the Windows Server 2003 computer. If the line is flat and at the very bottom or the very top of the graph, right-click the graph and select **Properties** from the pop-up menu. Otherwise, go to Step 27.

25. On the Windows Server 2003 computer, click the **Graph** tab. In the Maximum text box, enter **500** and click **OK**. The computer redraws the graph with the new scale. If the line on the graph is still flat, repeat the previous step and this step using 5000 and then 50,000 until the line is in the middle of the graph.

26. After a minute, look at the Average box at the bottom of the graph and record the number of bytes received per second. Multiply this number by 8 to find the number of bits received per second. Record the number of bits received per second and compare it to the bandwidth of the hub.

27. At the command prompt on the Windows XP computer, press **Ctrl+C** to stop the batch file. Type **Y** and press **Enter** when asked to terminate the batch job.

28. Plug the cables from both computers into the 100-Mbps or 10/100 hub. The lights on each NIC turn on.

29. At the command prompt on the Windows XP computer, type **test** and press **Enter**.

30. After a minute, record the number of bytes received per second. Multiply this number by 8 to find the number of bits received per second and compare it to the bandwidth of the hub.

31. At the command prompt, press **Ctrl+C** to stop the batch file. Type **Y** and press **Enter** when asked to terminate the batch job. Close the Performance window.

32. Compare the number of bits received per second on the 10-Mbps hub you recorded in Step 26 with the number of bits received per second on the 100-Mbps or 10/100 hub you recorded in Step 30.

33. Log off both computers.

Certification Objectives

Objectives for the Network+ Exam:

➤ Recognize the following media connectors and/or describe their uses: RJ-11, RJ-45, AUI, BNC, ST, SC

➤ Choose the appropriate media type and connectors to add a client to an existing network

➤ Specify the characteristics (e.g., speed, length, topology, cable type, etc.) of the following: 802.3 Ethernet standards, 10BaseT, 100BaseTX, 10Base2, 10Base5, 100BaseFX, Gigabit Ethernet

➤ Specify the main features of 802.2 (LLC), 802.3 (Ethernet), 802.5 (Token Ring), 802.11b (wireless), and FDDI networking technologies, including speed, access, method, topology, and media

Review Questions

1. What might cause a 100BaseTX network to experience an average throughput of less than 100 Mbps? (Choose all that apply.)

   a. heavy traffic on the network

   b. excessive noise

   c. too many protocols bound on the server

   d. a mix of different network operating systems on the servers

2. What is the maximum number of repeaters a data packet may traverse on a 100BaseT network?

   a. 2

   b. 3

    c. 4

    d. 5

3. Which of the following networks would be the most scalable?

    a. 10Base2

    b. 10Base5

    c. 10BaseT

    d. Token Ring

4. What does the "T" in 10BaseT and 100BaseT stand for?

    a. transmission

    b. transport layer

    c. twisted-pair

    d. transparent

5. Which of the following is not capable of full duplexing?

    a. 10BaseT

    b. 100BaseTX

    c. 100BaseT4

    d. 100BaseFX

6. What type of media do wireless networks use? (Choose all that apply.)

    a. UTP

    b. alpha wave

    c. infrared

    d. radio frequency

7. What type of cable is required for a 100BaseT network?

    a. CAT 3 or higher

    b. CAT 5 or higher

    c. CAT 6 or higher

    d. CAT 7 or higher

8. Where would you find a plenum cable?

    a. above the ceiling tiles in an office

    b. in an outdoor cable trench that leads to a building

    c. between a hub and a punch-down panel

    d. between a workstation and a wall jack

LAB 3.4 UNDERSTANDING HOW A CATEGORY 5 CABLE FAILS

Objectives

Verifying the integrity of network cabling is often an important first step in solving network problems. In the OSI model, the network media is at the Physical layer. If the network media is not functioning properly, then the layers above the Physical layer will not function properly either. It is important to keep in mind that damage to cabling may not be immediately obvious, and may result in odd or intermittent problems. For instance, a damaged cable may cause excess noise. While data may be transmitted through the cable, protocols at higher levels of the OSI model will need to retransmit data. The problem may also become worse over time, eventually preventing data from being transmitted through the cable at all.

Network cabling should be protected as much as possible. It can be damaged slowly over time by factors such as excessive heat or pressure, or it can be damaged quickly by a user's foot or a backhoe. The better protected network cabling is, the longer it will last.

In this lab you will simulate a failed cable by building an incorrectly made cable. While cables can be damaged in many different ways, it is also important to verify that network cabling is properly installed in the first place. If you do not verify proper installation of network cabling, you may find it difficult to distinguish between a problem with the original installation and cabling damaged after the installation. This can prevent you from finding the ultimate source of the problem and fixing it properly.

After completing this lab, you will be able to:

➤   Identify the problem associated with an incorrectly wired 10BaseT cable

Materials Required

This lab requires the following:

➤   At least 10 feet of Category 5 (or better) UTP cable

➤   Four RJ-45 connectors

➤   Two computers running Windows XP Professional, using Ethernet NICs with RJ-45 connectors, with File and Printer Sharing for Microsoft Networks installed, and with a workgroup named NETPLUSLAB

➤   One computer configured with an IP address of 172.16.30.1, and the other configured with an IP address of 172.16.30.2, both configured with a subnet mask of 255.255.255.0

➤   Access to both computers as the Administrator

➤   A network crimper

➤   A wire stripper

➤ A wire cutting tool

➤ Completion of Lab 3.2

Estimated completion time: **60 minutes**

3

ACTIVITY

1. Perform Steps 1 through 4 of Lab 3.2 for one end of the twisted-pair cable.

2. Repeat Steps 1 through 3 of Lab 3.2 for the other end of the twisted-pair cable.

3. On the second end of the twisted-pair cable, push the wires into the RJ-45 connector so that each wire is in its own slot and so that the colors match the pin numbers listed in Table 3-3. Using a crimping tool, punch down the end of the cable. This results in an incorrectly made cable.

Table 3-3 Pin numbers and color codes for creating an incorrect cable end

Pin number	Pair number	Color
1	4	Brown
2	4	White with brown stripes
3	1	White with blue stripes
4	3	White with orange stripes
5	3	Orange
6	1	Blue
7	2	White with green stripes
8	2	Green

4. Connect one end of the cable to each computer. If the network adapter lights on each computer do not illuminate, proceed with the next step. If they do, you accidentally made a correctly wired cable, and you need to begin this lab again.

5. On one computer, press **Ctrl+Alt+Del**. The Log On to Windows dialog box appears. Log on to the computer as the Administrator. The Windows XP desktop appears.

6. Click **Start**, then click **My Computer**. The My Computer window opens. Click **My Network Places**. The My Network Places window opens.

7. Click **Entire Network** below "Other Places" on the left side of the window. Double-click **Microsoft Windows Network**. Double-click the **NETPLUSLAB** icon. Notice that you cannot see the other computer in the list.

8. Log off the computer.

9. Using the wire cutting tool, cut the incorrectly wired end of the cable about one inch from the RJ-45 connector. The RJ-45 connector should drop off.

10. Rewire and recrimp the cable as described in Lab 3.2. Connect one end of the cable to the NIC in each of the computers.

11. Repeat Steps 5 through 7 again. You should now see the second computer appear in the list.

12. Log off the computer.

Certification Objectives

Objectives for the Network+ Exam:

➤ Recognize the following media connectors and/or describe their uses: RJ-11, RJ-45, AUI, BNC, ST, SC

➤ Given a wiring task, select the appropriate tool (e.g., wire crimper, media tester/ certifier, punch down tool, tone generator, optical tester, etc.)

➤ Given a network scenario, interpret visual indicators (i.e., link lights, collision lights, etc.) to determine the nature of the problem

➤ Specify the characteristics (e.g., speed, length, topology, cable type, etc.) of the following: 802.3 Ethernet standards, 10BaseT, 100BaseTX, 10Base2, 10Base5, 100BaseFX, Gigabit Ethernet

➤ Given a network troubleshooting scenario involving a wiring/infrastructure problem, identify the cause of the problem (i.e., bad media, interference, network hardware)

Review Questions

1. What pin number is used for transmitting a positive signal on an RJ-45 straight-through patch cable?

   a. 1

   b. 2

   c. 5

   d. 6

2. Which of the following could be a symptom of a damaged patch cable between a workstation and the wall jack on a 10BaseT network? (Choose all that apply.)

   a. The workstation cannot send or receive data to or from the network.

   b. The workstation and other workstations in the same office cannot send or receive data to or from the network.

    c. The workstation can send data to the network, but cannot receive data from the network.

    d. All workstations on the same segment can send data to the network, but cannot receive data from the network.

3. How does bend radius affect transmission?

    a. Transmission will not be successful until the bend radius has been reached.

    b. Transmission cannot occur at the bend radius.

    c. Transmission will be unreliable after the bend radius is exceeded.

    d. Transmission will be less secure after the bend radius is exceeded.

4. How many wire pairs are in a typical Category 3 cable?

    a. 2

    b. 3

    c. 4

    d. 6

5. Which of the following types of cable is most likely to be used on a Token Ring network?

    a. CAT 1

    b. CAT 3

    c. CAT 4

    d. CAT 7

6. What organization is responsible for establishing structured wiring standards?

    a. TIA/EIA

    b. ANSI

    c. ITU

    d. FCC

LAB 3.5 ADDING A HOST TO A WIRELESS NETWORK

Objectives

In this lab, you will add a host to a wireless network. Wireless networks allow a user to connect to the network without cabling. This makes it possible to use a networked computer in a cafeteria, outdoors, in a coffee shop, and many other places.

However, wireless networks come with a number of disadvantages. They do not have the throughput that Fast or Gigabit Ethernet networks provide. Throughput also varies depending on reception, and good reception may not be possible from all locations. Wireless signals are affected by sources of electronic noise, including the weather, fluorescent lights, and microwave ovens. Finally, wireless networks may not be as secure as cabled networks. An unsecured wireless access point may mean that anyone with a wireless card in the next building or in the parking lot could gain access to your network resources.

After completing this lab, you will be able to:

➤ Add a client to a wireless network

Materials Required

This lab will require the following:

➤ A computer (ideally a laptop) running Windows XP Professional with a wireless network card

➤ A wireless access point named "netplus" (or another name supplied by your instructor) configured with an IP address of 172.16.1.1 and a subnet mask of 255.255.255.0

➤ The wireless access point configured to give out DHCP addresses between 172.16.1.5 and 172.16.1.254 (or some portion of that range) and a subnet mask of 255.255.255.0

➤ Any additional settings needed to connect the Windows XP computer to this wireless access point

Estimated completion time: **25 minutes**

LAB ACTIVITY

ACTIVITY

1. Press **Ctrl+Alt+Del** on the Windows XP computer. The Log On to Windows dialog box opens. Log on as the Administrator. The Windows XP desktop appears.

2. Click **Start**, point to **All Programs**, point to **Accessories**, point to **Communications**, and click **Network Connections**. The Network Connections window opens.

3. Right-click **Wireless Network Connection**, and then select **Properties** from the pop-up menu that appears. The Wireless Network Connection Properties window opens.

4. Click the **Wireless Networks** tab. A list of available wireless networks appears under Available networks.

3

5. If you see the name of the wireless network, go to Step 9. If you do not see the name of the wireless network, go to Step 6.

6. Click **Add** under Preferred networks. The Wireless network properties dialog box opens.

7. Enter **netplus** (or the name of the wireless access point) in the Network name (SSID) text box. Configure any additional settings as indicated by your instructor. Figure 3-3 shows the Wireless network properties dialog box.

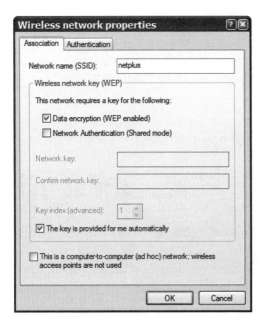

Figure 3-3   The Wireless network properties dialog box

8. Click **OK**. The Wireless network properties dialog box closes, and the name of the wireless access point appears under Available Networks.

9. Click **OK** to close the Wireless Network Connection Properties dialog box.

10. Now you can test your connectivity to the wireless network. Click **Start**, then click **Run**. The Run dialog box opens.

11. Type **cmd** and press **Enter**. A command prompt window opens.

12. Type **ping 172.16.1.1** and press **Enter**. The computer indicates that it has received four replies.

13. If the Windows XP computer is a laptop, type **ping -t 172.16.1.1** and press **Enter**. The ping command begins running continuously, and will not stop until you end it. Pick up the laptop and walk away from the wireless access point. How far can you walk away from the wireless access point before the computer prints that it is unable to reach 172.16.1.1?

14. Press **Ctrl+C** to stop the `ping` command.

15. Log off the computer.

Certification Objectives

Objectives for the Network+ Exam:

➤ Specify the main features of 802.2 (LLC), 802.3 (Ethernet), 802.5 (Token Ring), 802.11b (wireless), and FDDI networking technologies, including speed, access, method, topology, and media

➤ Identify the purpose, features, and functions of the following network components: hubs, switches, bridges, routers, gateways, CSU/DSU, network interface cards/ISDN adapters/system area network cards, wireless access points, modems

Review Questions

1. In which of the following ways does a wireless LAN differ from an Ethernet LAN?

   a. A wireless LAN requires additional protocols in the TCP/IP suite.

   b. A wireless LAN uses completely different protocols than an Ethernet LAN.

   c. A wireless LAN uses different techniques at the Physical layer to transmit data.

   d. A wireless LAN uses different techniques at the Data Link layer to transmit frames.

2. Which of the following are potential disadvantages of wireless LANs as compared to cabled LANs? (Choose all that apply.)

   a. Controlling access to a wireless LAN is more difficult.

   b. Issues such as the location of buildings and the weather may affect connectivity to a wireless LAN.

   c. The additional protocols required by wireless LANs creates additional overhead.

   d. Signal strength may be affected by many sources of electronic noise.

3. How is a wireless NIC different from a NIC that requires a cable?

   a. A wireless NIC contains an antenna.

   b. A wireless NIC contains a chip, which does additional processing at higher levels of the OSI model.

   c. A wireless NIC requires an external power source.

   d. A wireless NIC requires an external antenna.

3

4. You have been hired as a network consultant by the East Coast Savings bank. East Coast Savings would like to implement a wireless LAN, but with high standards of security. What sort of restrictions would you recommend placing on the wireless LAN?

   a. Wireless LAN users have the same access as users attached to the Ethernet network.

   b. Wireless LAN users may surf the Web, but may not access the rest of the bank's network.

   c. Wireless LAN users may surf the Web, but may not access the rest of the bank's network without special security software.

   d. Wireless LAN users must use their own wireless ISP.

5. Why is a wireless signal susceptible to noise?

   a. Wireless NICs are usually poorly made.

   b. Wireless transmissions cannot be shielded like transmissions along an Ethernet cable.

   c. Wireless NICs do not support the network protocols necessary for error correction.

   d. Wireless NICs rely on the upper levels of the OSI model for error correction.

4

NETWORK PROTOCOLS

Labs included in this chapter

► Lab 4.1 Configuring IP Addresses and Subnet Masks

► Lab 4.2 Installing Additional Network Protocols

► Lab 4.3 Automatically Assigning IP Addresses with DHCP

► Lab 4.4 Changing the Binding Order on a Multiprotocol Network

► Lab 4.5 Disabling Unnecessary Protocols

Net+ Exam Objectives	
Objective	**Lab**
Identify IP addresses (IPv4, IPv6) and their default subnet masks	4.1, 4.3
Define the purpose, function, and/or use of the following protocols within TCP/IP: IP, TCP, UDP, FTP, TFTP, SMTP, HTTP, HTTPS, POP3/IMAP4,TELNET, ICMP, ARP, NTP	4.1, 4.3
Differentiate between the following network protocols in terms of routing, addressing schemes, interoperability, and naming conventions: TCP/IP, IPX/SPX, NetBEUI, and AppleTalk	4.4, 4.5
Given a network configuration, select the appropriate NIC and network configuration settings (DHCP, DNS, WINS, protocols, NETBIOS/hostname, etc.)	4.1, 4.2

LAB 4.1 CONFIGURING IP ADDRESSES AND SUBNET MASKS

Objectives

In order to address a TCP/IP host properly, you need both an IP address and a subnet mask. The subnet mask is used to further divide a network. This allows a network administrator to control access or traffic between two sub-networks (or subnets). A router is required to route network traffic between the two subnets. For instance, you might wish to prevent users from directly accessing a Web server. If you put the users and the Web server on different subnets, you can then use a router to control user access to the Web server.

An IP address consists of four numbers separated by dots. Each individual number in the address is called an octet. For instance, in the IP address 10.172.11.145, the first octet is 10, the second octet is 172, and so on. IP addresses have traditionally been divided into classes based on the first octet. The first octet of Class A addresses is between 1 and 126, the first octet of Class B addresses is between 128 and 191, and the first octet of Class C addresses is between 191 and 223. Addresses whose first octet is 127 or 224 and above are reserved.

Subnet masks can be used to conserve IP addresses. The size of a subnet mask determines the number of hosts that can be placed on a network. Using subnet masks, you can allocate IP address blocks that fit the number of hosts you have. The default subnet mask of a Class B network is 255.255.0.0, and it can have up to 65,534 hosts. A Class A network has a default subnet mask of 255.0.0.0, and it can have up to 16,777,214 hosts. Without subnetting, you would be unable to divide these very large networks into smaller networks. With subnetting, you can carve a larger network into many different subnets. For instance, suppose you were assigned a Class B network. If you subdivided this network into smaller networks with subnet masks of 255.255.255.0 (the default subnet mask for Class C networks), you would be able to divide the Class B network into 256 smaller networks.

After completing this lab, you will be able to:

➤ Configure IP addresses and subnet masks on Windows XP, both configured as members of the NETPLUS workgroup

➤ Discuss the purpose of subnet masks

Materials Required

This lab will require the following:

➤ Two computers running Microsoft Windows XP, both configured as members of the NETPLUS workgroup

➤ Access to each computer as the Administrator

➤ Both computers connected to a hub with Category 5 (or better) UTP cables

Estimated completion time: **20 minutes**

LAB ACTIVITY

ACTIVITY

1. On one of the computers, press **Ctrl+Alt+Del** to display the Log On to Windows dialog box. Log on to the computer as the Administrator. The Windows XP desktop appears. Repeat with the other computer.

2. On one computer, click **Start**, then click **Control Panel**. Click **Network** and **Internet Connections**, and then click **My Network Places**. The My Network Places window opens.

3. Click **View network connections**.

4. Right-click **Local Area Connection** and select **Properties** from the pop-up menu. The Local Area Connection Properties window opens.

5. Double-click **Internet Protocol (TCP/IP)**. The Internet Protocol (TCP/IP) Properties dialog box opens.

6. Click the **Use the following IP address** option button.

7. Enter **172.20.1.1** in the IP address text box.

8. Enter **255.255.255.0** in the Subnet mask text box. See Figure 4-1.

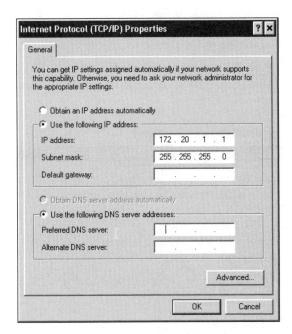

Figure 4-1 Internet Protocol (TCP/IP) Properties dialog box

9. Click **OK** twice. The Local Area Connection Properties window closes.

10. Now you will configure the second computer in a different network. Repeat Steps 2 through 9 on the second computer, using 172.20.2.1 as the IP address and 255.255.255.0 as the subnet mask. Table 4-1 shows the IP addresses and subnet masks on each computer.

Table 4-1   IP address and subnet mask assignments in different networks

Computer	IP address	Subnet mask
First computer	172.20.1.1	255.255.255.0
Second computer	172.20.2.1	255.255.255.0

11. You now have configured the two computers on two different subnets. To demonstrate this, on the second computer click **Start**, then click **Run**. The Run dialog box opens.

12. Type **cmd** and press **Enter**. A command prompt window opens.

13. In the command prompt window, type **ping 172.20.1.1** and press **Enter**. You see a message indicating that the remote computer is unreachable. The message appears on the screen four times.

14. Repeat Steps 11 through 13 on the first computer, attempting to ping 172.20.2.1.

15. Now you will change the subnet mask so that both computers are on the same network. Repeat Steps 2 through 9 on the first computer, keeping the IP address the same but changing the subnet mask to 255.255.0.0.

16. Repeat Steps 2 through 9 on the second computer, keeping the IP address the same but changing the subnet mask to 255.255.0.0. Table 4-2 summarizes the new IP address assignments for the network.

Table 4-2   New IP address assignments in the same network

Computer	IP address	Subnet mask
First computer	172.20.1.1	255.255.0.0
Second computer	172.20.2.1	255.255.0.0

17. Repeat Steps 11 through 13 on the second computer, attempting to ping 172.20.1.1. The computer receives four replies, indicating that there is network connectivity between the two computers.

18. Repeat Steps 11 through 13 on the first computer, attempting to ping 172.20.2.1.

19. Log off both computers.

Certification Objectives

Objectives for the Network+ Exam:

➤ Identify IP addresses (IPv4, IPv6) and their default subnet masks

➤ Define the purpose, function, and/or use of the following protocols within TCP/IP: IP, TCP, UDP, FTP, TFTP, SMTP, HTTP, HTTPS, POP3/IMAP4, TELNET, ICMP, ARP, NTP

➤ Given a network configuration, select the appropriate NIC and network configuration settings (DHCP, DNS, WINS, protocols, NETBIOS/host name, etc.)

Review Questions

1. What is the class of network that you configured as shown in Table 4-1?
   a. Class A
   b. Class B
   c. Class C
   d. Class D

2. What is the purpose of a subnet mask?
   a. to indicate which protocols a particular network uses
   b. to further subdivide a network
   c. to mask, or prevent access to, portions of a network
   d. to limit the protocols used in a particular network

3. A network has a subnet mask of 255.255.255.0. How many usable IP addresses can this network contain?
   a. 65,535
   b. 65,534
   c. 256
   d. 254

4. Assuming that it has the default subnet mask, why can't you assign the IP address 192.168.54.255 to a host?
   a. This address is reserved for multicast.
   b. This address is reserved for experimental uses.
   c. This address describes the network.
   d. This address is the broadcast address.

5. Which of the following commands can you use in Windows to display information about the subnet mask configured for a particular NIC?
   a. ipconfig
   b. ping
   c. cmd
   d. netstat

6. You are a network consultant working for a small sporting goods company. The company would like to restrict access to its accounting server by implementing traffic filtering. What is one step required to accomplish this?

   a. Place the server on the same subnet as user workstations.

   b. Implement traffic filtering on both the server and user workstations.

   c. Place the server on a different subnet from user workstations.

   d. Place a switch between the server and user workstations.

LAB 4.2 INSTALLING ADDITIONAL NETWORK PROTOCOLS

Objectives

Typically, a network administrator tries to minimize the number of network protocols used in a network. Additional network protocols can create additional network overhead. Furthermore, it's necessary to configure servers, clients, and network devices for each additional protocol, and to manage addressing for each protocol.

However, it is not always possible to use just one network protocol. Many legacy applications do not support TCP/IP. For instance, many mainframe applications support only SNA. You may need to configure SNA support in order for your users to employ such applications. The difficulty of implementing an additional network protocol will depend on the specific protocol and the complexity of the network. In this lab, you will configure IPX/SPX for two computers. In a simple network such as the one in this lab, little additional configuration is required.

After completing this lab, you will be able to:

➤   Install additional network protocols for Windows XP Professional and Windows Server 2003 computers

Materials Required

This lab will require the following:

➤   The network required for Lab 1.3

Estimated completion time: **15-20 minutes**

ACTIVITY

1. On the Windows Server 2003 computer, press **Ctrl+Alt+Del**. The Log On to Windows dialog box appears. Log on to the Windows Server 2003 computer as the Administrator. The Windows Server 2003 desktop appears.

2. Click **Start**, point to **Control Panel**, point to **Network Connections**, then click **Local Area Connection**. The Local Area Connection Status window opens.

3. Click **Properties**. The Local Area Connection Properties window opens.

4. Now you will configure the computers so that they cannot communicate through TCP/IP. Double-click **Internet Protocol (TCP/IP)**. The Internet Protocol (TCP/IP) Properties dialog box opens.

5. Make sure that the **Use the following IP address** option button is selected. In both the **IP address** text box and the **Preferred DNS Server** text box, type **1.1.1.1**. If there is an entry in the Default gateway text box, remove it. Click **OK**. Because the two computers no longer have IP addresses on the same network segment, they will be unable to communicate with each other through TCP/IP without the use of a router. (Note that the TCP/IP protocol cannot be removed.)

6. Click **Install**. The Select Network Component Type dialog box opens, as shown in Figure 4-2.

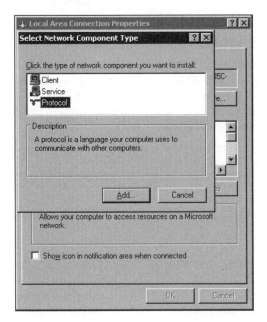

Figure 4-2   Select Network Components dialog box

7. Double-click **Protocol**. The Select Network Protocol dialog box opens.

8. Double-click **NWLink IPX/SPX/NetBIOS Compatible Transport Protocol**. The computer installs the protocol.

9. Click **Close**, and then click **Close** again. The Local Area Connection Status window closes.

10. On the Windows XP computer, press **Ctrl+Alt+Del** to display the Log On to Windows dialog box. Log on as the Administrator of the NETPLUSLAB domain. The Windows XP desktop appears.

11. Click **Start**, then click **My Computer**. The My Computer windows opens. Click **My Network Places**. The My Network Places window opens.

12. Click **Entire Network**. An icon for Microsoft Windows Network appears. Double-click the **Microsoft Windows Network** icon. An icon for netpluslab appears. Double-click **Server 1**. After a few seconds, you see an error message indicating that \\SERVER1\sysvol is not accessible and that the two computers cannot communicate. Click **OK**.

13. Click **View network connections** below the "Network Tasks" heading.

14. Right-click **Local Area Connection** and select **Properties** from the pop-up menu, and then click **Install**. The Select Network Component Type dialog box opens.

15. Double-click **Protocol**. The Select Network Protocol dialog box opens.

16. Double-click **NWLink IPX/SPX/NetBIOS Compatible Transport Protocol**. The computer installs the IPX/SPX protocol.

17. Click **Close**. The Local Area Connection properties window closes.

18. Click **My Network Places**.

19. Click **Entire Network**. An icon for Microsoft Windows Network appears. Double-click the **Microsoft Windows Network** icon. An icon for netpluslab appears. Double-click the **netpluslab** icon. Icons for computers appear, including Server1. Double-click the **Server1** icon.

20. In the **User name** text box, enter **netplus@netpluslab.net**. In the Password text box, enter the password for this account. Click **OK**. The folder opens, indicating that this computer can communicate with the other computer using IPX/SPX.

21. Log off both computers.

Certification Objectives

Objectives for the Network+ Exam:

➤ Given a network configuration, select the appropriate NIC and network configuration settings (DHCP, DNS, WINS, protocols, NETBIOS/host name, etc.)

Review Questions

1. In this lab, what is the most likely explanation for the fact that you did not configure addressing for the IPX/SPX protocol but the two computers were still able to communicate with each other?

    a. No addressing is required for IPX/SPX.

    b. Addressing is always performed automatically for IPX/SPX.

    c. The network number of the address was assigned automatically, and the host portion of an IPX address is the MAC address.

    d. IPX/SPX is not a routable protocol.

2. At which layer of the OSI model does IPX/SPX operate?

    a. Physical

    b. Data Link

    c. Transport

    d. Network

3. Which of the following is a valid TCP/IP address?

    a. 1.1.1.1

    b. EF-34-AA-0B-2A-C6

    c. 543.78.100.92

    d. FF-FF-FF-FF-FF-FF

4. Which of the following is a valid IPX address?

    a. 10.193.207.111

    b. FEED0000:02608C3E97FF

    c. FEEGH00:02608C301290

    d. FEE0.09A1.786A.1108

5. Which of the following are potential disadvantages of using multiple protocols in a network? (Choose all that apply.)

    a. extra overhead

    b. additional client configuration

    c. management of addressing for the new protocol

    d. additional configuration of network devices

6. Which of the following is a valid reason to add an additional protocol to a network?

    a. to ensure that, if one protocol fails, the second protocol will still be valid

    b. to increase the odds that a new client will support at least one protocol

    c. to ensure that clients can communicate with a legacy application

    d. to prevent overuse of the primary network protocol

Lab 4.3 Automatically Assigning IP Addresses with DHCP

Objectives

In this lab you will assign IP addresses to client workstations automatically with a Dynamic Host Configuration Protocol (DHCP) server. DHCP allows you to assign IP addresses from a central location, without having to configure each workstation individually. In all but the smallest networks, this will save you time. You can also configure additional information, such as the default gateway and any DNS or WINS servers to be used.

DHCP works by assigning a pool of IP addresses to a network. When a workstation requests an IP address, the DHCP server assigns one of the available addresses from the pool. Most network administrators do not use DHCP to address their servers, routers, or other network devices. You may find it useful to set aside a range of IP addresses on each network for devices with static IP addresses. Servers and most network devices typically have static IP addresses, and are not often moved. However, you can use DHCP to assign static addresses based on a device's MAC address.

To configure the Windows DHCP server, you create a DHCP scope. Each scope consists of a range of IP addresses to be assigned, addresses to be excluded from the scope, and other information to be assigned to clients. Multiple DHCP scopes are typically used when a DHCP server needs to assign addresses for multiple subnets.

After completing this lab, you will be able to:

➤ Configure the DHCP server on Windows Server 2003

➤ Understand DHCP and dynamic addressing

Materials Required

This lab will require the following:

➤ A computer running Windows Server 2003 Enterprise Edition named *SERVER1*, configured as a DNS server and a domain controller for the netpluslab.net domain, with an IP address of 192.168.54.1 and a subnet mask of 255.255.255.0

➤ Access to the computer as the Administrator

➤ DHCP installed on *SERVER1* but not configured

➤ A computer running Windows XP Professional in the NETPLUSLAB.NET domain, without a specified IP address

➤ Access to the Windows XP computer as the Administrator

➤ Both computers connected to a hub with straight-through Category 5 (or better) UTP cables

Estimated completion time: **30 minutes**

LAB ACTIVITY

ACTIVITY

1. On SERVER1, press **Ctrl+Alt+Del** to display the Log On to Windows dialog box. Log on as the Administrator. The Windows Server 2003 desktop appears.

2. Click **Start**, point to **Administrative Tools**, then click **DHCP**. The DHCP window opens.

3. Click **server1.netpluslab.net[192.168.54.1]** in the left pane of the window. Right-click **server1.netpluslab.net[192.168.54.1]** and select **New Scope** from the pop-up menu. The New Scope Wizard opens.

4. Click **Next**.

5. Enter **Net Plus Lab** in the Name text box. Enter **Test** in the Description text box. Click **Next**.

6. Now you will configure the DHCP server to assign clients IP addresses from 192.168.54.10 to 192.168.54.200. This range allows for servers and network devices with static IP addresses from 192.168.54.1 to 192.168.54.9 and 192.168.54.201 to 192.168.54.254. In the Start IP address text box, enter **192.168.54.10**. In the End IP address text box, enter **192.168.54.200**. In the Subnet mask text box, enter **255.255.255.0**, if necessary. Click **Next**. Figure 4-3 shows the New Scope Wizard.

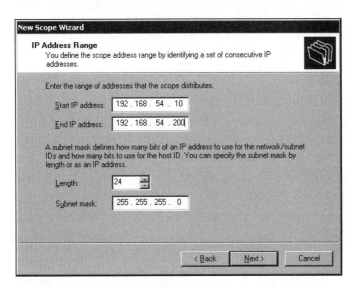

Figure 4-3 New Scope Wizard

7. Now you will exclude the IP address 192.168.54.100 from the DHCP scope. In the Start IP address text box, enter **192.168.54.100**. This allows you to reserve static IP addresses for existing servers or network devices in the middle of the range of IP addresses to be used for the DHCP scope. Click **Add**. The computer excludes the address from the DHCP scope. Click **Next**.

8. Now you can assign the amount of time that a client can use an IP address assigned to it from the DHCP server before it needs to renew it. Enter **10** in the Days text box. Click **Next**.

9. Now you have the opportunity to configure further options. Click the **Yes, I want to configure these options now** option button. Click **Next**.

10. Now you can specify the default gateway used by clients. Click **Next**, as this network has no default gateway.

11. Now you can specify information about domain name resolution for clients. In the Parent domain text box, enter **netpluslab.net**. In the IP address text box, enter **192.168.54.1** and press **Add**. Clients will now use this server as their DNS server. Click **Next**.

12. In this window you can specify WINS servers. Click **Next**.

13. Now you must activate the DHCP scope. Make sure that the **Yes, I want to activate this scope now** option button is selected and click **Next**. Click **Finish**.

14. Note that the server1.netpluslab.net[192.168.54.1] icon is a white circle with a red arrow in the center. Right-click **server1.netpluslab.net[192.168.54.1]** in the left pane, and select **Authorize** from the pop-up menu. Wait a few seconds and press **F5**. If the server1.netpluslab.net[192.168.54.1] icon in the left pane is not a white circle with a green arrow in the center, click **F5** every few seconds until it is. A green arrow indicates that the scope is active, while a red arrow indicates that it is not. The DHCP server is now authorized to assign IP addresses in the netpluslab.net domain.

15. On the Windows XP computer, press **Ctrl+Alt+Del**. The Log On to Windows dialog box appears. Log on as the Administrator. The Windows XP desktop appears.

16. Click **Start**, then click **My Computer**. The My Computer windows opens. Click **My Network Places**. The My Network Places window opens.

17. Click **View network connections** below the "Network Tasks" heading.

18. Right-click the **Local Area Connection** icon, and select **Properties** from the pop-up menu. The Local Area Connection window opens.

19. Double-click **Internet Protocol (TCP/IP)**. The Internet Protocol (TCP/IP) Properties dialog box opens.

4

20. Click the **Obtain an IP address automatically** and the **Obtain DNS server address automatically** option buttons. Click **OK**, then click **OK** again to close the Local Area Connection Properties window.

21. Click **Start**, then click **Run**. The Run dialog box opens.

22. Type **cmd** and then press **Enter**. A command prompt window opens.

23. Type **ipconfig** and press **Enter**. What is the current IP address of this computer?

24. Type **ipconfig /release** and press **Enter**. The computer releases any current address assigned by DHCP.

25. Type **ipconfig /renew** and press **Enter**. The computer obtains an IP address from the DHCP server, and prints it. What is the new IP address?

26. Type **ipconfig /all** and press **Enter**. Record the name or address of the DNS server, the DHCP server, and the time the DHCP lease expires.

27. Log off both computers.

Certification Objectives

Objectives for the Network+ Exam:

➤ Identify IP addresses (IPv4, IPv6) and their default subnet masks

➤ Define the purpose, function, and/or use of the following protocols within TCP/IP: IP, TCP, UDP, FTP, TFTP, SMTP, HTTP, HTTPS, POP3/IMAP4, TELNET, ICMP, ARP, NTP

Review Questions

1. What was the IP address the Windows XP computer obtained in Step 25?

2. When does the DHCP lease you obtained in this lab expire?

3. Which of the following are valid methods of assigning IP addresses to workstations, servers and network devices? (Choose all that apply.)

   a. manual configuration

   b. DHCP

   c. BOOTP

   d. POST

4. You would like to assign a WINS server to each workstation. Can you accomplish this via DHCP?

5. Your colleague placed a second DHCP server on the network by mistake. What might happen as a result? (Choose all that apply.)

    a. The second DHCP server might lease duplicate addresses to some hosts.

    b. The second DHCP server might give out incorrect settings to its clients.

    c. DHCP may stop working on the first DHCP server.

    d. You may need to configure IP addresses on some hosts manually.

6. Which of the following information could not be given out by a DHCP server?

    a. WINS server address

    b. DNS server address

    c. default gateway

    d. additional network protocols to be used

LAB 4.4 CHANGING THE BINDING ORDER ON A MULTIPROTOCOL NETWORK

Objectives

The process of associating a network protocol with a NIC is called binding. For Windows computers on multiprotocol networks, the order in which a protocol is bound to a NIC determines how each computer will communicate with other devices. Windows maintains a list of the protocols bound to each NIC. Each computer sending information over the network will attempt to use the first protocol in the list first. If this fails, it will attempt to use the second, and so on. Windows also maintains a list of the types of the network providers that can be accessed by the computer for each network client used by the computer.

Binding order can affect network performance. For instance, suppose that TCP/IP is the most commonly used protocol on a network (which will be the case in many if not most networks). If each computer attempts to use IPX/SPX first and fails, it will take each computer longer to use network services. In most cases, the protocol that is used most often should be bound to the NIC first, so that it is used first. Adjusting the network provider order can also affect network performance. The network provider order determines the order in which network clients will be used to access network resources.

After completing this lab, you will be able to:

➤ Change the protocol binding order and the network provider order on Microsoft Windows XP and Server 2003 computers

➤ Discuss how the binding order affects network performance

Materials Required

This lab will require the following:

➤ The network configured at the end of Lab 4.2

➤ Internet Protocol (TCP/IP) at the bottom of the binding order and Microsoft Windows Network in the middle of the provider order (which is the default after NWLink IPX/SPX/NetBIOS Compatible Transport Protocol has been installed)

4

Estimated completion time: **30 minutes**

LAB ACTIVITY

ACTIVITY

1. On the Windows XP computer, press **Ctrl+Alt+Del**. The Log On to Windows dialog box appears. Log on as the Administrator. The Windows XP desktop appears.

2. Click **Start**, point to **All Programs**, point to **Accessories**, point to **Communications**, then click **Network Connections**. The Network Connections window opens.

3. On the menu bar, click **Advanced**, then click **Advanced Settings**. The Advanced Settings window opens. See Figure 4-4.

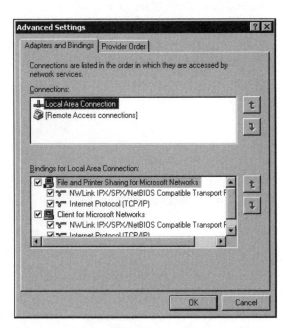

Figure 4-4   Advanced Settings window

4. The computer lists the network protocol bindings used by the computer for each network client used. What are the protocols bound to this computer's NIC, and in which order will Windows use them? Below the "File and Printer Sharing for Microsoft Networks" heading, click **Internet Protocol (TCP/IP)**. The up arrow on the right becomes green. Click the up arrow until Internet Protocol (TCP/IP) moves up to first in the binding order.

5. Below the "Client for Microsoft Networks" heading, scroll down if necessary and click **Internet Protocol (TCP/IP)** to highlight it. The up arrow on the right becomes green. Click the up arrow until Internet Protocol (TCP/IP) moves up to first place in the binding order.

6. Click the **Provider Order** tab.

7. Below "Network Providers," select **Microsoft Windows Network**. The up arrow on the right becomes green. Click the up arrow until Microsoft Windows Network moves up to first place in the binding order.

8. Click **OK** to close the Advanced Settings window. You have finished changing the binding order and the network provider order on the Windows XP computer.

9. On the Windows Server 2003 computer, press **Ctrl+Alt+Del** to display on the Log On to Windows dialog box. Log on as the Administrator. The Windows Server 2003 desktop appears.

10. Click **Start**, point to **Control Panel**, point to **Network Connections**, and right-click **Network Connections** in the Start menu. Select **Open** from the pop-up menu. The Network Connections window opens.

11. Repeat Steps 3 through 8 on the Windows Server 2003 computer. You have finished changing the binding order and the network provider order on a Windows Server 2003 computer.

12. Log off both computers.

Certification Objectives

Objectives for the Network+ Exam:

➤ Differentiate between the following network protocols in terms of routing, addressing schemes, interoperability, and naming conventions: TCP/IP, IPX/SPX, NetBEUI, and AppleTalk

Review Questions

1. Which network protocols did you see on the two computers, and in what order were they originally bound?

2. Suppose you are running both IPX/SPX and TCP/IP on a network that relies on a Windows Server 2003 computer to supply users with applications and data sharing space and a NetWare 4.11 server to manage a tape backup device. List the best binding order for the Windows Server 2003 computer.

3. For which of the following network components is binding order a factor in performance? (Choose all that apply.)

    a. workstation

    b. server

    c. hub

    d. switch

4. You have configured a Windows Server 2003 computer with TCP/IP and NetBEUI. TCP/IP is second in the binding order. What will happen to a TCP/IP packet that is sent to the computer's NIC?

    a. The packet will be rejected because TCP/IP is second in the binding order.

    b. The computer will process the packet immediately using TCP/IP.

    c. The computer will attempt to process the packet with NetBEUI, then with TCP/IP.

    d. The computer will process the packet immediately using NetBEUI.

5. Which binding policy will optimize performance on a Windows-based network?

    a. The most frequently used network interface cards should be at the top of the order.

    b. The most infrequently used interfaces should be at the top of the order.

    c. The most frequently used protocols should be at the top of the order.

    d. Binding order does not affect performance on a Windows-based network.

Lab 4.5 Disabling Unnecessary Protocols

Objectives

The goal of this lab is to help you learn how to disable protocols that are not being used. You will often be able to configure multiple network clients to use only one or two network protocols. Disabling or removing a protocol will reduce network traffic and the load on your servers. On a computer with multiple NICs, you may find it useful to disable a protocol on one network interface card and leave it enabled on another. The clients on the network attached to one NIC might need that protocol, while the clients on the network attached to the other NIC do not.

After completing this lab, you will be able to:

➤ Disable unnecessary protocols

Materials Required

This lab will require the following:

➤ The network required for Lab 4.4

Estimated completion time: **15-20 minutes**

LAB ACTIVITY

ACTIVITY

1. On the Windows XP computer, press **Ctrl+Alt+Del**. The Log On to Windows dialog box appears. Log on to the Windows XP computer as the Administrator. The Windows XP desktop appears.

2. Click **Start**, point to **All Programs**, point to **Accessories**, point to **Communications**, and click **Network Connections**. The Network Connections window opens.

3. Right-click the **Local Area Connection** icon and select **Properties** from the pop-up menu. The Local Area Connection Properties window opens.

4. Click **NWLink IPX/SPX/NetBIOS Compatible Transport Protocol** to highlight it.

5. Click **Uninstall**. A dialog box opens, indicating that uninstalling a network component removes it from all network connections. Figure 4-5 shows the process of uninstalling a network protocol.

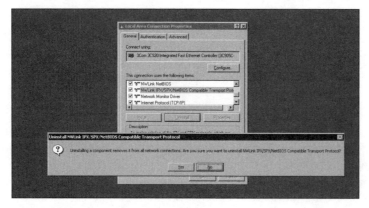

Figure 4-5   Uninstalling a protocol

6. Click **Yes** to remove the protocol. The computer removes NWLink IPX/ SPX/NetBIOS Compatible Transport Protocol and NWLink NetBIOS. The Local Network dialog box opens, indicating that you must shut down the computer before the changes will take effect.

7. Click **Yes**. The computer reboots.

8. On the Windows Server 2003 computer, press **Ctrl+Alt+Del** to display the Log On to Windows dialog box. Log on as the Administrator. The Windows Server 2003 desktop appears.

9. Click **Start**, point to **Control Panel**, point to **Network Connections**, then click **Local Area Connection**. The Local Area Connection Status window opens.

10. Click the **Properties** button. The Local Area Connection Properties window opens.

11. Repeat Steps 4 through 7. You have successfully removed the IPX/SPX protocol from the Windows Server 2003 computer.

12. Log off both computers.

Certification Objectives

Objectives for the Network+ Exam:

➤ Differentiate between the following network protocols in terms of routing, addressing schemes, interoperability, and naming conventions: TCP/IP, IPX/SPX, NetBEUI, and AppleTalk

Review Questions

1. True or False? It is prudent to install and bind all four major protocol suites on your server, regardless of whether they are going to be used.

2. Why would a network administrator choose to disable one of two network interface cards on a server?

   a. because it is infrequently used

   b. because it is faulty

   c. because it is not as fast as the other

   d. because it is incapable of handling certain protocols

3. A computer uses both the IPX/SPX and TCP/IP protocols. Which of the following would be true if IPX/SPX were disabled?

   a. Clients would not be able to access the server's resources via IPX/SPX.

   b. Clients would not be able to access the server at all.

   c. Only those clients running TCP/IP would be able to access the server's resources.

   d. Clients would be able to access the server's resources via both TCP/IP and IPX/SPX, but TCP/IP-based services would be slower.

4. Why would a network administrator choose to unbind a protocol on a server?

   a. because it is only occasionally used, and as long as it remains bound it is using server resources

   b. because it is no longer used, and as long as it remains bound it is using server resources

   c. because it is interfering with traffic using other protocols

   d. because it has proven to be unstable with certain applications

5. Besides TCP/IP, what must be bound to a client's NIC before the client can log on to a Windows Server 2003 server?

   a. Client for Microsoft Networks

   b. Gateway Services for NetWare

   c. IPX/SPX

   d. NWLink

6. Why is NetBEUI not routable?

   a. because it does not contain a subprotocol at the Application layer of the OSI model

   b. because it does not contain Network layer addressing information

   c. because it is incompatible with modern routing techniques

   d. because its data frames are too large and slow to be practically routed

NETWORKING HARDWARE

Labs included in this chapter

➤ Lab 5.1 Configuring Transmission and Duplex Settings

➤ Lab 5.2 Creating a Multi-homed Computer by Installing Two NICs

➤ Lab 5.3 Activating Routing and Remote Access in Windows Server 2003

➤ Lab 5.4 Activating a Routing Protocol in Windows Server 2003

➤ Lab 5.5 Configuring a Simple Firewall

Net+ Exam Objectives	
Objective	**Lab**
Identify the purpose, features, and functions of the following network components: hubs, switches, bridges, routers, gateways, CSU/DSU, network interface cards, wireless access points, modems	5.1, 5.2, 5.3, 5.4
Identify the OSI layers at which the following network components operate: hubs, switches, bridges, routers, network interface cards	5.2, 5.3
Given a network configuration, select the appropriate NIC and network configuration settings (DHCP, DNS, WINS, protocols, NetBIOS/host name, etc.)	5.2, 5.3
Given output from a diagnostic utility (e.g., Tracert, Ping, Ipconfig, etc.), identify the utility and interpret the output	5.1, 5.3, 5.4
Identify the purpose, benefits, and characteristics of using a firewall	5.5
Specify the main features of 802.2 (LLC), 802.3 (Ethernet), 802.5 (Token Ring), 802.11b (wireless) and FDDI networking technologies, including Speed, Access, Method, Topology, Media	5.1

Lab 5.1 Configuring Transmission and Duplex Settings

Objectives

On Ethernet networks, duplex and transmission settings are perhaps the most important settings for a NIC, aside from the network address. Ordinarily these settings are configured automatically through the process of autonegotiation with attached switches. However, autonegotiation sometimes results in incorrect settings. A NIC whose transmission speed is set incorrectly will not operate at the correct speed. Duplex mismatches are a common source of errors on Ethernet networks, and may force a computer to retransmit large numbers of frames because of collisions. Depending on traffic and the settings on the computer and the switch or hub, a duplex mismatch may or may not be easily noticed.

Typically duplex and transmission settings are most important on servers. Compared to a workstation, a server is less likely to be moved, more likely to require high throughput, and more likely to be connected to a switch. Additionally, checking duplex and transmission settings on workstations requires more work, as an organization is likely to have fewer servers.

After completing this lab, you will be able to:

➤ Examine and configure transmission and duplex settings on a NIC

Materials Required

This lab will require the following:

➤ A computer running Windows Server 2003 Enterprise Edition with at least one 10/100 NIC configured with an IP address of 192.168.54.1 and a subnet mask of 255.255.255.0

➤ Access to the computer as an Administrator

➤ A computer running Windows XP Professional with a 10/100 NIC configured with an IP address of 192.168.54.2 and a subnet mask of 255.255.255.0

➤ Drivers for the NIC installed on the Windows Server 2003 computer allowing configuration of speed and duplex settings, and knowledge of the settings for a 100-Mbps full duplex connection; to find out, click Start, point to Control Panel, point to Network Connections, then click Local Area Connection; from the Local Area Connection Status dialog box, click Properties; from the Local Area Connection Properties window, click Configure, then click the Advanced tab; look for Media Type, Link Speed & Duplex or a similar option

➤ A 10/100 Ethernet hub and the straight-through CAT 5 UTP cables required to connect the two computers to the hub

Estimated completion time: **45 minutes**

LAB ACTIVITY

ACTIVITY

1. Plug one end of each cable into the hub. Plug the other end of each cable into one of the computers.

2. On the Windows Server 2003 computer, press **Ctrl+Alt+Del** to open the Log On to Windows dialog box. Log on as the Administrator. The Windows Server 2003 desktop appears.

3. Click **Start**, point to **Control Panel**, point to **Network Connections**, and click **Local Area Connection**. The Local Area Connection Status dialog box opens.

4. Click **Properties**. The Local Area Connection Properties dialog box opens.

5. Click **Configure** under the name of the network card. The Properties dialog box for the NIC opens.

6. Click the **Advanced** tab. The Advanced tab opens. Figure 5-1 shows the Properties dialog box for a typical NIC.

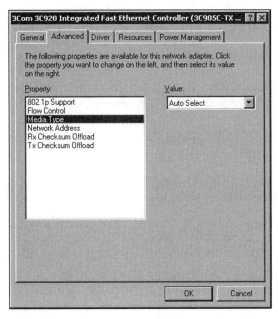

Figure 5-1   Properties dialog box for a typical NIC

7. The precise options may vary depending on the driver for the network card. Select **Media Type**, **Link Speed & Duplex** or the option indicated by your instructor in the Property box. Record the current value for this option. (While it will vary depending on the NIC driver used, typically it will be Auto Select or Auto Detect.)

8. In the Value drop-down menu, select **100 Mbps Full–Duplex** or the equivalent option as indicated by your instructor. Click **OK**. The Properties dialog box closes. If the Local Area Connection Status dialog box also closes, go to Step 10.

9. Click **OK** to close the Local Area Connection Properties dialog box, and then click **Close**.

10. Click **Start**, point to **All Programs**, point to **Accessories**, then click **Command Prompt**. A command prompt window opens.

11. Type **ping 192.168.54.2** and press **Enter**. The computer indicates that it has received four replies from the remote computer. Do you see any red error lights on the hub? (You may not, because this network will not have a lot of traffic.)

12. Repeat Steps 3 through 9. When you repeat Step 8, use the value that you recorded in Step 7 instead of 100 Mbps Full–Duplex.

13. Log off the computer.

Certification Objectives

Objectives for the Network+ Exam:

➤ Identify the purpose, features, and functions of the following network components: hubs, switches, bridges, routers, gateways, CSU/DSU, network interface cards, wireless access points, modems

➤ Given output from a diagnostic utility (e.g., Tracert, Ping, Ipconfig, etc.), identify the utility and interpret the output

➤ Specify the main features of 802.2 (LLC), 802.3 (Ethernet), 802.5 (Token Ring), 802.11b (wireless) and FDDI networking technologies, including Speed, Access, Method, Topology, Media

Review Questions

1. What effect might an incorrect duplex setting have on a NIC? (Choose all that apply.)

    a. errors

    b. collisions

    c. retransmitted frames

    d. incorrect theoretical transmission speed

2. In the same dialog box in which you configured transmission speed and duplex settings, it is also possible to change the physical address of a NIC. What might happen if you were to do so?

    a. No devices could connect to that NIC because of its new physical address.

    b. TCP/IP communication would be normal immediately after the change.

    c. IPX/SPX communication would be normal after the ARP cache entries on other hosts timed out.

    d. TCP/IP communication would be normal after the ARP cache entries on other hosts timed out.

3. True or False? Changing the duplex setting on a NIC is the same as changing its physical address.

4. You have just attached a server to a new network. However, the server's throughput is lower than expected. Why might this be? (Select all that apply.)

    a. The server is running the wrong routing protocol.

    b. The server's duplex setting is incorrect, and many frames are retransmitted.

    c. The server's transmission speed setting is incorrect.

    d. The server's NIC's physical address is incorrectly configured.

5. What effect do duplex settings have on a server's routing protocols?

    a. None, the routing protocols operate at the Transport Layer.

    b. None, the routing protocols operate at the Network Layer.

    c. Mismatched duplex settings cause collisions and retransmissions.

    d. Mismatched duplex settings cause TCP/IP to fail altogether.

LAB 5.2 CREATING A MULTI-HOMED COMPUTER BY INSTALLING TWO NICS

Objectives

Network adapters (also called network interface cards, or NICs) are connectivity devices that enable a workstation, server, printer, or other node to receive and transmit data over the network media. In most modern network devices, NICs contain the data transceiver, which is the device that transmits and receives data signals.

NICs operate at both the Physical layer and Data Link layer of the OSI model, because they apply data signals to the wire and assemble or disassemble data frames. They do not, however, analyze the data from higher layers. A router, on the other hand, operates at the Network layer of the OSI model and can interpret higher-layer logical addressing information.

In this lab, you will perform the first step in creating a multi-homed computer consisting of a single computer with two NICs. A multi-homed computer has more than one NIC. Multi-homed computers called routers are used to interconnect dissimilar networks; the presence of two NICs in a computer allows that computer to connect to two different networks. Other types of networks may be connected by using different types of interfaces.

After completing this lab, you will be able to:Physically install NICsMake a multi-homed computer using two NICsConfigure TCP/IP properties on NICs

Materials Required

This lab will require the following:

➤ A computer running Windows Server 2003 Enterprise Edition named *SERVER1* without any NICs installed

➤ At least two PCI bus slots available on the Windows Server 2003 computer

➤ Access to the Windows Server 2003 computer as an Administrator

➤ Two Ethernet PCI NICs with RJ-45 connectors listed on the Windows Server Catalog hardware compatibility list (HCL); at the time of this writing, you can find the Windows Server Catalog by connecting to the Internet and pointing your browser to the following URL: *http://www.microsoft.com/windows/server/catalog*

➤ Two Ethernet hubs compatible with the NICs

➤ Two straight-through CAT 5 (or better) UTP cables

➤ A toolkit with a Phillips-head screwdriver, a ground mat, and a ground strap

---

Estimated completion time: **60 minutes**

LAB ACTIVITY

ACTIVITY

1. Power off the computer.

2. Unplug the power cord from the computer, then place the computer on the ground mat.

3. Place the ground strap on your wrist and attach it to the ground mat underneath the computer.

4. Remove any screws from the computer's case.

5. Remove the computer case.

6. Choose a vacant PCI slot on the system board where you will insert the NIC. Remove the metal slot cover from the slot you will use.

7. Place the NIC in the slot, pushing it firmly and straight down into place.

8. Attach the NIC to the system unit with the Phillips-head screwdriver. This will secure the NIC in place.

9. Replace the cover.

10. Reinsert the screws on the cover.

11. Connect one end of one cable to the NIC. Connect the other end of the same cable to one of the hubs.

12. Plug in the computer and turn it on. Plug in the hub. Link lights on both the hub and the back of the NIC turn green. On some NICs, there may also be a yellow light, or a flashing yellow light. If the link lights do not illuminate, verify that the cables are connected properly.

13. After the Windows Server 2003 computer is running, look at the lights on the NIC and at the port lights on the hub. They should be on. If they are not on, check the cabling. You may also need to turn off the computer, unplug it, and verify that the NIC is firmly seated inside the computer.

14. Press **Ctrl+Alt+Del**. The Log On to Windows dialog box appears. Log onto the server as the Administrator. The Windows Server 2003 desktop appears, and a dialog box indicating that Windows Server 2003 has discovered new hardware opens briefly. A wizard may open, attempting to install new hardware. If so, click **Cancel** to close the wizard.

15. Click **Start**, point to **Control Panel**, point to **Network Connections**, then click **Local Area Connection**. The Local Area Connection Status dialog box opens.

16. Click the **Properties** button. The Local Area Connection Properties dialog box opens.

17. Double-click **Internet Protocol (TCP/IP)**. The Internet Protocol (TCP/IP) Properties dialog box opens.

18. Select the **Use the following IP address** option button. The IP Address, Subnet mask, and Default gateway text boxes are highlighted.

19. In the IP Address text box, type **172.16.1.1**.

20. In the Subnet mask text box, type **255.255.255.0**.

21. Leave the Default gateway text box blank.

22. Click **OK**. A dialog box may appear, indicating that the DNS server list is empty and that the computer will configure itself as the DNS server. If so, click **OK** again. You return to the Local Area Connection Properties dialog box.

23. Click **OK** again to close the Local Area Connection Properties dialog box. You return to the Local Area Connection Status dialog box.

24. Click **Close** to close the Local Area Connection Status dialog box.

25. Repeat Steps 1 through 24 with the second NIC. The second NIC should appear as Local Area Connection 2. In Step 19, use an IP address of 192.168.54.1. You have now built a multi-homed computer. You will finish making this computer a router in Lab 5.3.

26. Log off the computer.

Certification Objectives

Objectives for the Network+ Exam:

➤ Identify the purpose, features, and functions of the following network components: hubs, switches, bridges, routers, gateways, CSU/DSU, network interface cards, wireless access points, modems

➤ Identify the OSI layers at which the following network components operate: hubs, switches, bridges, routers, network interface cards

➤ Given a network configuration, select the appropriate NIC and network configuration settings (DHCP, DNS, WINS, protocols, NetBIOS/host name, etc.)

Review Questions

1. Which of the following devices operates at the Physical layer of the OSI model? (Choose all that apply.)
    a. NIC
    b. hub
    c. bridge
    d. router

2. What type of address does a router interpret?
    a. physical address
    b. MAC address
    c. Block ID
    d. network address

3. Which of the following connectivity devices takes the most time to interpret the data frames it receives?

    a. hub

    b. bridge

    c. MAU

    d. router

4. On a typical 100BaseT network, where would you find transceivers?

    a. in the NICs

    b. in the operating systems

    c. in the UPSs

    d. in cabling

5. Which of the following is a difference between a router and a hub?

    a. A router is less sophisticated than a hub.

    b. A router operates at the Transport layer of the OSI model, while a hub operates at the Data Link layer of the OSI model.

    c. A router operates at the Network layer of the OSI model, while a hub operates at the Physical layer of the OSI model.

    d. A router regenerates signals, while a hub interprets addressing information to ensure that data are directed to their proper destination.

6. In which of the following networking scenarios would a router be the optimal connectivity device?

    a. a home network with five users who want to share documents that are stored on one of the five workstations

    b. a WAN that connects a college physics department with a classroom in a high school on the other side of town

    c. a LAN that connects 10 users, a server, and a printer at a small business

    d. a peer-to-peer LAN that connects eight users to provide a shared database

7. What is the most likely purpose of the hubs in this lab?

    a. to connect the computer to different networks

    b. to determine by checking the link lights whether or not the NIC has been installed correctly

    c. to determine by checking the link lights whether or not you have configured the IP addresses on the NICs correctly

    d. to allow the NICs to operate at the Network layer

5

Lab 5.3 Activating Routing and Remote Access in Windows Server 2003

Objectives

In this lab, you will configure a multi-homed server to be a simple router, and add a static route to its routing table. When a router receives a packet from a computer or another router, it looks in its routing table to see where it must send the packet. A routing table consists of a list of all the networks the router knows about, and the next hop for each of these networks. Each route consists of a destination network and the next hop where the router should send packets to reach the destination. The next hop may be the IP address of the next router on the path to the destination, or the network interface card closest to it. A router has separate routing tables for each routable protocol (such as TCP/IP or IPX/SPX) it runs.

For instance, suppose a router receives a packet with a destination address of 10.100.17.29. It looks in its routing table for a route that matches this address. It finds the route, and sees that packets for 10.100.17.29 should be sent out to the router at 10.100.17.1. Then it sends the packet to 10.100.17.1.

When the router at 10.100.17.1 receives the packet, it looks at its routing table for a matching route. The matching route tells the router to send the packet out its Ethernet NIC. It sends the packet out its Ethernet NIC, where it is received by the destination computer. In this manner, routers can send packets over long paths consisting of many hops.

In order to fill its routing table, a router must learn the routes it needs to use. One way in which routers learn routes is by looking at the addresses on their own interfaces. Network administrators can also add routes directly into a routing table. Routes configured by a network administrator are known as static routes.

Note that most network administrators will use dedicated routing hardware whenever possible, rather than a software router such as the one you will configure in this lab. Dedicated routing hardware will typically be faster, more stable, and have more features than a software router.

After completing this lab, you will be able to:

➤ Activate and configure Routing and Remote Access on a Windows Server 2003 server

➤ Show the routing table of a Windows Server 2003 server configured as a network router

➤ Add a static route to a Windows Server 2003 server configured as a network router

Materials Required

This lab will require the following:

➤ The network built at the end of Lab 5.2

➤ A computer named *SERVER1* running Windows Server 2003 Enterprise Edition with two NICs

➤ One NIC on the *SERVER1* computer configured with an IP address of 192.168.54.1 and a subnet mask of 255.255.255.0

➤ The other NIC on the *SERVER1* computer configured with an IP address of 172.16.1.1 and a subnet mask of 255.255.255.0

➤ Two computers running Windows XP Professional with NICs compatible with the hubs

➤ One of the Windows XP computers named *WORKSTATION1* and configured with an IP address of 192.168.54.2 and a default gateway of 192.168.54.1

➤ The other Windows XP computer named *WORKSTATION2* and configured with an IP address of 172.16.1.2 and a default gateway of 172.16.1.1

➤ Access to both Windows XP computers as the local Administrator

➤ Two straight-through CAT 5 (or better) UTP cables

Estimated completion time: **75 minutes**

LAB ACTIVITY

ACTIVITY

1. Plug in each NIC in *SERVER1* to one of the hubs. On *SERVER1*, press **Ctrl+Alt+DEL** to display the Log On to Windows dialog box. Log on as the Administrator. The Windows Server 2003 desktop appears.

2. On the Windows Server 2003 computer, click **Start**, point to **Administrative Tools**, and then click **Routing and Remote Access**.

3. In the left pane of the dialog box, click the name of the server to select it. Click **Action**, and then click **Configure and Enable Routing and Remote Access**. The Routing and Remote Access Server Setup Wizard appears.

4. Click **Next**. The Configuration dialog box appears, listing several options for configuring this computer as a router.

5. Select the **Custom configuration** option, and then click **Next**. The Custom Configuration dialog box appears.

6. Click the **LAN routing** check box to place a check in it. Click **Next**.

7. Click **Finish**. The Routing and Remote Access Server Setup Wizard saves your settings and starts the Routing and Remote Access Service.

8. A dialog box opens, indicating that the Routing and Remote Access Service has been installed. Click **Yes** to start the service. A dialog box indicating that the service is initializing appears briefly. Close the Routing and Remote Access dialog box.

9. Plug the RJ-45 connector of one of the CAT 5 cables into one of the hubs. Plug the other end of the cable into the NIC in the back of one of the Windows XP Professional computers.

10. Repeat the previous step, connecting the other computer to the other hub. The Windows XP computers should each be plugged into different hubs, while *SERVER1* should be plugged into both hubs. This will allow traffic from *WORKSTATION1* to travel through *SERVER1* to *WORKSTATION2*. Figure 5-2 shows the network cabling.

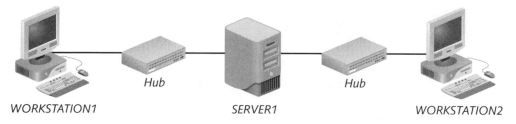

Hub   SERVER1   Hub

WORKSTATION1   WORKSTATION2

Figure 5-2   Network cabling for Lab 5.3

11. On *WORKSTATION1*, press **Ctrl+Alt+Del** to display the Log On to Windows dialog box. Log on to *WORKSTATION1* as the Administrator. The Windows XP desktop appears.

12. Click **Start**, point to **All Programs**, point to **Accessories**, and then click **Command Prompt**. A command prompt window appears.

13. Type **ping 172.16.1.2** and press **Enter**. If the output does not indicate that the computer has received four replies from 172.16.1.2, repeat Steps 9 and 10 before continuing, switching the hubs to which each computer is attached.

14. Repeat Steps 11 and 12 with *WORKSTATION2*. The Windows Server 2003 computer is now acting as a router. This means that it accepts packets from *WORKSTATION1*, and uses its routing table to determine where to send the packets so that they reach their destination, *WORKSTATION2*.

15. At the command prompt, type **ping 192.168.54.2** and press **Enter**. The output indicates that this computer has received four replies from the other computer. You have successfully used the Windows Server 2003 computer as a router.

16. Next, you will configure a secondary IP address on *WORKSTATION2*. Click **Start**, point to **All Programs**, point to **Accessories**, point to **Communications**, and then click **Network Connections**. The Network Connections dialog box opens.

17. Right-click the **Local Area Connection** icon, and then click **Properties** in the pop-up menu.

18. Double-click **Internet Protocol (TCP/IP)**. The Internet Protocol (TCP/IP) Properties dialog box appears. Click **Advanced**. The Advanced TCP/IP Settings window appears.

19. Click the **Add** button beneath the IP addresses heading at the top of the dialog box. The TCP/IP Address dialog box opens.

20. Type **10.1.1.1** in the IP address text box. Type **255.0.0.0** in the Subnet mask text box.

21. Click **Add**. You have just configured this computer with a second IP address, which it can also use to communicate with other computers. You return to the Advanced TCP/IP Settings dialog box.

22. Click **OK** to close the Advanced TCP/IP Settings dialog box, click **OK** to close the Internet Protocol TCP/IP Properties dialog box, and then click **OK** to close the Local Area Connection Properties dialog box.

23. In the command prompt window for *WORKSTATION1*, type **ping 10.1.1.1** and press **Enter**. You see a reply (printed four times on the screen) indicating that the destination host is unreachable.

24. Next, you will check to see if a route exists on the Windows Server 2003 computer so that you can reach the secondary IP address on *WORKSTATION2* from *WORKSTATION1*. On the Windows Server 2003 computer, click **Start**, point to **All Programs**, point to **Accessories**, and then click **Command Prompt**.

25. Type **route print** and press **Enter**. The computer prints a list of its interfaces and its routing table. Notice that there is no route to any IP address or network beginning with 10. See Figure 5-3 for an example of a routing table on a Windows Server 2003 computer like *SERVER1* in this lab.

Figure 5-3 Routing table

26. Type **ping 10.1.1.1** and press **Enter**. The computer responds with "Destination host unreachable" four times.

27. Now you will configure a static route on *SERVER1* so that *WORKSTATION1* can reach 10.1.1.1. Type **route add 10.0.0.0 mask 255.0.0.0 172.16.1.2** and press **Enter**. This tells the router to add a route to any machine with a network number of 10.0.0.0 and a subnet mask of 255.0.0.0 through the computer with the IP address of 172.16.1.2.

28. Type **ping 10.1.1.1** and press **Enter**. The computer responds with "Reply from 10.1.1.1" four times.

29. Type **route print** and press **Enter**. The computer prints its routing table. In the Network Destination column, you should see the route you added in Step 27, 10.0.0.0.

30. Return to the command prompt window you opened earlier on *WORKSTATION1*. Type **ping 10.1.1.1** and press **Enter**. The computer responds with "Reply from 10.1.1.1" four times. You have now successfully used the static route you configured on the Windows Server 2003 computer.

31. Finally, you will look at the route used by packets to reach 10.1.1.1. Type **tracert 10.1.1.1** and press **Enter**. The computer prints the route packets take to reach the address 10.1.1.1.

32. Log off all three computers.

Certification Objectives

Objectives for the Network+ Exam:

➤ Identify the purpose, features, and functions of the following network components: hubs, switches, bridges, routers, gateways, CSU/DSU, network interface cards, wireless access points, modems

➤ Identify the OSI layers at which the following network components operate: hubs, switches, bridges, routers, network interface cards

➤ Given a network configuration, select the appropriate NIC and network configuration settings (DHCP, DNS, WINS, protocols, NetBIOS/host name, etc.)

➤ Given output from a diagnostic utility (e.g., Tracert, Ping, Ipconfig, etc.), identify the utility and interpret the output

5

Review Questions

1. What is the purpose of a routing table on a TCP/IP-based network?

   a. to associate the NetBIOS names of nodes with their IP addresses

   b. to associate the IP addresses of nodes with their host names

   c. to associate the IP addresses of nodes with their locations on the network

   d. to associate the host names of nodes with their MAC addresses

2. Which of the following most fully describes what a successful response from the ping command indicates?

   a. that a node is powered on

   b. that a node is physically connected to the network

   c. that a node is running the Windows Server 2003 operating system

   d. that a node is connected to the network and is running TCP/IP successfully

3. What does the tracert command show?

   a. the path taken by packets to the destination address

   b. the MAC address of the destination address

   c. whether or not the remote host supports TCP/IP

   d. the operating system run by the host at the destination address

4. What command would you use to add a node's IP address, subnet mask, and network location interface to a routing table?

   a. route add

   b. add host

   c. add node

   d. route open

5. In the default `ping` command on a computer running Windows Server 2003 or Windows XP Professional, how many replies will you receive if the test is successful?

    a. 1

    b. 2

    c. 3

    d. 4

6. What menu option sequence would you choose to set up Routing and Remote Access Service on a Windows Server 2003 computer?

    a. Start, Control Panel, Network Connections, Routing and Remote Access

    b. Start, Administrative Tools, Routing and Remote Access

    c. Start, All Programs, Accessories, Routing and Remote Access

    d. Start, Control Panel, Routing and Remote Access

Lab 5.4 Activating a Routing Protocol in Windows Server 2003

Objectives

Configuring more than a handful of static routes on a network is time-consuming and error prone. Many networks consist of hundreds or even thousands of routes. For instance, at the time of this writing the Internet routing table consists of over 100,000 routes. If you used static routes to maintain the routing tables on your routers, you would need to configure each static route on each router. Imagine configuring 500 or more routes on 50 routers! Additionally, each time you added a new network, you would need to configure a new route on each router.

In order to simplify network administration, most networks of any size use a routing protocol to help routers learn routes. A router running a routing protocol tells connected routers, or neighbors, about the networks it knows about. In turn, it learns all the routes its neighbors know about. In this way, it can discover all the routes in the network. Routing protocols also allow routers to find the best routes to a destination. Finally, routing protocols allow routers to recover from outages. If a router fails, other routers will learn this from information sent by the routing protocol. If another route to the destination is available, they will use it.

In this lab, you will configure Routing Information Protocol (RIP) version 2 on a computer running Windows Server 2003. RIP is a relatively simple routing protocol, which is supported on many network devices and servers. However, keep in mind that routing protocols can be quite complex, and that mistakes with routing protocols can cause large outages.

After completing this lab, you will be able to:

➤ Explain the function of various routing protocols

➤ Install a routing protocol on a Windows Server 2003 computer

Materials Required

This lab will require the following:

➤ A computer named *SERVER1* running Windows Server 2003 Enterprise Edition with two NICs

➤ One NIC on the *SERVER1* computer configured with an IP address of 192.168.54.1 and a subnet mask of 255.255.255.0

➤ The other NIC on the *SERVER1* computer configured with an IP address of 172.16.1.1 and a subnet mask of 255.255.255.0

➤ A computer named *SERVER2* running Windows Server 2003, with a NIC, an IP address of 192.168.54.2, a subnet mask of 255.255.255.0, and no default gateway

➤ Routing and Remote Access disabled on both computers

➤ Two Ethernet hubs

➤ Three straight-through CAT 5 (or better) UTP cables

➤ Access as Administrator to both computers

Estimated completion time: **45 minutes**

ACTIVITY

1. Connect each hub to each of the NICs in *SERVER1* with CAT 5 cables.

2. Connect the NIC in *SERVER2* to one of the hubs with the remaining CAT 5 cable.

3. On *SERVER2*, press **Ctrl+Alt+Del** to open the Log On to Windows dialog box. Log onto the computer as the Administrator. The Windows Server 2003 desktop appears.

4. Click **Start**, point to **All Programs**, point to **Accessories**, and click **Command Prompt**. A command prompt window opens.

5. Now you will verify that you have network connectivity with *SERVER1*. Type **ping 192.168.54.1** and press **Enter**. The computer indicates that it has received four replies. If instead you see a time out error (or other error), *SERVER2* is plugged into the wrong hub. Take the cable plugged into *SERVER2*'s NIC, remove the end attached to the hub, and plug it into the other hub. Repeat this step.

6. Now you will attempt to reach the IP address of *SERVER1* 's other NIC. Type **ping 172.16.1.1** and press **Enter**. You see four messages indicating that the destination host is unreachable.

7. Type **route print** and press **Enter** to show the computer's routing table. Record the networks listed in the Network Destination column, and the corresponding subnet masks in the Netmask column.

8. On *SERVER1*, press **Ctrl+Alt+Del** to open the Log On to Windows dialog box. Log onto the computer as the Administrator. The Windows Server 2003 desktop appears.

9. Click **Start**, point to **All Programs**, point to **Administrative Tools**, and click **Routing and Remote Access**. The Routing and Remote Access dialog box opens.

10. In the left pane, select *SERVER1*. Click **Action**, and then click **Configure and Enable Routing and Remote Access**. The Routing and Remote Access Server Setup Wizard appears.

11. Click **Next**. The Configuration dialog box appears, listing several options for configuring this computer as a router.

12. Select the **Custom configuration** option, and then click **Next**. The Custom Configuration dialog box appears.

13. Click the **LAN routing** check box to place a check in it. Click **Next**.

14. Click **Finish**. The Routing and Remote Access Server Setup Wizard saves your settings and starts the Routing and Remote Access Service.

15. A dialog box opens, indicating that the Routing and Remote Access Service has been installed. Click **Yes** to start the service. Dialog boxes indicating that the service is initializing appear briefly.

16. In the left pane of the Routing and Remote Access dialog box, click the **plus sign (+)** next to the SERVER1 (local) icon. A tree of options appears below the SERVER1 icon. Click the **plus sign (+)** next to the IP Routing icon. More options appear underneath the IP Routing icon, including an icon named General.

17. Right-click the **General** icon, and then click **New Routing Protocol** in the pop-up menu. The New Routing Protocol dialog box opens. Figure 5-4 shows the New Routing Protocol dialog box.

18. Click **RIP Version 2 for Internet Protocol**, and then click **OK**. A RIP icon appears in the left pane on the same tree as the General icon while the Windows Server 2003 computer installs the Routing Information Protocol.

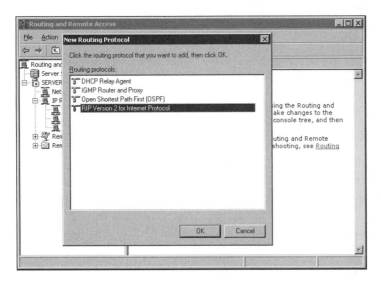

Figure 5-4   Adding a new routing protocol

19. Right-click the new **RIP** icon in the tree in the left pane, and then click **New Interface**. The New Interface for RIP Version 2 for Internet Protocol dialog box appears.

20. Click **Local Area Connection**, and then click **OK** to add the interface. The RIP Properties – Local Area Connection Properties dialog box appears.

21. Click **OK** to close the dialog box and finish adding the interface. If necessary, select RIP in the left pane. An icon for Local Area Connection appears in the right pane of the Routing and Remote Access dialog box.

22. Repeat Steps 19 through 21 for Local Area Connection 2.

23. Right-click the **SERVER1 (local)** icon. On the pop-up menu, point to **All Tasks**, then click **Restart**. A dialog box appears briefly indicating that the Routing and Remote Access Service is restarting.

24. Enable Routing and Remote Access on *SERVER2* by repeating Steps 9 through 23. After RIP for IP is installed on both computers, they will dynamically share their routing tables within a minute.

25. Wait one minute. In the left pane of the Routing and Remote Access dialog box on *SERVER2*, right-click the **RIP** icon, and then click **Show Neighbors**. The SERVER2 – RIP Neighbors dialog box opens, showing the IP address of *SERVER1*. If you do not see the IP address of *SERVER1* in this dialog box, wait another minute and repeat this step.

26. In the command prompt window on *SERVER2*, type **ping 172.16.1.1** and press **Enter**.

27. Type **route print** and press **Enter**. What additional routes do you see now that you didn't see in Step 9?

Certification Objectives

Objectives for the Network+ Exam:

➤ Identify the purpose, features, and functions of the following network components: hubs, switches, bridges, routers, gateways, CSU/DSU, network interface cards, wireless access points, modems

➤ Given output from a diagnostic utility (e.g., Tracert, Ping, Ipconfig, etc.), identify the utility and interpret the output

Review Questions

1. What does RIP stand for?
   a. Regulated Interaction Protocol
   b. Routing Information Protocol
   c. Response Interpretation Protocol
   d. Registered Installation Protocol

2. True or False? In order to determine the best path to transfer data, routers communicate using routing protocols such as TCP/IP.

3. What additional routes did you find in Step 27?

4. Which routing protocol is commonly used for Internet backbones?
   a. OSPF
   b. RIP for IP
   c. EIGRP
   d. BGP

5. Under what circumstances might the best path not equal the shortest distance between two nodes? (Choose all that apply.)
   a. when a communications link has been recently added to the network
   b. when a communications link is suffering congestion
   c. when a router experiences routing protocol errors
   d. when the media on the shortest path is slower than the media on the best path

6. Which protocol was developed by Cisco Systems and has a fast convergence time but is supported only on Cisco routers?

   a. OSPF

   b. RIP for IP

   c. EIGRP

   d. BGP

7. What does "OSPF" stand for?

   a. open shortest path first

   b. overhead system path forwarding

   c. overlook system packet forwarding

   d. open session peer first

LAB 5.5 CONFIGURING A SIMPLE FIREWALL

Objectives

A firewall is a gateway used to connect two or more different networks. More importantly, a firewall controls the types of traffic allowed to cross it. Many firewalls can control traffic with varying degrees of ease anywhere from the Data Link layer up to the Application layer. The distinction between a firewall and a router is fuzzy. Many routers can also filter traffic. Like a router, a firewall may be a dedicated piece of hardware, or software configured on a server. The function of a firewall also overlaps somewhat with that of a router. A firewall may use a handful of static routes, or it may run a routing protocol like a router. However, a firewall will typically not have as many features as a full-blown router. Typically, a firewall is considered a device whose primary purpose is to restrict traffic.

One common use for a firewall is to connect an organization's network with the Internet. The firewall is often configured to allow all traffic originating from within the organization's network onto the Internet, while allowing only requested Internet traffic into the organization's network. The Internet is thought of as being "outside" the firewall, while the organization's network is thought of as being "inside." Exceptions may be made for some traffic inside the firewall. For instance, Internet users may be allowed to connect to a Web server inside the firewall. Firewalls may also often perform Network Address Translation, which you will learn about in Chapter 11.

After completing this lab, you will be able to:

➤ Configure a simple firewall on a Windows Server 2003 computer

Materials Required

In this lab, you will need the following:

➤ The network built at the end of Lab 5.3

Estimated completion time: **30 minutes**

LAB ACTIVITY

ACTIVITY

1. On *WORKSTATION1*, press **Ctrl+Alt+Del** to open the Log On to Windows dialog box. Log on as the Administrator. The Windows XP desktop appears.

2. Click **Start**, point to **All Programs**, point to **Accessories**, then click **Command Prompt**. A command prompt window opens.

3. Type **ping 172.16.1.2** and press **Enter**. The computer indicates that it has received four replies from the remote computer.

4. Now you will prevent *WORKSTATION1* from pinging *WORKSTATION2*. On the Windows Server 2003 computer, press **Ctrl+Alt+Del** to open the Log On to Windows dialog box. Log on as the Administrator. The Windows Server 2003 desktop appears.

5. Click **Start**, point to **Administrative Tools**, then click **Routing and Remote Access**. The Routing and Remote Access dialog box opens.

6. Right-click **SERVER1** in the left pane of the Routing and Remote Access dialog box. In the pop-up menu, select **Disable Routing and Remote Access**. A dialog box opens, indicating that you are disabling Routing and Remote Access and that you will need to reconfigure it later if you wish to use it again.

7. Click **Yes**.

8. Right-click **SERVER1** in the left pane again. Select **Configure and Enable Routing and Remote Access** in the pop-up menu. The Routing and Remote Access Server Setup Wizard opens.

9. Click **Next**. The Configuration dialog box opens.

10. Select the **Custom configuration** option and click **Next**. The Custom Configuration dialog box opens.

11. Select the **NAT and basic firewall** and **LAN routing** check boxes. Click **Next**.

12. Click **Finish**. A dialog box opens, indicating that the Routing and Remote Access Service has been installed and asking if you would like to start it. Click **Yes**. A dialog box opens briefly indicating that the Routing and Remote Access Service is starting.

13. If the tree below SERVER1 (local) in the left pane of the Routing and Remote Access dialog box is not already expanded, click the **plus sign (+)** next to SERVER1 (local). The tree expands beneath it.

14. Click the **plus sign (+)** next to IP Routing (if the tree beneath it has not already been expanded).

15. Right-click **NAT/Basic Firewall** in the left pane underneath IP Routing. Select **New Interface** from the pop-up menu.

16. Double-click **Local Area Connection 2**. The Network Address Translation Properties dialog box opens.

17. Select the **Basic firewall only** option. Figure 5-5 shows the Network Address Translation Properties dialog box.

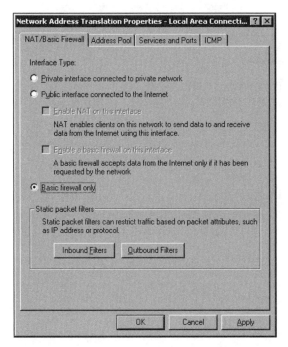

Figure 5-5   Network Address Translation Properties dialog box

18. Click the **Inbound Filters** button. The Inbound Filters dialog box opens.

19. Click **New**. The Add IP Filter dialog box opens.

20. Select the **Destination network** check box. In the IP address text box, enter **172.16.0.0**. In the Subnet mask text box, enter **255.255.255.0**. Select **ICMP** in the Protocol drop-down menu. Click **OK**. The Add IP Filter dialog box closes.

21. Make sure that the **Receive all packets except those that meet the criteria below** option button is selected. Click **OK** twice to return to the Routing and Remote Access dialog box.

22. Right-click **SERVER1 (local)**. On the pop-up menu, point to **All Tasks**, then click **Restart**. A dialog box opens briefly, indicating that the Routing and Remote Access Service is restarting.

23. At the command prompt on *WORKSTATION1*, type `ping 172.16.1.2` and press **Enter**. The computer indicates (four times) that the request timed out.

Certification Objectives

Objectives for the Network+ Exam:

➤ Identify the purpose, benefits, and characteristics of using a firewall

Review Questions

1. Which of the following could serve as firewalls? (Choose all that apply.)

   a. a modem

   b. a Windows Server 2003 computer

   c. a hub

   d. a Linux server

2. True or False? A firewall can run a routing protocol like a router.

3. What is the highest level of the OSI model in which a firewall can operate?

   a. Data Link

   b. Network

   c. Transport

   d. Application

4. A gateway connects two different types of networks, two different types of communications protocols, or two different computer architectures. Which of the following is *not* considered a gateway?

   a. a router connecting a Token Ring

   b. a computer translating application data from TCP/IP to IPX/SPX

   c. a computer translating voice signals into data and transmitting it over a TCP/IP network

   d. a file and print server communicating with clients using both TCP/IP and IPX/SPX

5. You have configured a device that runs the OSPF routing protocol, but whose primary purpose is to prevent unwanted Internet traffic from reaching your company's LAN. Which of the following is true about this device?

   a. It is a router, because it runs a routing protocol.

   b. It is a router, because its primary purpose is to control traffic.

   c. It is a firewall, because it runs a routing protocol.

   d. It is a firewall, because its primary purpose is to control traffic.

5

TOPOLOGIES AND ACCESS METHODS

Labs included in this chapter

➤ Lab 6.1 The Parallel Backbone

➤ Lab 6.2 Building a Daisy Chain

➤ Lab 6.3 Configuring Ethernet Frame Types

➤ Lab 6.4 Examining Ethernet Frames

Net+ Exam Objectives	
Objective	**Lab**
Recognize the following logical or physical network topologies given a schematic diagram or description: star, bus, mesh, ring, wireless	6.1, 6.2
Recognize the following media connectors and/or describe their uses: RJ-11, RJ-45, AUI, BNC, ST, SC	6.1, 6.2
Choose the appropriate media type and connectors to add a client to an existing network	6.2
Identify the purpose, features, and functions of the following network components: hubs, switches, bridges, routers, NICs	6.1, 6.2
Specify the main features of 802.2 (LLC), 802.3 (Ethernet), 802.5 (Token Ring), 802.11b (wireless), and FDDI networking technologies, including: speed, access, method, topology, media	6.3, 6.4
Given a network configuration, select the appropriate NIC and network configuration settings (DHCP, DNS, WINS, protocols, NetBIOS/host name, etc.)	6.1, 6.3

LAB 6.1 THE PARALLEL BACKBONE

Objectives

In this lab, you will build a network that includes a variation of the parallel backbone. In a parallel backbone, each network segment has two or more connections to the central router or switch. If one connection fails, each segment can still connect to the rest of the network through the other connection.

The disadvantage to using a parallel backbone is cost. Depending on the type of devices used in the network and on the logical topology, it may require additional cabling, additional network devices, or additional configuration of network devices. As a network administrator, you must often choose between price and reliability. In most networks, only the most important devices have redundant network connections. For instance, a failure of the server that handles a company's billing may cost the company a substantial amount of money. The cost of a parallel backbone may be offset by the money that could be lost during such an outage. For a workstation, however, a parallel backbone may not be cost effective.

After completing this lab, you will be able to:

➤ Create a parallel backbone network

Materials Required

This lab will require the following:

➤ Two computers running Windows Server 2003 Enterprise Edition, one named *SERVER1* and the other named *SERVER2*, each with two NICs with RJ-45 connectors but without IP addresses configured

➤ Routing and Remote Access deactivated on both computers

➤ Access as the Administrator to both computers

➤ Two 10/100 Ethernet hubs

➤ Four straight-through CAT 5 (or better) UTP cables

Estimated completion time: **60 minutes**

ACTIVITY

1. Power on the two computers and the two hubs.

2. Plug one of the cables into a NIC in *SERVER1*. Plug the other end of the cable into one of the hubs. The link light on both the hub and on the NIC illuminate.

3. Plug another cable into the second NIC in *SERVER1*. Plug the other end of this cable into the other hub (that is, the hub you did not use in Step 2). Both NICs on *SERVER1* are now connected to different hubs. The link lights on the hub and on the NIC illuminate.

4. Plug a third cable into a NIC on *SERVER2*. Plug the other end of this cable into one of the hubs.

5. Plug the fourth cable into the second NIC on *SERVER2*. Plug the other end of this cable into the other hub. Both NICs on *SERVER2* are now plugged into different hubs, and each server is now connected to each hub. Figure 6-1 shows the network cabling for this lab.

6

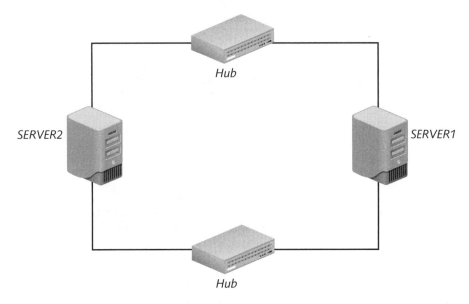

Figure 6-1   Network cabling for Lab 6.1

6. On *SERVER1*, press **Ctrl+Alt+Del** to open the Log On to Windows dialog box. Log onto the server as the Administrator. The Windows Server 2003 desktop appears.

7. Click **Start**, point to **Control Panel**, point to **Network Connections**, then click **Local Area Connection**. The Local Area Connection Status window opens.

8. Click **Properties**. The Local Area Connection Properties window opens.

9. Double-click **Internet Protocol (TCP/IP)**. The Internet Protocol (TCP/IP) Properties window opens.

10. Select the **Use the following IP address** option button. Enter **192.168.54.1** in the IP Address text box and **255.255.255.0** in the Subnet mask text box. Select the **Use the following DNS Server addresses** option button, and enter **192.168.54.1** in the Preferred DNS server text box.

11. Click the **Advanced** button. The Advanced TCP/IP Settings window opens.

12. Click **Add** beneath the IP addresses text box. The TCP/IP Address dialog box opens.

13. Now you will configure a secondary IP address. Enter **10.1.1.1** in the IP address text box and **255.255.255.0** in the Subnet mask text box.

14. Click the **Add** button. The dialog box closes, and the new IP address appears below "IP addresses" in the Advanced TCP/IP Settings text box.

15. Click **OK** three times to close the Local Area Connection Properties window. Click **Close** to close the Local Area Connection Status window.

16. Click **Start**, point to **Control Panel**, point to **Network Connections**, then click **Local Area Connection 2**. The Local Area Connection 2 Status window opens.

17. Click **Properties**. The Local Area Connection 2 Properties window opens.

18. Double-click **Internet Protocol (TCP/IP)**. The Internet Protocol (TCP/IP) Properties window opens.

19. Select the **Use the following IP address** option. Enter **192.168.56.1** in the IP Address text box and **255.255.255.0** in the Subnet mask text box. Select the **Use the following DNS Server addresses** option button, and enter **192.168.54.1** in the Preferred DNS server text box.

20. Click **OK** twice to close the Local Area Connection 2 Properties window. Click **Close** to close the Local Area Connection 2 Status window.

21. Click **Start**, point to **All Programs**, point to **Administrative Tools**, and click **Routing and Remote Access**. The Routing and Remote Access window opens.

22. Right-click **SERVER1 (local)** in the left pane of the Routing and Remote Access window. Select **Configure and Enable Routing and Remote Access** from the pop-up menu. The Routing and Remote Access Setup Wizard opens.

23. Click **Next**.

24. Select the **Custom configuration** option. Click **Next**.

25. Click the **LAN routing** text box in order to select it. Click **Next**.

26. Click **Finish**. A dialog box opens, indicating that the service has been installed and asking if you would like to start the service. Click **Yes**. The service starts.

27. If necessary, click the **plus sign (+)** next to SERVER1(local) to expand the tree. In left pane of the Routing and Remote Access window, click the **plus sign (+)** to expand the tree below IP Routing if the tree is not already expanded. Right-click **General**, then select **New Routing Protocol** from the pop-up menu. The New Routing Protocol dialog box opens.

28. Double-click **RIP Version 2 for Internet Protocol**. The dialog box closes, and RIP appears below IP Routing in the tree in the left pane of the Routing and Remote Access window.

29. Right-click **RIP** in the tree in the left pane. Select **New Interface** from the pop-up menu. The New Interface for RIP Version 2 for Internet Protocol dialog box opens.

30. Double-click **Local Area Connection**. The RIP Properties – Local Area Connection Properties window opens.

31. Click **OK**.

32. Repeat Steps 29 through 31 for Local Area Connection 2.

33. Right-click **SERVER1 (local)** in the left pane. A pop-up menu opens. Point to **All Tasks**, then click **Restart**. The Routing and Remote Access service restarts.

34. On *SERVER2*, repeat Steps 6 through 10 and 15 through 33. (Note that when repeating Step 15, it will be necessary to click **OK** only twice.) However, use **192.168.54.2** in the IP address text box and Preferred DNS server text boxes in Step 10, and **192.168.56.2** in the IP address text box and **192.168.54.2** in the Preferred DNS server text box in Step 19.

35. On *SERVER2*, click **Start**, point to **All Programs**, point to **Accessories**, then click **Command Prompt**. A command prompt window opens.

36. Type **ping 10.1.1.1** and press **Enter**. You see a message indicating that the computer has received four replies from the remote computer. (If the ping command is unsuccessful, switch the cables attached to *SERVER2*'s NICs, and verify that the link light on each NIC and hub is illuminated as expected.)

37. Remove one of the cables attached to *SERVER2*. (However, leave all of the cables attached to *SERVER1*.)

38. Type **ping 10.1.1.1** and press **Enter**. You see a message indicating that the computer has received four replies from the remote computer despite the removal of the cable.

39. Log off both computers.

6

Certification Objectives

Objectives for the Network+ Exam:

➤ Recognize the following logical or physical network topologies given a schematic diagram or description: star, bus, mesh, ring, wireless

➤ Recognize the following media connectors and/or describe their uses: RJ-11, RJ-45, AUI, BNC, ST, SC

➤ Identify the purpose, features, and functions of the following network components: hubs, switches, bridges, routers, NICs

➤ Given a network configuration, select the appropriate NIC and network configuration settings (DHCP, DNS, WINS, protocols, NetBIOS/host name, etc.)

Review Questions

1. What is an advantage of using a parallel backbone over a collapsed backbone?

   a. A collapsed backbone requires too many connecting devices.

   b. A parallel backbone uses redundant connections, and is more reliable.

   c. A collapsed backbone uses redundant connections, costing more money.

   d. A parallel backbone uses fewer redundant connections, which costs less money.

2. What is the purpose of using the routing protocol in this lab?

   a. Each server can choose a different path when the current path fails.

   b. The network administrator does not have to configure static routes.

   c. It has no purpose.

   d. Each server saves the appropriate IP addresses in their ARP cache.

3. Which of the following is true about the use of parallel backbones in real-life networks?

   a. Parallel backbones are used when redundant connections are not possible.

   b. Parallel backbones are used whenever possible because they are so inexpensive.

   c. Parallel backbones only work in Ethernet networks.

   d. Parallel backbones are used for important servers and networks because they are more expensive to build.

4. In this lab, you configured the hubs and the two servers in a ring. How does the topology in this lab differ from a ring topology such as Token Ring? (Choose all that apply.)

   a. Each host transmits when necessary.

   b. A single workstation or server in a simple ring topology could take down the entire ring.

   c. Each host passes a token to the next host.

   d. The topology in this lab was an example of an active topology.

5. Which of the following network technologies has built-in redundancies?

   a. Token Ring

   b. Gigabit Ethernet

   c. FDDI

   d. 10Base2 Ethernet

6

LAB 6.2 BUILDING A DAISY CHAIN

Objectives

In this lab, you will create a daisy chain, which is simply a linked series of devices. You would most likely have several workstations or servers connected to each hub in the daisy chain. Because the hubs are modular and only require CAT 5 or better cables, the sort of network built in this lab is cheap and quick.

In any daisy chain, however, you run the risk of expanding the network beyond its physical limitations. That is, your daisy chain might exceed the maximum length for the network technology used. For instance, on a 10BaseT network connecting more than five network segments together with more than four hubs violates the standards, while on a 100BaseTX network connecting more than three network segments with more than two hubs violates the standards. On a Gigabit Ethernet network, you can use only one hub. Depending on the network devices involved, overextending a daisy chain can result in serious problems. On a network such as the one in this lab, for instance, it can result in high error rates, data transmission problems, or reduced throughput. These problems may also be intermittent and hence more difficult to identify and troubleshoot.

Ordinarily, you must use a crossover cable in order to connect two hubs or switches together. However, many switches and hubs have an uplink port. An uplink port allows you to use a straight-through cable instead. One end of the straight-through cable is attached to an uplink port, and the other end is attached to an ordinary switch or hub port. In other cases, the hub or switch may have a button that determines whether the uplink port functions as an uplink port or as an ordinary port.

After completing this lab, you will be able to:

➤ Identify common enterprise backbone topologies

➤ Build a simple version of a common enterprise backbone

Materials Required

This lab will require the following:

➤ Four Ethernet hubs set at a common speed

➤ Five straight-through CAT 5 (or better) UTP cables

➤ Three cross-over CAT 5 (or better) UTP cables, if required, to connect the hubs

➤ A computer running Microsoft Windows XP Professional named *WORKSTATION1*, with an RJ-45 NIC running at the same speed as the hubs and with an IP address of 192.168.54.2 and a subnet mask of 255.255.255.0

➤ A computer running Microsoft Windows XP Professional named *WORKSTATION2*, with an RJ-45 NIC running at the same speed as the hubs and with an IP address of 192.168.54.3 and a subnet mask of 255.255.255.0

➤ Access as an Administrator to both computers

Estimated completion time: **45 minutes**

LAB ACTIVITY

ACTIVITY

1. Power on each hub and each computer.

2. Plug one of the CAT 5 cables into a port in one of the hubs. Plug the other end of this cable into the uplink port of one of the other hubs. On both hubs a link light illuminates. If the hubs do not have uplink ports or if the lights do not illuminate, use a crossover cable to connect the hubs instead. The uplink port is designed to allow two hubs to be connected with a straight-through cable, but not all hubs have uplink ports.

3. Connect one of the remaining two hubs to one of the two hubs you connected in Step 2. Connect the remaining hub to the hub you just connected. Now you have a chain of four hubs. Each connection on each hub should have an illuminated link light.

4. Plug the RJ-45 connector from one of the CAT 5 cables into a data port on one of the hubs on the end. Plug the other end into the NIC in the back of one of the computers. A link light illuminates on both the hub and the NIC.

5. Repeat Step 4 by connecting the other computer into the hub at the other end of the chain. Figure 6-2 shows the network cabling for this lab.

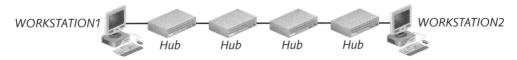

WORKSTATION1   Hub   Hub   Hub   Hub   WORKSTATION2

Figure 6-2   Network cabling for Lab 6.2

6. On *WORKSTATION1*, press **Ctrl+Alt+Del** to open the Log On to Windows dialog box. Log onto the computer as the Administrator. The Windows XP desktop appears.

7. Click **Start**, point to **All Programs**, point to **Accessories**, and click **Command Prompt**. A command prompt window opens.

8. Type **ping 192.168.54.3** and press **Enter**. You see a message indicating that the computer has received four replies. (If you see an error message instead, go on to the next step.)

9. Repeat the previous step, examining the lights on each hub for errors. (Typically a light on a hub will blink red or will not blink at all if the hub is experiencing errors.) Do you see any error lights on any of the hubs?

10. Log off the computer.

Certification Objectives

Objectives for the Network+ Exam:

➤ Recognize the following logical or physical network topologies given a schematic diagram or description: star, bus, mesh, ring, wireless

➤ Recognize the following media connectors and/or describe their uses: RJ-11, RJ-45, AUI, BNC, ST, SC

➤ Choose the appropriate media type and connectors to add a client to an existing network

➤ Identify the purpose, features, and functions of the following network components: hubs, switches, bridges, routers, NICs

Review Questions

1. Does the network you built in this lab meet the requirements for the hubs that you used? Why or why not?

2. What type of port connects one hub to another in a daisy-chain fashion?

   a. output port

   b. patch panel port

   c. uplink port

   d. external port

3. When connecting hubs in a daisy-chain fashion on a 10BaseT network, what is the maximum number of hubs you may connect?

   a. 2

   b. 3

   c. 4

   d. 5

4. When connectivity devices are connected in a daisy-chain fashion, what type of backbone do they create?

   a. parallel

   b. serial

   c. collapsed

   d. distributed

5. What type of network access method is used on a ring network?

   a. CSMA/CA

   b. CSMA/CD

   c. demand priority

   d. token passing

6. Which of the following is the most popular hybrid topology used on modern Ethernet networks?

   a. star-wired bus

   b. star-wired ring

c. ring-wired star

d. bus-wired star

7. What is risky about daisy-chaining hubs on a 100BaseT network? (Choose all that apply.)

    a. Too many hubs may cause errors in addressing data for their proper destination.

    b. Too many hubs may cause the network to exceed its maximum length.

    c. Too many hubs will increase the attenuation of a data signal.

    d. Too many hubs will increase the possibility for errors in data encryption and decryption.

6

LAB 6.3 CONFIGURING ETHERNET FRAME TYPES

Objectives

In most networks, the Ethernet frame type is determined automatically by the NIC and no configuration is necessary. In some cases, however, you may find it necessary to configure the NIC manually to use a particular frame type. Depending on the protocols in question, use of multiple protocols may require multiple frame types. For instance, while recent versions of NetWare use IP by default, the default frame type used when IPX/SPX is configured is Ethernet_802.2. However, Ethernet_II is the most commonly used frame type on all modern networks. NetWare servers also support a variety of frame types, and the default has changed over the years. Additionally, NetWare servers may be configured to use multiple frame types in order to support the use of multiple IPX networks on the same NIC. You may also need to use different frame types to support legacy operating systems or applications.

There are a total of four Ethernet frame types. Besides Ethernet_II and Ethernet_802.2, Ethernet networks may also use Ethernet_802.3 and Ethernet_SNAP. In general, you should minimize the number of frame types in use in your network. The use of multiple frame types requires each NIC to examine each incoming frame in order to determine its type. This delays processing of the frame slightly.

While newer versions of NetWare primarily use IP, older versions of NetWare used IPX/SPX. The IPX/SPX protocol stack is similar to the TCP/IP stack in some ways. For instance, IPX is a connectionless, best effort protocol similar to IP, while SPX is a connection-oriented protocol similar to TCP.

After completing this lab, you will be able to:

➤   Examine and change Ethernet frame settings for computers running Windows Server 2003 or Windows XP Professional

Materials Required

This lab will require the following:

➤ A computer running Windows Server 2003 Enterprise Edition named *SERVER1*, with a NIC configured with an IP address of 192.168.54.1 and a subnet mask of 255.255.255.0, and with the NWLink IPX/SPX/NetBIOS Compatible Transport Protocol installed

➤ A computer running Windows XP Professional named *WORKSTATION1*, with a NIC configured with an IP address of 192.168.54.2 and a subnet mask of 255.255.255.0, and with the NWLink IPX/SPX/NetBIOS Compatible Transport Protocol installed

➤ The Win32 version of the network protocol analyzer Ethereal (available from *www.ethereal.com*) installed on the Windows Server 2003 computer

➤ Access to both computers as an Administrator

➤ Both computers connected to a hub with straight-through CAT5 (or better) UTP cables

Estimated completion time: **45 minutes**

LAB ACTIVITY

ACTIVITY

1. On *SERVER1*, press **Ctrl+Alt+Del** to open the Log On to Windows dialog box. Log onto the computer as the Administrator. The Windows Server 2003 desktop appears.

2. Click **Start**, point to **Control Panel**, point to **Network Connections**, and click **Local Area Connection**. The Local Area Connection Status dialog box opens.

3. Click **Properties**. The Local Area Connection Properties dialog box opens.

4. Double-click **NWLink IPX/SPX/NetBIOS Compatible Transport Protocol**. The NWLink IPX/SPX/NetBIOS Compatible Transport Protocol Properties dialog box opens.

5. Select the **Manual frame type detection** option.

6. Click the **Add** button. The Manual Frame Detection dialog box opens.

7. From the Frame type drop-down menu, select **Ethernet SNAP**. Click **OK**.

8. Click **OK** twice to close the Local Area Connection Properties dialog box. Click **Close** to close the Local Area Connection Status dialog box.

9. On *WORKSTATION1*, press **Ctrl+Alt+Del** to open the Log On to Windows dialog box. Log onto the computer as the Administrator. The Windows XP desktop appears.

10. Click **Start**, point to **All Programs**, point to **Accessories**, point to **Communications**, and click **Network Connections**. The Network Connections dialog box opens.

11. Right-click the **Local Area Connection** icon. Select **Properties** from the pop-up menu. The Local Area Connection Properties dialog box opens.

12. Double-click **NWLink IPX/SPX/NetBIOS Compatible Transport Protocol**. The NWLink IPX/SPX/NetBIOS Compatible Transport Protocol Properties dialog box opens.

13. In the Frame type drop-down menu, select **Ethernet SNAP**. Click **OK** twice to close the Local Area Connection Properties dialog box.

14. On the Windows Server 2003 computer, click **Start**, point to **All Programs**, point to **Ethereal**, and click **Ethereal**. The Ethereal Network Analyzer opens.

15. Click **Capture**, then click **Start**. The Ethereal: Capture Options window opens.

16. Click **OK**. Ethereal begins to capture frames. The Ethereal: Capture window opens, displaying statistics about the number of captured frames.

17. Now you will generate some frames while Ethereal captures them in the background. Click **Start**, point to **All Programs**, point to **Accessories**, and click **Command Prompt**. A command prompt window opens.

18. Type **ping 192.168.54.2** and press **Enter**. You see a message indicating that the computer has received four replies.

19. Now look at the Ethereal: Capture window, which lists the frames captured by protocol. When some IPX frames have been captured, click **Stop**. This may take several minutes. A list of captured frames is displayed in the top pane, while details about the protocol highlighted in the top pane are shown in the bottom two panes. The Ethereal Network Analyzer window is shown in Figure 6-3.

20. Scroll through the frames in the top pane until you see a frame marked IPX or NBIPX in the Protocol column. Click the frame to highlight it. Detailed information about the frame appears in the bottom two panes of the window.

21. In the middle pane, click the **plus sign (+)** next to IEEE 802.3 Ethernet and next to Logical-Link Control. What type of Ethernet frame does this appear to be?

22. Scroll through the frames until you find a frame listed as ICMP in the Protocol column. Click the frame to highlight it. Detailed information about the frame appears in the bottom two panes.

23. In the middle pane, click the **plus sign (+)** next to Ethernet II. What sort of frame is this? How does it differ from the frame you saw in Step 21?

24. Log off both computers.

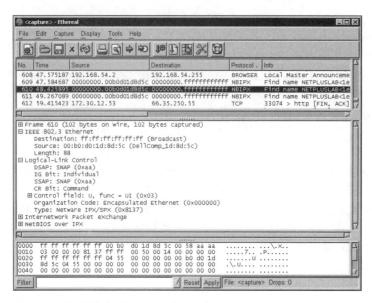

Figure 6-3   Ethereal Network Analyzer

Certification Objectives

Objectives for the Network+ Exam:

➤   Specify the main features of 802.2 (LLC), 802.3 (Ethernet), 802.5 (Token Ring), 802.11b (wireless), and FDDI networking technologies, including: speed, access, method, topology, media

➤   Given a network configuration, select the appropriate NIC and network configuration settings (DHCP, DNS, WINS, protocols, NetBIOS/host name, etc.)

Review Questions

1. Which of the following are reasons one might use multiple frame types on a network? (Choose all that apply.)

   a. to support multiple servers

   b. to support a legacy operating system

   c. to ensure that data arrive at their intended destination

   d. to support multiple network protocols

2. How is the frame type used by a NIC most likely to be configured?

   a. automatically by auto-detection

   b. manually

   c. by any servers on the network

   d. by any routes on the network

3. Which of the following is a disadvantage of using multiple frame types on a network?

    a. It requires additional configuration of network addressing.

    b. A NIC cannot automatically determine the network address of received frames.

    c. Routers cannot determine the best path to a host.

    d. Each NIC must examine each frame to determine the frame type.

4. Which of the following is true about the major types of Ethernet frames?

    a. Each frame operates at the Network layer.

    b. Each frame contains the destination and source MAC addresses.

    c. Each frame has a different maximum size.

    d. Each frame uses a preamble at the end of the frame to signal the end of the frame.

5. What is one reason you might use multiple frame types on a NetWare network?

    a. to support multiple IPX networks on the same NIC

    b. to support multiple applications on the same server

    c. to support the use of the IP protocol

    d. to prevent monopolization of the network by any single frame type

6

LAB 6.4 EXAMINING ETHERNET FRAMES

Objectives

In this lab you will examine the parts of an Ethernet frame in greater detail. Every Ethernet frame contains a number of fields, including the 7-byte preamble (which tells the NIC that it is about to receive data), the 1-byte start-of-frame delimiter (which indicates that the frame is about to start), the 14-byte header (containing the destination MAC address, the source MAC address, and another field that depends on the frame type), 46 to 1500 bytes of data, and the 4-byte Frame Check Sequence (FCS) field (which uses a Cyclic Redundancy Check (CRC) to determine if the data in the frame has been corrupted). If the data field is not at least 46 bytes long, it will be padded by the sending host until it is 46 bytes long. Only the header, the data and any padding, and the FCS field are used to determine the size of the frame.

The dominant Ethernet frame type in modern networks is Ethernet_II. The most important difference between the Ethernet_II frame and other types of Ethernet frames is the type field in the header. This field contains a code for the protocol used, such as IP, IPX, ARP, etc., and makes it possible for Ethernet_II frames to carry multiple types of protocols. (The

Ethernet_SNAP frame type also has a type field. However, it also uses additional fields, resulting in extra overhead.)

Note that neither Ethereal nor most other software protocol analyzers can capture the preamble and the FCS field. On most operating systems, these fields are discarded before they reach the operating system. In order to see these fields, you may need to use a dedicated hardware protocol analyzer such as RADCOM's PrismLite Integrated WAN/LAN/ATM Protocol Analyzer.

After completing this lab, you will be able to:

➤ Distinguish between the parts of an Ethernet frame

Materials Required

This lab will require the following:

➤ A computer running Windows Server 2003 Enterprise Edition with a NIC, configured with a name of *SERVER1*, an IP address of 192.168.54.1, and a subnet mask of 255.255.255.0

➤ A computer running Windows XP Professional with a NIC, configured with a name of *WORKSTATION1*, an IP address of 192.168.54.2, and a subnet mask of 255.255.255.0

➤ The network protocol analyzer Ethereal (available from *www.ethereal.com*) installed on the Windows Server 2003 computer

➤ Access to both computers as an Administrator

➤ Both computers connected to a hub with straight-through CAT5 (or better) UTP cables

---

Estimated completion time: **45 minutes**

LAB ACTIVITY

ACTIVITY

1. On the Windows Server 2003 computer, press **Ctrl+Alt+Del** to open the Log On to Windows dialog box. Log onto the computer as the Administrator. The Windows Server 2003 desktop appears.

2. Click **Start**, point to **All Programs**, point to **Ethereal**, and click **Ethereal**. The Ethereal Network Analyzer opens.

3. Click **Capture**, then click **Start**. The Ethereal: Capture Options window opens.

4. Click **OK**. The Ethereal: Capture window opens, displaying the number of frames of each type captured.

5. Click **Start**, point to **All Programs**, point to **Accessories**, and click **Command Prompt**. A command prompt window opens.

6. Type `ping -t 192.168.54.2` and press **Enter**. The computer begins pinging 192.168.54.2 and will continue to do so until you stop it.

7. Now look at the Ethereal: Capture window. When the total number of frames captured is greater than 10, click **Stop**. A list of captured frames appears in the top pane, and details about the highlighted frame appear in the bottom two panes. Figure 6-4 shows an example of a captured frame.

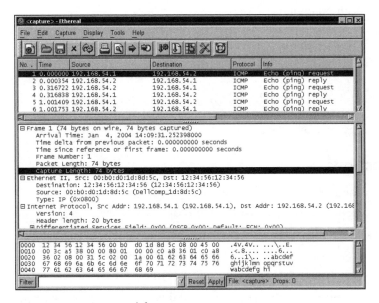

Figure 6-4   Captured frame

8. Click a frame listed as **ICMP** in the Protocol column to highlight it. Detailed information about the frame appears in the bottom two panes.

9. In the middle pane, click the **plus sign (+)** sign next to Ethernet II to expand the tree below it. Record the source and destination addresses.

10. Record the destination and source addresses in the Internet Protocol part of the frame. (This is part of the data field of the frame.) Was this frame sent from the Windows Server 2003 computer, or was it sent from the Windows XP computer?

11. In the command prompt window, press **Ctrl+C** to stop the **ping** command, then type **ipconfig /all** and press **Enter**. What is the MAC address for this host? Does it match one of the addresses you recorded in Step 9?

12. Type **arp -a** and press **Enter**. Look for the IP address of the other computer. Does its associated MAC address match one of the addresses you recorded in Step 9?

13. Look at the type field below "Ethernet II." What is this frame's type? Does it match the protocol listed in Ethereal's protocol column?

14. Log off both computers.

Certification Objectives

Objectives for the Network+ Exam:

➤ Specify the main features of 802.2 (LLC), 802.3 (Ethernet), 802.5 (Token Ring), 802.11b (wireless), and FDDI networking technologies, including: speed, access, method, topology, media

Review Questions

1. What is the purpose of the checksum?
   a. to ensure that data arrives in the proper sequence
   b. to ensure that data is properly encrypted and decrypted
   c. to ensure that data arrives at its intended destination
   d. to ensure that data arrives whole and intact

2. How many times is a checksum calculated when a frame of data is sent from a source computer to a destination computer that resides on the same segment?
   a. 1
   b. 2
   c. 3
   d. 4

3. What type of address identifies the source of data in a frame?
   a. MAC
   b. logical
   c. network
   d. host

4. What is the purpose of padding in an Ethernet frame?

    a. to ensure that the data in the frame is exactly 1500 bytes long

    b. to ensure that the data in the frame is no more than 46 bytes long

    c. to signal that the frame has ended

    d. to ensure that the data in the frame is at least 46 bytes long

5. What is the minimum size of an Ethernet frame?

    a. 56 bytes

    b. 64 bytes

    c. 128 bytes

    d. 256 bytes

6. Which parts of an Ethernet frame are Ethereal and other protocol analyzers unlikely to capture? (Choose all that apply.)

    a. the header

    b. the Frame Check Sequence

    c. the padding

    d. the preamble

6

7

WANs and Remote Connectivity

Labs included in this chapter

➤ Lab 7.1 Pricing WAN Services

➤ Lab 7.2 Connecting to an Internet Service Provider in Windows Server 2003

➤ Lab 7.3 Configuring a Remote Access Server

➤ Lab 7.4 Creating a VPN with the Point-to-Point Tunneling Protocol

➤ Lab 7.5 Configuring Terminal Services on Windows Server 2003

Net+ Exam Objectives	
Objective	**Lab**
Identify the purpose, features, and functions of the following network components: hubs, switches, bridges, routers, gateways, CSU/DSU, network interface cards/ISDN adapters/system area network cards, wireless access points, modems	7.2
Recognize the following media connectors and/or describe their uses: RJ-11, RJ-45, AUI, BNC, ST, SC	7.2, 7.3
Choose the appropriate media type and connectors to add a client to an existing network	7.2, 7.3
Identify the basic characteristics (e.g., speed, capacity, media) of the following WAN technologies: packet switching vs. circuit switching, ISDN, FDDI, ATM, Frame Relay, SONET/SDH, T1/E1, T1/T3, OCx	7.1
Define the function of the following remote access protocols and services: RAS, PPP, PPTP, ICA	7.2, 7.3, 7.4
Given a remote connectivity scenario (e.g., IP, IPX, dial-up, PPPoE, authentication, physical connectivity, etc.), configure the connection	7.2, 7.3
Identify the basic capabilities (i.e., client support, interoperability, authentication, file and print services, application support, and security) of the following server operating systems: UNIX/Linux, NetWare, Windows, Macintosh	7.3, 7.4, 7.5

Lab 7.1 Pricing WAN Services

Objectives

In this lab, you will price several options for WAN services. Many organizations use multiple types of WAN links for redundancy and to eliminate single points of failure on the network. For example, an organization might use T-1s to connect its two largest remote offices to its central office, and it might use ISDN lines as backups in case either T-1 fails. To connect its smaller offices to the central office, an organization might use ISDN lines as the primary link and a dial-up modem as the backup link. Many organizations will also have a backup link for their Internet connection.

You can use these services to connect an organization to the Internet, as well as to connect offices in one location to offices in another. The pricing of Internet services is often more complicated, as you must purchase both a WAN link and Internet access itself. Depending on the type of WAN link, however, many WAN service providers will be able to offer both the WAN connection and the Internet access. Many telephone companies, for example, will install a T-1 and provide Internet access with the T-1 service.

WAN topologies can also have a huge impact on price. The star, partial mesh, and full mesh WAN topologies are used most commonly. Independent of the cost of the actual WAN, the star topology is the cheapest. A star topology consists of one link from a central office to each satellite office. For each new office you add, you need to add only one new link. However, a star topology offers no redundancy in case of a link failure. In a partial mesh topology, some (but not all) of the satellite offices are interconnected. If one link fails, there will often (but not always) be a backup link. The price of adding an office rises depending on the number of satellite offices and on the degree to which they are linked. In a full mesh, all offices are connected to each other. The price of adding an office increases with the number of offices. With a large number of offices, a full mesh WAN topology will cost many times what a star topology for the same number of offices would cost. Other WAN topologies, such as the bus and ring topologies, do not scale well and are rarely used for WANs with more than a handful of locations.

After completing this lab, you will be able to:

➤ Compare WAN links in terms of cost and speed

➤ Compare WAN topologies in terms of price and redundancy

➤ Identify WAN hardware components

Materials Required

This lab will require the following:

➤ Pencil and paper

➤ If some of the services discussed in this lab are not offered in your area, representative pricing provided by your instructor for those services

Estimated completion time: **60-90 minutes**

7

LAB ACTIVITY

ACTIVITY

1. Call a local Internet service provider or telephone company and ask to speak with someone about the cost and availability of high-speed Internet links for businesses. Identify the name of the organization you called.

2. Explain that you are doing research for a school project on the pricing of Internet links. Give your name, the name of the networking class you are taking, and the name of your school.

3. For T-1 service, ask if the service is available in your area. If the service is available, ask if there are any geographic restrictions on the service. For instance, some services may not be available in all areas because the necessary infrastructure has not yet been built. Record the geographic availability of the service.

4. If the service is available, ask for the bandwidth of the service and record it below. T-1 service should be available in most areas. If T-1 service is not available, go to Step 8.

5. Ask for the monthly cost of the service. Make sure to ask if you would be billed a flat fee, or whether your bill would change depending on how much you used the service. Record the monthly costs.

6. Ask if any additional equipment is required for the service and if the company provides it. Additionally, ask if the hardware charge is a flat fee or a monthly charge. If so, ask for the typical price of the additional equipment. Record the cost of additional equipment expected.

7. Ask about any initial setup fees that you might be charged. Typical setup fees include the installation of the T-1 line itself. Record the cost of the setup fees.

8. Repeat Step 3 through Step 7, this time referencing DSL.

9. Repeat Step 3 through Step 7, this time referencing ISDN.

10. Repeat Step 3 through Step 7, this time referencing a PSTN connection with a modem.

11. For each service, calculate the cost of any setup and installation fees and the cost of equipment required (excluding monthly charges for hardware). Record the setup, installation, and equipment costs.

12. For each service, calculate the cost of two years of monthly service, including any monthly charges for hardware. If the service is billed based on usage, estimate the cost based on medium usage. Record the cost of two years of service.

13. For each service, compare the costs calculated in Step 11 and Step 12.

14. Now you will examine the effects of different WAN topologies on WAN pricing. For the T-1 service, calculate the cost of T-1 service connecting each office in Figure 7-1 in the star topology shown. Use the two-year monthly service fees you calculated in Step 12.

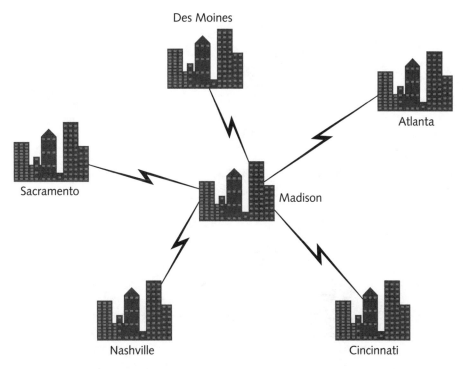

Figure 7-1   Star WAN topology

15. For the T-1 service, calculate the cost of T-1 service connecting each office in Figure 7-2 in the partial mesh topology shown. Use the two-year monthly service fees you calculated in Step 12.

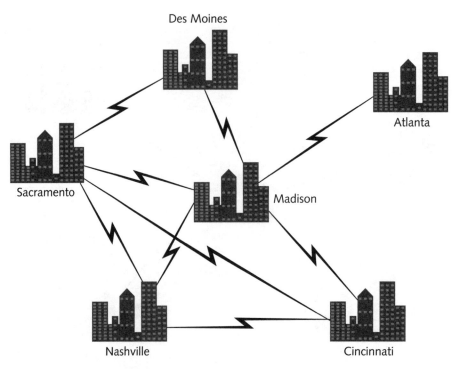

Des Moines

Atlanta

Sacramento

Madison

Nashville

Cincinnati

Figure 7-2   Partial mesh WAN topology

16. For the T-1 service, calculate the cost of T-1 service connecting each office in Figure 7-3 in the full mesh topology shown. Use the two-year monthly service fees you calculated in Step 12.

Certification Objectives

Objectives for the Network+ Exam: Identify the basic characteristics (e.g., speed, capacity, media) of the following WAN technologies: packet switching vs. circuit switching, ISDN, FDDI, ATM, Frame Relay, SONET/SDH, T1/E1, T1/T3, OCx

Review Questions

1. Which of the following best describes the function of a CSU?

    a. It transmits several signals over a single channel.

    b. It separates a single channel into multiple channels.

    c. It terminates a digital signal and ensures connection integrity.

    d. It converts the digital signal used by connectivity devices into the digital signal sent through the cabling.

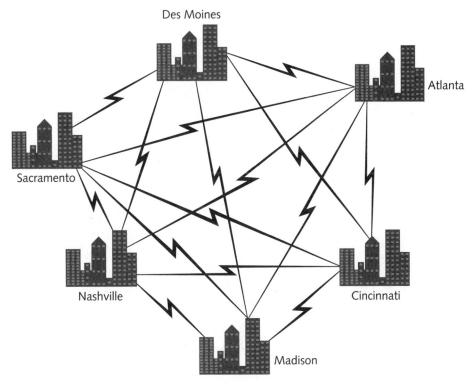

Figure 7-3   Full mesh WAN topology

2. Which of the following WAN topologies is the least expensive to build?

    a. star-wired ring

    b. full mesh

    c. partial mesh

    d. star

3. Which of the following WAN topologies gives the most redundancy?

    a. bus

    b. partial mesh

    c. full mesh

    d. star

4. What is the maximum number of channels that a single T1 can contain?

    a. 12

    b. 24

    c. 48

    d. 64

5. What is the maximum throughput of a T3 line?

   a. 1.544 Mbps

   b. 45 Mbps

   c. 672 Mbps

   d. 275 Mbps

6. What does DSL use to achieve higher throughput than PSTN over the same lines?

   a. full duplexing

   b. data modulation

   c. message switching

   d. framing

7. Which of the following WAN links is most reliable?

   a. DSL

   b. PSTN

   c. ISDN

   d. SONET

8. Which of the following is the most expensive type of connection to install and lease?

   a. DSL

   b. ISDN

   c. T1

   d. T3

LAB 7.2 CONNECTING TO AN INTERNET SERVICE PROVIDER IN WINDOWS SERVER 2003

Objectives

In this lab, you will make a connection to an ISP. Although higher-speed connections such as DSL or cable allow many people to connect more quickly to the Internet, dial-up connections to the Internet are still more common and are available in most areas. Dial-up access using the Public Switched Telephone Network (PSTN), also known as the Plain Old Telephone Service (POTS), remains popular because it is ubiquitous, inexpensive, and easy to use. In your work as a networking professional, you will find it valuable to understand how to configure and troubleshoot dial-up connections because so many of your clients will rely on such connections for network access.

In many small networks, many or all users need at least occasional access to the Internet. Sharing a single Internet connection is cheaper and easier to configure than giving users their own modems and ISP accounts. Using Internet Connection Sharing (ICS), you can configure one modem on one computer and the rest of the office can connect through that computer. ICS will automatically configure the server to give DHCP addresses to workstations. Furthermore, you can configure the ICS server to dial the ISP connection whenever a workstation requests information on the Internet. However, a dial-up connection can quickly become congested as you add users.

Additionally, ICS will automatically configure Network Address Translation (NAT) for the ISP connection. NAT allows an ICS server and any workstation using the ICS server to connect to the Internet to appear to the ISP as one IP address. Otherwise, you would need to arrange with the ISP for each workstation to have its own IP address. This would require additional configuration, as well as additional expense in many cases.

After completing this lab, you will be able to:

➤ Configure a dial-up connection to an ISP

➤ Share a dial-up Internet connection with a workstation

Materials Required

This lab will require the following:

➤ A computer running Windows Server 2003 Enterprise Edition named *SERVER1* with a NIC configured with an IP address of 192.168.54.1 and a subnet mask of 255.255.255.0; no secondary IP addresses must be configured for this NIC

➤ Routing and Remote Access disabled on *SERVER1*

➤ A modem installed and configured on *SERVER1*, without any location or Internet connection information configured

➤ Access to an analog outside phone line, or a digital to analog converter (to prevent the digital phone lines from ruining the modems)

➤ If dialing an additional number, such as 9, is required to access that outside line, knowledge of that number

➤ The phone number of an ISP's dial-up pool, and a user name and password for a valid account that does not require any advanced settings

➤ A computer running Windows XP Professional with a NIC, configured with a name of *WORKSTATION1* and to receive an IP address through DHCP

➤ Access as the Administrator to both computers

➤ Both computers connected to an Ethernet hub with straight-through CAT 5 or better UTP cables

Estimated completion time: **30 minutes**

LAB ACTIVITY

ACTIVITY

1. Plug the RJ-11 connector on one end of the phone cable into the modem attached to *SERVER1*. Plug the other end into the wall jack for the phone line.

2. On *SERVER1*, press **Ctrl+Alt+Del** to display the Log On to Windows dialog box. Log onto the server as the Administrator. The Windows Server 2003 desktop appears.

3. Click **Start**, point to **Control Panel**, point to **Network Connections**, and click **New Connection Wizard**. The New Connection Wizard opens.

4. Click **Next**. The wizard asks you to select a network connection type.

5. Make sure that the **Connect to the Internet** option is selected, and click **Next**. The wizard asks you how you want to connect to the Internet.

6. If necessary, select the **Connect using a dial-up modem** option and click **Next**. The wizard asks you to select a name for your connection.

7. Enter **Netplus Lab** in the ISP Name text box. Click **Next**. The wizard asks you to enter the phone number of the ISP.

8. Enter the phone number of the ISP in the Phone number text box. Include any additional digits needed, such as a 1, the area code, or any numbers (often a 9) required to use an outside phone line. Click **Next**. The wizard asks you to specify whether or not the connection can be used by any user.

9. If necessary, select the **Anyone's use** option. Click **Next**. The wizard asks you to enter account information for the ISP.

10. Enter the user name in the User name text box, and enter the account's password in the Password and Confirm password text boxes. Click **Next**. The wizard indicates that you have successfully completed it, and summarizes the options that you have selected.

11. Click **Finish**. The New Connection Wizard closes, and the Connect Netplus Lab dialog box opens. (If the Connect Netplus Lab dialog box does not open, click **Start**, point to **Control Panel**, point to **Network Connections**, and then click **Netplus Lab**.)

12. Click **Properties**. The Netplus Lab Properties dialog box opens.

13. Click the **Advanced** tab. The Advanced tab of the Netplus Lab Properties dialog box opens.

14. Click the **Allow other network users to connect through this computer's Internet connection** check box to place a check mark in it. The "Establish a dial-up connection whenever a computer on my network attempts to access the Internet" check box also becomes checked. See Figure 7-4.

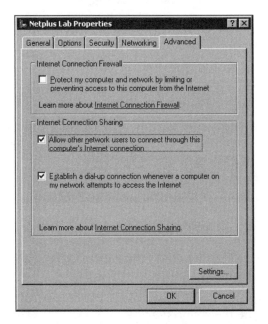

Figure 7-4   Netplus Lab Properties dialog box

15. If the Home networking connection drop-down box is present, select **Local Area Connection**. If not, go to the next step. (The Home networking connection drop-down box will only be available if the computer has more than one network card.)

16. Click **OK**. A dialog box may appear, indicating that when Internet Connection Sharing is enabled, the NIC will be automatically configured with an IP address of 192.168.0.1 and that it might lose contact with other devices on the network.

17. Click **Yes**. The Netplus Lab Properties dialog box reappears.

18. On *WORKSTATION1*, press **Crtl+Alt+Del** to display the Log On to Windows dialog box. Log on as the Administrator. The Windows XP desktop appears.

19. Click **Start**, point to **All Programs**, point to **Accessories**, and point to **Command Prompt**. A command prompt window opens.

20. Type **ipconfig /renew** and press **Enter**. The computer obtains a new IP address for the server. Record the new IP address here.

21. Click **Start**, then click **Internet Explorer**. Internet Explorer opens.

22. In the Address bar, type **www.microsoft.com** and press **Enter**. The modem attached to *SERVER1* dials the ISP connection, and the Microsoft home page opens.

23. Log off both computers.

Certification Objectives

Objectives for the Network+ Exam:

➤ Identify the purpose, features, and functions of the following network components: hubs, switches, bridges, routers, gateways, CSU/DSU, network interface cards/ISDN adapters/system area network cards, wireless access points, modems

➤ Recognize the following media connectors and/or describe their uses: RJ-11, RJ-45, AUI, BNC, ST, SC

➤ Choose the appropriate media type and connectors to add a client to an existing network

➤ Define the function of the following remote access protocols and services: RAS, PPP, PPTP, ICA

➤ Given a remote connectivity scenario (e.g., IP, IPX, dial-up, PPPoE, authentication, physical connectivity, etc.), configure the connection

Review Questions

1. What are two differences between PPP and SLIP?
   a. SLIP can handle only asynchronous transmission, while PPP can handle both asynchronous and synchronous transmission.
   b. SLIP encapsulates traffic according to its original Network layer protocol, while PPP masks SLIP traffic as IP-based data.
   c. SLIP cannot carry Network layer protocols other than TCP/IP, while PPP can carry any Network layer protocol.
   d. SLIP is compatible with only NetWare servers, while PPP is compatible with both NetWare and Windows computers.

2. Which of the following is one primary difference between PPP and PPTP?
   a. PPP can handle only asynchronous transmission, while PPTP can handle both asynchronous and synchronous transmission.
   b. PPP encapsulates traffic according to its original Network layer protocol, while PPTP masks PPP traffic as IP-based data.

    c. PPP cannot carry Network layer protocols other than TCP/IP, while PPTP can carry any Network layer protocol.

    d. PPP is compatible with only NetWare servers, while PPTP is compatible with both NetWare and Windows computers.

3. Which of the following is the most secure remote access protocol?

    a. SLIP

    b. PPP

    c. RAS

    d. PPTP

4. Which of the following best describes the asynchronous communications method?

    a. Data that are transmitted and received by nodes must conform to a timing scheme.

    b. Data that are transmitted and received by nodes do not have to conform to any timing scheme.

    c. Data that are transmitted and received by nodes are subject to resequencing by each connectivity device through which they pass.

    d. Data that are transmitted and received by nodes require an additional sequencing bit to ensure that they are reassembled in the proper order.

5. If your ISP uses DHCP to assign TCP/IP information to a dial-up connection, which of the following must you still specify in your connection parameters?

    a. the type of server into which you are dialing

    b. your workstation's IP address

    c. the network's DHCP server address

    d. the network's subnet mask

LAB 7.3 CONFIGURING A REMOTE ACCESS SERVER

Objectives

In this lab, you will create a remote access server (RAS) and connect to it from a client. With a remote access server, users may access network resources from home or on the road. A salesperson, for example, might be on the road a large percentage of the time and have no network access besides her dial-up connection. By dialing into a dial-up server with Routing and Remote Access Server (RRAS), a remote user can check e-mail, share files, and use the network just as if she were locally connected to the network.

In Windows Server 2003, keep in mind that you need to specifically enable a user to dial in remotely to a Windows Server 2003 computer. Even if the server has a modem and is configured to accept incoming calls, it may reject a call if a user does not have dial-in permission.

After completing this lab, you will be able to:

➤ Configure RRAS to allow a Windows Server 2003 computer to accept dial-up connections

Materials Required

This lab will require the following:

➤ A computer running Windows Server 2003 Enterprise Edition with a name of *SERVER1*, a workgroup of NETPLUS, and Routing and Remote Access installed but not activated

➤ Two NICs on *SERVER1*, one configured with an IP address of 192.168.54.1 and a subnet mask of 255.255.255.0 and the other configured with an IP address of 172.16.1.1 and a subnet mask of 255.255.255.0

➤ A shared folder on *SERVER1* named NETPLUS containing at least one text file

➤ A computer running Windows XP Professional named *WORKSTATION1*

➤ Access as the Administrator to both computers

➤ A user account named netplus configured on *SERVER1* with the rights needed to dial into the server

➤ Modems installed and configured on both machines

➤ Access to two outside analog phone lines in the same or different locations, or to two digital to analog converters (to prevent digital phone lines from ruining the modems)

➤ Knowledge of the telephone number of the phone line to which the Windows Server 2003 computer is attached

➤ Two phone cords with RJ-11 connectors on both ends that are long enough to reach the wall outlet

Estimated completion time: **60 minutes**

LAB ACTIVITY

ACTIVITY

1. Connect one end of a phone cord to the back of the modem installed on *SERVER1*, and connect the other end to the wall outlet.

2. Repeat the previous step with the Windows XP computer.

3. On *SERVER1*, press **Ctrl+Alt+Del** to display the Log On to Windows dialog box. Log onto the computer as the Administrator. The Windows Server 2003 desktop appears.

4. Click **Start**, point to **Administrative Tools**, then click **Routing and Remote Access**. The Routing and Remote Access dialog box opens.

5. Right-click the **SERVER1 (local)** icon in the left pane of the dialog box. From the pop-up menu, click **Configure and Enable Routing and Remote Access**. The Routing and Remote Access Server Setup Wizard opens.

6. Click **Next**. The wizard asks you for information on how to configure the Routing and Remote Access Service.

7. If necessary, select the **Remote access (dial-up or VPN)** option. Click **Next**.

8. Click the **Dial-up** check box to select it. Click **Next**. The wizard shows you information about the interfaces that dial-up users will connect to.

9. Make sure that **Local Area Connection** is highlighted, and click **Next**. The wizard asks you to choose how IP addresses will be assigned to remote clients. Figure 7-5 shows you an example of this dialog box in the Routing and Remote Access Server Setup Wizard.

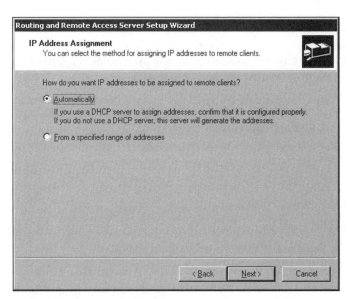

Figure 7-5   Assigning addresses to remote clients

10. Make sure that the **Automatically** option button is selected, and click **Next**. The wizard asks you how you would like to configure authentication.

11. Make sure that the **No, use Routing and Remote Access to authenticate connection requests** option is selected, and click **Next**. The computer indicates that you have completed the wizard.

12. Click **Finish**. A dialog box appears indicating that to support the relaying of DHCP messages from remote access clients, you must configure the DHCP Relay Agent.

13. Click **OK**. Dialog boxes appear indicating that the service is initializing. The Routing and Remote Access Server Setup Wizard closes.

14. On *WORKSTATION1*, click **Start**, point to **All Programs**, point to **Accessories**, point to **Communications**, and click **New Connection Wizard**. The New Connection Wizard opens, and the Location Information dialog box opens on top of it. If the Location Information dialog box does not open, go to Step 17.

15. Select your country from the drop-down menu. Enter your area code in the "What area code (or city code) are you in now?" text box. If you need to enter a number to specify a carrier code or access an outside line, enter them in the appropriate text boxes. Click **OK**. The Location Information dialog box closes, and the Phone and Modem Options dialog box opens.

16. Click **OK**. The Phone and Modem Options dialog box closes, leaving the New Connection Wizard open.

17. Click **Next**. The wizard asks what sort of connection type you would like to configure.

18. Select the **Connect to the network at my workplace** option. Click **Next**. The wizard asks how you would like to connect.

19. Select the **Dial-up connection** option and click **Next**. The wizard asks you to specify a name for the connection. Enter **Netplus Lab** in the Company Name box. Click **Next**. The wizard asks you for the phone number for the connection.

20. Enter the phone number of *SERVER1* in the Phone number text box. Click **Next**. The wizard asks you whether the account should be configured for all accounts or only this account.

21. Click **Next**. The computer indicates that you have completed the wizard.

22. Click **Finish**. The New Connection Wizard closes.

23. Click **Start**, point to **All Programs**, point to **Accessories**, point to **Communications**, and click **Network Connections**. The Network Connections dialog box opens.

24. Right-click the **Netplus Lab** icon and select **Connect** from the pop-up menu.

25. In the User name text box, enter **netplus**, In the Password text box, enter the password for this account given to you by your instructor. Click **Connect**. The modem connects to the remote access server.

26. A dialog box indicating that you have connected successfully opens. Click **OK**. You have successfully logged on to the remote access server.

27. Click **Start**, then click **My Computer**.

28. On the menu bar, click **Tools**, then click **Map Network Drive**. The Map Network Drive dialog box opens.

29. In the Folder text box, enter **\\192.168.54.1\NETPLUS**. Click **Connect using a different user name**. The Connect As dialog box opens.

30. Type **Administrator** in the User name text box, and enter the password for the Administrator account on SERVER1 in the Password text box. Click **OK**. The Connect As dialog box closes.

31. Click **Finish**. The Map Network Drive dialog box appears briefly, indicating that the computer is attempting to map the network drive. After it closes, an icon for the mapped network drive appears underneath Network Drives in the My Computer window.

32. Double-click the icon for the mapped network drive. A folder containing the name of at least one text file appears.

33. Double-click a text file. The text file opens.

34. Close the text file and log off both computers.

Certification Objectives

Objectives for the Network+ Plus exam:

➤ Recognize the following media connectors and/or describe their uses: RJ-11, RJ-45, AUI, BNC, ST, SC

➤ Choose the appropriate media type and connectors to add a client to an existing network

➤ Define the function of the following remote access protocols and services: RAS, PPP, PPTP, ICA

➤ Given a remote connectivity scenario (e.g., IP, IPX, dial-up, PPPoE, authentication, physical connectivity, etc.), configure the connection

➤ Identify the basic capabilities (i.e., client support, interoperability, authentication, file and print services, application support, and security) of the following server operating systems: UNIX/Linux, NetWare, Windows, Macintosh

Review Questions

1. Which of the following best describes a modem's function?

    a. to encapsulate Data Link layer protocols as Network Layer protocols before transmitting data over the PSTN

    b. to separate data into frames as it is transmitted from the computer to the PSTN, and then strip data from frames as it is received from the PSTN

    c. to encrypt data as it is transmitted from the computer to the PSTN, and then decrypt data as it is received from the PSTN

    d. to convert a source computer's digital pulses into analog signals for the PSTN, and then convert analog signals back into digital pulses for the destination computer

2. What is another common term for "Public Switched Telephone Network"?

    a. Plain Old Telephone Service

    b. Basic Rate Telephone Service

    c. Limited Access Telephone Service

    d. Transcontinental Public Telephone Service

3. Which of the following types of dial-up connections would result in the best performance from the client's perspective?

    a. a PPP dial-up connection to an RRAS server that allowed the client to launch an application from the RRAS server

    b. a PPTP dial-up connection to an RRAS server that allowed the client to launch an application from another server on the LAN

    c. a SLIP dial-up connection to an RRAS server that allowed the client to log on to an application server on the LAN and run an application from that application server

    d. a PPTP dial-up connection to an RRAS server that allowed the client to log on to a Citrix terminal server and use ICA to run an application

4. What does RAS stand for?

    a. remote authentication service

    b. remote access server

    c. remote accounting service

    d. remote addressing server

5. Why do most remote clients (for example, those that dial into an RRAS server) use DHCP and not static IP addressing? (Choose all that apply.)

   a. because using DHCP allows more efficient use of a limited number of IP addresses

   b. because using DHCP ensures that the client is authorized to access the network

   c. because using DHCP ensures that the client is assigned a valid IP address

   d. because using DHCP allows the client to use the same IP address each time he or she dials into the LAN

7

LAB 7.4 CREATING A VPN WITH THE POINT-TO-POINT TUNNELING PROTOCOL

Objectives

While a remote access server allows users to dial in and use network resources, dialing into a remote access server can be quite expensive if many of the users have to dial long distance. One way to reduce the cost of using a remote access server is to create a virtual private network (VPN). In a VPN, users connect to the remote access server over an encrypted channel through a public network, typically the Internet. Remote users have the same access that they had when dialing in directly to the remote access server. However, instead of paying long distance fees per minute, an organization pays for its users' Internet connections and the Internet connectivity of its remote access server.

A VPN can be thought of as an imaginary cable, which is connected from one end of the VPN to the other end. In many types of VPNs, a virtual network interface is created on both ends of the VPN, just as if they were directly linked by the same cable even though the two endpoints might be across the Internet. Each virtual network interface has an IP address just as a normal interface does. However, this IP address is associated with a logical NIC and not a physical NIC. For this reason, an IP address like this is often called a virtual IP address.

In this lab, you will create a VPN using the Point-to-Point Tunneling Protocol (PPTP). PPTP creates virtual NICs on the server and client. Traffic between each virtual NIC is encrypted so that a malicious user with a protocol analyzer cannot view the contents. Although there may be many network devices between the client and the server, the PPTP tunnel makes the client and server seem as if they are both attached to the same hub.

Other protocols, including IPSec, can also be used to carry VPN traffic. VPNs run on a wide variety of hardware, including servers with several different operating systems, routers, firewalls, and dedicated VPN hardware such as Cisco's VPN 3000 Series Concentrators. As VPN traffic requires additional processing and can use a lot of CPU time, many devices will offload processing of VPN traffic onto a special chip or module.

After completing this lab, you will be able to:

➤ Configure a VPN with PPTP between a client computer and a Windows Server 2003 computer

Materials Required

This lab will require the following:

➤ A computer running Windows Server 2003 Enterprise Edition named *SERVER1* with two NICs, one configured with an IP address of 192.168.54.1 and a subnet mask of 255.255.255.0 and the other configured with an IP address of 172.16.1.1 and a subnet mask of 255.255.255.0

➤ Routing and Remote Access disabled on the Windows Server 2003 computer

➤ A shared folder on *SERVER1* containing at least one text file

➤ A computer running Windows XP Professional named *WORKSTATION1* with a NIC configured with an IP address of 192.168.54.3 and a subnet mask of 255.255.255.0

➤ Each NIC on both computers connected with straight-through CAT 5 (or better) UTP cables to a single hub

➤ Access to both computers as the Administrator

➤ An account on *SERVER1* with a known password and sufficient rights to dial into *SERVER1*

Estimated completion time:	**30 minutes**

LAB ACTIVITY

ACTIVITY

1. On *SERVER1*, press **Ctrl+Alt+Del** to display the Log On to Windows dialog box. Log on as the Administrator. The Windows Server 2003 desktop appears.

2. Click **Start**, point to **Administrative Tools**, then click **Routing and Remote Access**. The Routing and Remote Access dialog box opens.

3. In the left pane of the dialog box, right-click **SERVER1 (local)**. From the pop-up menu, select **Configure and Enable Routing and Remote Access**. The Routing and Remote Access Server Setup Wizard opens.

4. Click **Next**. The wizard displays configuration options for the Routing and Remote Access service.

5. Select the **Virtual Private Network (VPN) access and NAT** option. Click **Next**. The wizard asks you to select at least one interface that connects this server to the Internet.

6. Select **Local Area Connection** and click **Next**. The wizard asks you to select options for IP address assignment.

7. If necessary, select the **Automatically** option and click **Next**. The wizard asks you to select options for managing multiple remote access servers.

8. If necessary, select **No, use Routing and Remote Access to authenticate connection requests** and click **Next**. The wizard indicates that you have finished.

9. Click **Finish**. A Routing and Remote Access dialog box may open, indicating that you must make further configuration changes in order to support the relay of DHCP messages. If not, go to Step 11.

10. Click **OK**. A dialog box opens, indicating that the Routing and Remote Access Service is starting. The dialog box closes, and the tree underneath SERVER1 (local) has expanded.

11. Right-click **Ports** on the tree underneath SERVER1 (local), and select **Properties** from the pop-up menu. The Ports Properties dialog box opens. See Figure 7-6.

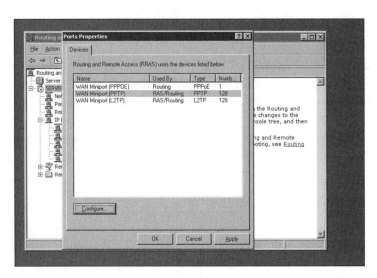

Figure 7-6   The Ports Properties dialog box

12. Click **WAN Miniport (PPTP)** to select it. Click **Configure**. The Configure Device – WAN Miniport (PPTP) dialog box opens.

13. Click the **Demand-dial routing connections (inbound and outbound)** check box in order to remove the check. Click **OK** twice.

14. Right-click **SERVER1 (local)**. From the pop-up menu, point to **All Tasks**, then click **Restart**. The Routing and Remote Access service restarts.

15. On *WORKSTATION1*, press **Ctrl+Alt+Del** to display the Log On to Windows dialog box. Log on as the Administrator. The Windows XP desktop appears.

16. Click **Start**, and then click **Control Panel**. The Control Panel window opens.

17. Click the **Network and Internet Connections** category.

18. Click the **Set up or change your Internet connection** icon. The Internet Properties dialog box opens, with the Connections tab displayed.

19. Click **Setup**. The New Connection Wizard opens. If no location information has been configured previously, the Location Information dialog box opens on top of it. If the Location Information dialog box does not open, go to Step 21.

20. Enter the area code. Click **OK** to close the Location Information dialog box.

21. In the New Connection Wizard, click **Next**. The wizard asks you to select network connection types.

22. Select **Connect to the network at my workplace**, and click **Next**. The wizard asks you to select the type of connection.

23. Select **Virtual Private Network connection**, then click **Next**. The wizard asks you to enter a company name.

24. Enter **NetPlus** in the Company Name box. Click **Next**. The wizard asks you to configure settings for dialing the initial connection to the Internet or other public network. If the wizard instead asks for the name or IP address of the VPN server, go to Step 26.

25. Select the **Do not dial the initial connection** option button. Click **Next**. The wizard instead asks for the name or IP address of the VPN server.

26. Enter **192.168.54.1** in the Host name or IP address text box. Click **Next**. The wizard indicates that you have finished.

27. Click **Finish**. The New Connection Wizard closes.

28. Click the **Network Connections** icon. The Network Connections window opens.

29. Double-click the **NetPlus** icon.

30. Enter the user name and password for the account that can dial into *SERVER1* in the User name and Password text boxes. Click **Connect**. The Connecting NetPlus dialog box opens, indicating that the computer is being registered on the network.

31. Click **Start**, point to **All Programs**, point to **Accessories**, then click **Command Prompt**. A command prompt window opens.

32. Type **ipconfig** and press **Enter**. The computer displays the IP address for each NIC on the computer, including the virtual NIC. (Note that the virtual NIC is named PPP adapter NetPlus.) What is the IP address of the virtual interface?

33. On *SERVER 1*, click **Start**, point to **All Programs**, point to **Accessories**, then click **Command Prompt**. A command prompt window opens.

34. Type **ipconfig** and press **Enter**. The computer displays the IP address for each NIC on the computer, including the virtual NIC for the VPN. (Note that the name of the virtual NIC is PPP Adapter RAS Server (Dial In) Interface.) What is the IP address of the virtual interface on *SERVER 1*?

35. On WORKSTATION1, click **Start**, then click **My Computer**.

36. On the menu bar, click **Tools**, then click **Map Network Drive**. The Map Network Drive dialog box opens.

37. In the Folder text box, enter **\\192.168.54.1\NETPLUS**. Click **Connect using a different name**. The Connect As dialog box opens.

38. Type **Administrator** in the User name text box, and enter the password for the Administrator account in the Password text box. Click **OK**. The Connect As dialog box closes.

39. Click **Finish**. The Map Network Drive dialog box appears briefly, indicating that the computer is attempting to map the network drive. After it closes, an icon for the mapped network drive appears underneath Network Drives in the My Computer window.

40. Double-click the icon for the mapped network drive. A folder containing the name of at least one text file appears.

41. Double-click a text file. The text file opens.

42. Close the text file and log off both computers.

Certification Objectives

Objectives for the Network+ Exam:

➤ Define the function of the following remote access protocols and services: RAS, PPP, PPTP, ICA

➤ Identify the basic capabilities (i.e., client support, interoperability, authentication, file and print services, application support, and security) of the following server operating systems: UNIX/Linux, NetWare, Windows, Macintosh

Review Questions

1. What is one reason an organization might employ a VPN rather than simply allow users to dial directly into their remote access server?

    a. VPNs always provide better performance than direct-dial connections.

    b. VPNs allow more users to connect to the LAN simultaneously.

    c. VPNs are less expensive for connecting a large number of remote users.

    d. VPNs prevent the need for firewalls between access servers and the Internet.

2. In this lab, you connected a workstation with a server using a VPN. Which of the following is true about the VPN connection you created in this lab?

    a. It uses physical IP addresses.

    b. It uses virtual IP addresses on the workstation end.

    c. It uses virtual IP addresses on both ends.

    d. It requires a modem for connection.

3. Which of the following transmission methods is most apt to be used by VPN clients?

    a. PSTN

    b. T-1

    c. Frame Relay

    d. SONET

4. What does the "T" in PPTP stand for?

    a. Tunneling

    b. Transmission

    c. Transport

    d. Telecommunications

5. Which of the following protocol suites could be used to transmit data over a VPN that relies on PPTP? (Choose all that apply.)

    a. IPX/SPX

    b. TCP/IP

    c. NetBEUI

    d. AppleTalk

LAB 7.5 CONFIGURING TERMINAL SERVICES ON WINDOWS SERVER 2003

Objectives

The primary remote administration tool for Windows Server 2003 is Terminal Services. Terminal Services allows a network administrator to log onto a remote Windows Server 2003 computer more or less as if the network administrator were at the console. This can be invaluable for administration. For instance, suppose that a problem with a particular server occurs while you are at home. Without some means of accessing the computer remotely, you must go to the computer in order to fix the problem. With Terminal Services, however, you can connect to the computer remotely and fix the problem without ever leaving home.

By default, Terminal Services on Windows Server 2003 is configured in Remote Administration mode. You can also configure it in Application Server mode. Application Server mode allows users to log onto the server and run applications. This has several advantages. First, network administrators can manage applications from one location. Otherwise, each application must be managed for each user's computer. Second, Terminal Services allows a network administrator to take over a particular user's session. This allows you to see exactly what the user sees. Finally, computers connecting to a computer running Terminal Services in Application Server mode, or a terminal server, may use a wide variety of hardware and operating systems. The terminal server does the bulk of the processing for applications run in Terminal Services. As a result, users may use older or less powerful computers.

One disadvantage of allowing users to connect to a terminal server is cost. Using Terminal Services in Application Server Mode requires additional licensing, while running Terminal Services in Remote Administration mode does not. In this lab you will activate temporary licensing for Terminal Services, which allows the use of Terminal Services for 120 days without the purchase of additional licensing. Additionally, managing applications on a terminal server is more complicated than managing the same applications on a user's desktop.

Finally, Windows XP allows users to log onto their computers through Remote Desktop. However, you may not have more than one user, local or remote, logged onto the same computer at the same time. Remote Desktop should not be confused with Remote Desktop Connection, the client used to connect to Terminal Services on remote Windows Server 2003 computers and Remote Desktop on remote Windows XP computers.

After completing this lab, you will be able to:

➤ Configure Terminal Services on Windows Server 2003

7

Materials Required

This lab will require the following:

➤ A computer running Windows Server 2003 Enterprise Edition configured with a name of *SERVER1* and a NIC configured with an IP address of 192.168.54.1 and a subnet mask of 255.255.255.0

➤ Access to the Internet for *SERVER1* for activation of Terminal Server Licensing, or prior activation of Terminal Server Licensing

➤ A computer named *WORKSTATION1* running Windows XP Professional, with a NIC configured with an IP address of 192.168.54.3 and a subnet mask of 255.255.255.0

➤ Access as the Administrator to each computer

➤ Each computer connected to a hub with straight-through CAT 5 or better UTP cables

➤ Terminal Services Licensing installed on the Windows Server 2003 computer

➤ Terminal Services not installed on *SERVER1*

➤ Four ordinary user accounts with known passwords on *SERVER1*, each with sufficient permissions to log on interactively to *SERVER1* using Terminal Services

Estimated completion time: **45 minutes**

LAB ACTIVITY

ACTIVITY

1. If Terminal Server Licensing on *SERVER1* has previously been activated, go to Step 10. If not, the following steps require some form of Internet access for *SERVER1* and may be done with *SERVER1* attached to another network if necessary. On *SERVER1*, press **Ctrl+Alt+Del** to display the Log On to Windows dialog box. Log onto the computer as the Administrator. The Windows Server 2003 desktop appears.

2. Click **Start**, point to **Administrative Tools**, and then click **Terminal Server Licensing**. The Terminal Server Licensing window opens, with an icon for *SERVER1* in the right pane of the window. In the Activation status column, the activation status of *SERVER1* is Not activated.

3. If a dialog box appears indicating that no license servers can be found, click **OK**, then right-click **All servers** in the left pane of the window and click **Connect**. The Connect to License Server dialog box opens. Enter **SERVER1** and click **OK**.

4. Right-click the icon for SERVER1. From the pop-up menu, select **Activate Server**. The Terminal Server License Server Activation Wizard opens.

5. Click **Next**. The wizard asks you to select a connection method.

6. Click **Next**. The wizard asks you for company information.

7. Fill in your name in the First name and Last name text boxes. Enter the name of your school in the Company text box, and select your country from the Country or Region drop-down menu. Click **Next**. The wizard asks you to fill in optional information, including your e-mail address.

8. Click **Next**. A dialog box appears briefly indicating that the computer is looking for the Microsoft activation server, then the computer indicates that you have completed the Terminal Server License Server Activation Wizard.

9. Click the **Start Terminal Server Client Licensing Wizard now** check box to remove the check from it. Click **Finish**. The wizard closes, and the Activation Status of the SERVER1 icon is now Activated. Close the Terminal Server Licensing window.

10. If necessary, reattach *SERVER1* to the lab network.

11. On *WORKSTATION1*, press **Ctrl+Alt+Del** to display the Log On to Windows dialog box. Log onto the computer as the Administrator. The Windows XP desktop appears.

12. Click **Start**, point to **All Programs**, point to **Accessories**, point to **Communications**, and click **Remote Desktop Connection**. The Remote Desktop Connection dialog box opens. Figure 7-7 shows the Remote Desktop Connection dialog box.

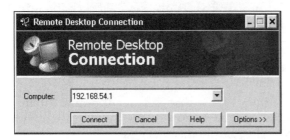

Figure 7-7 Remote Desktop Connection dialog box

13. Enter **192.168.54.1** in the Computer text box. Click **Connect**. The Log On to Windows dialog box appears for *SERVER1*. Log on to the remote computer as the Administrator. The Windows Server 2003 desktop appears.

14. Minimize the Remote Desktop Connection wizard by clicking the horizontal line on the bar at the top of the screen.

15. Repeat Steps 12 through 14 twice. On the second repetition, a Logon Message dialog box appears indicating that the terminal server has exceeded the maximum number of connections. Click **OK** in the Logon Message dialog box, then click **Close**.

16. Now you will install Terminal Services as an Application Server. On *SERVER1*, click **Start**, point to **Control Panel**, and then click **Add or Remove Programs**. The Add or Remove Programs dialog box opens.

17. Click the **Add/Remove Windows Components** icon on the left side of the dialog box. The Windows Setup dialog box appears asking you to please wait, and then the Windows Component Wizard opens.

18. Click the **Terminal Server** check box to place a check in it. (You will need to scroll down to see it.) Click **Next**. The wizard indicates that you have chosen to install Terminal Server on this computer. The Configuration Warning dialog box opens. Click **Yes**.

19. Click **Next**. The wizard asks you to choose security options.

20. Click **Next** to select the default. The wizard indicates that it is configuring components, and finally that you have successfully completed it.

21. Click **Finish**. The Windows Setup dialog box appears briefly, asking you to wait. Then the System Settings Change dialog box appears, indicating that you must restart the computer in order for the changes you made to take effect and asking you if you want to restart the computer now.

22. Click **Yes** to reboot the computer. The computer reboots.

23. Press **Ctrl+Alt+Del** to display the Log On to Windows dialog box. Log on to the computer as the Administrator. The Windows Server 2003 desktop appears. Close the Terminal Server help window, if necessary.

24. Click **Start**, point to **Administrative Tools**, and then click **Terminal Services Configuration**. The Terminal Services Configuration window opens.

25. In the left pane of the window, click the **Server Settings** folder. Icons for server settings appear in the right pane of the window.

26. Now you will configure the server so that users can log on to multiple sessions. Right-click the **Restrict each user to one session** icon. From the pop-up menu, click **No**. The pop-up menu closes.

27. On *WORKSTATION1*, repeat Steps 12 through 14. Repeat twice more, logging in each time as a different ordinary user.

28. On *SERVER1*, click **Start**, point to **Administrative Tools**, and click **Terminal Services Manager**. The right pane of the window shows all the users currently logged onto the server and their sessions.

29. Right-click one of the sessions and click **Disconnect** from the pop-up menu. A Terminal Service Manager dialog box opens, indicating that each selected session will be disconnected.

30. Click **OK**. The session is disconnected, and the text underneath the Session heading reads Disconnected.

31. Repeat Steps 29 and 30 for each of the remaining sessions.

32. On *WORKSTATION1*, check to see if any of the sessions are open.

33. Log off both computers.

Certification Objectives

Objectives for the Network+ Exam:

➤ Identify the basic capabilities (i.e., client support, interoperability, authentication, file and print services, application support, and security) of the following server operating systems: UNIX/Linux, NetWare, Windows, Macintosh

Review Questions

1. Which of the following are reasons you might implement Terminal Services instead of a remote access server? (Choose all that apply.)

   a. no modems required on Terminal Server

   b. central configuration and control of applications on the Terminal Server

   c. no modems required on clients

   d. no need to configure security on the Terminal Server

2. What is the difference between configuring a Windows Server 2003 computer to accept Remote Desktop Connection and configuring it to run Terminal Services?

   a. Remote Desktop Connection requires additional licensing.

   b. Terminal Services requires each client to have a modem.

   c. Terminal Services allows no more than two simultaneous connections.

   d. Terminal Services allows more than two simultaneous connections.

3. What is one way a network administrator can effectively troubleshoot a user's problem in a Terminal Services session that can't be done with a remote access server?

   a. by speaking with the user over the phone

   b. by examining the Terminal Server's error logs

   c. by taking over the user's session temporarily

   d. by rebooting the server

4. Which of the following is a potential disadvantage of Terminal Services?

   a. It requires additional licensing.

   b. It requires the client to be running Windows XP.

   c. It requires the client to have a high-speed connection such as a T-1.

   d. It requires the server to have a minimum of 1 GB RAM.

5. True or False? You cannot log onto a Windows XP computer using a Remote Desktop connection.

NETWORK OPERATING SYSTEMS AND WINDOWS SERVER 2003-BASED NETWORKING

Labs included in this chapter

➤ Lab 8.1 Creating a New Domain Tree

➤ Lab 8.2 Delegating Administrative Rights

➤ Lab 8.3 Adding a Domain to a Forest

➤ Lab 8.4 Setting User Permissions with Groups

➤ Lab 8.5 Remotely Managing a Computer with Active Directory

Net+ Exam Objectives	
Objective	**Lab**
Identify the basic capabilities (i.e., client support, interoperability, authentication, file and print services, application support, and security) of the following server operating systems: UNIX/Linux, NetWare, Windows, Macintosh	8.1, 8.2, 8.3, 8.4, 8.5

LAB 8.1 CREATING A NEW DOMAIN TREE

Objectives

In Windows Server 2003, Active Directory allows you to manage computers and users throughout an organization. An Active Directory implementation is usually called a forest. Each forest consists of one or more domain trees. Each domain tree (often just called a tree) contains one or more domains arranged in a hierarchical manner. Each domain tree typically corresponds to an organization. For example, child domains inside the domain tree might correspond to the Sales, Marketing, and Manufacturing departments. If a forest consists of more than one domain tree, the other domain trees might correspond to related but separate organizations which nonetheless need to share resources. For instance, a conglomerate might own several companies that share only a handful of network resources. Each of these companies might correspond to a different domain tree within the forest.

When creating a new forest, you might create happyfuntoys.com as the first domain tree in the forest. You might then create the following child domains for each location: cleveland.happyfuntoys.com, milwaukee.happyfuntoys.com, shanghai.happyfuntoys.com, and so on. Each child domain might have additional child domains. Each department in each location might have its own child domain: marketing.cleveland.happyfuntoys.com, manufacturing.cleveland.happyfuntoys.com, accounting.cleveland.happyfuntoys.com, and so on. The forest might contain another tree for a sister company, educationalfuntoys.com, which would have its own child domains: toledo.educationalfuntoys.com, berlin.educationalfuntoys.com, boston.educationalfuntoys.com, and so on. You can then configure each child domain so that its users and computers can use the network resources in the rest of the tree that they need, and each tree so that its users and computers can use the resources they need in the other tree. As you might expect, an Active Directory forest can quickly become complicated, and you should carefully plan any Active Directory forest you create before you make it.

Active Directory requires DNS. If DNS is not configured properly or is not functioning properly, then Active Directory will not work properly. When you first create a domain tree, however, Windows offers you the opportunity to configure the DNS server for the new domain tree.

After completing this lab, you will be able to:

➤ Create a new domain tree

➤ Create a new forest

➤ Add a client computer to the domain

Materials Required

This lab will require the following:

➤ A computer running Windows Server 2003 Enterprise Edition named *SERVER1* and configured with an IP address of 192.168.54.1 and a subnet mask of 255.255.255.0, not configured as a domain controller

➤ A computer running Windows XP Professional named *WORKSTATION1*, configured with an IP address of 192.168.54.3 and a subnet mask of 255.255.255.0 and using 192.168.54.1 as its preferred DNS server

➤ Both computers connected to a hub with straight-through CAT 5 (or better) UTP cables

➤ Access to both computers as the Administrator

➤ The Windows Server 2003 installation CD-ROM

8

Estimated completion time: **40 minutes**

LAB ACTIVITY

ACTIVITY

1. On *SERVER1*, press **Ctrl+Alt+Del** to display the Log On to Windows dialog box. Log onto the server as the Administrator.

2. Click **Start**, then click **Run**. The Run dialog box opens.

3. Type **dcpromo** and press **Enter**. The Active Directory Installation Wizard opens.

4. Click **Next**. The wizard describes some of the limitations older versions of Windows will have with Windows Server 2003.

5. Click **Next**. The wizard asks you what sort of domain controller type you would like to configure.

6. Make sure that the **Domain controller for a new domain** option is selected and click **Next**. The wizard asks what sort of domain you would like to create.

7. Make sure the **Domain in a new forest** option is selected and click **Next**. The wizard asks for the DNS name of the new domain.

8. Type **netpluslab.net** and click **Next**. Figure 8-1 shows the Active Directory Installation Wizard.

9. The wizard asks you to specify the NetBIOS name for the new domain. Accept the default entry, NETPLUSLAB, by clicking **Next**. The wizard asks you to specify the location of database and log files for Active Directory.

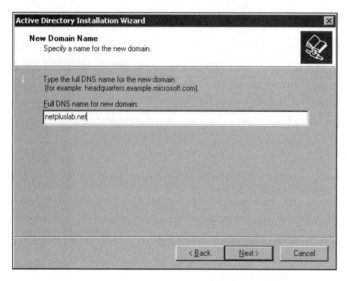

Figure 8-1   The Active Directory Installation Wizard

10. Select the defaults by clicking **Next**. The wizard asks you to choose a folder to be shared as the system volume.

11. Accept the default entry by clicking **Next**. The wizard asks about the DNS installation on the computer.

12. Select the **Install and configure the DNS server on this computer, and set this computer to use this DNS server as its preferred DNS server** option. Click **Next**. The wizard asks you to select default permissions for user and group objects.

13. Make sure the **Permissions compatible only with Windows 2000 or Windows Server 2003 operating systems** option is selected and click **Next**. The wizard asks you to select a Directory Services Restore Mode Administrator Password.

14. Enter the password **Passw0rd** (or another password selected by your instructor) in the Restore Mode Password and the Confirm password text boxes. Click **Next**. The computer summarizes the options you have selected.

15. Click **Next**. If prompted, insert the Windows Server 2003 installation CD into the CD-ROM drive and click **OK**. A dialog box appears, indicating that the wizard is configuring Active Directory. This may take several minutes, so do not click buttons or press keys until it has completed. After a few minutes, the computer indicates that you have completed the Active Directory Installation Wizard.

16. Click **Finish**. A dialog box appears, indicating that you must reboot the server before the configuration changes you made can become active.

17. Click **Restart Now**. The server reboots.

18. After the server reboots, press **Ctrl+Alt+Del** to display the Log On to Windows dialog box. Log on as the Administrator. (Now the account is for the Administrator for the *netpluslab.net* domain.) The Windows Server 2003 desktop appears.

19. Click **Start**, point to **All Programs**, point to **Accessories**, then click **Command Prompt**. A command prompt window opens.

20. Now you will verify that the Active Directory Installation Wizard has configured DNS. Type **ipconfig /all** and press **Enter**. The computer prints detailed information about its IP configuration, including its IP address and the DNS servers it uses. What is the IP address used by this computer, and what are the DNS servers now used by this server?

8

21. Now you will confirm that the computer has added an entry for itself in DNS. Type **nslookup server1.netpluslab.net** and press **Enter**. What is the IP address for server1.netpluslab.net? Does it match the IP address for this computer that you saw in the previous step?

22. On *WORKSTATION1*, press **Ctrl+Alt+Del** to display the Log On to Windows dialog box. Log on as the Administrator. The Windows XP desktop appears.

23. Click **Start**, point to **All Programs**, point to **Accessories**, point to **Communications**, and click **Network Connections**. The Network Connections window opens.

24. Click **Advanced** on the menu bar, then click **Network Identification**. The System Properties window opens.

25. Click **Network ID**. The Network Identification Wizard opens.

26. Click **Next**. The wizard asks how you wish to use the computer.

27. Make sure the **This computer is part of a business network, and I use it to connect to other computers at work** option button is selected, and click **Next**. The wizard asks what sort of network you use.

28. Make sure the **My company uses a network with a domain** option button is selected and click **Next**. The wizard summarizes information required to add the computer to a domain.

29. Click **Next**. The wizard asks for account information

30. In the User name text box, enter **Administrator**. Since the wizard is requesting account information for the new domain you have just created, in the Password text box enter the password for this account on *SERVER1* (as this

account is now the Administrator account for the *netpluslab.net* domain). In the Domain text box, enter **netpluslab.net**. Click **Next**. The wizard asks you for information concerning the domain to which the computer itself belongs.

31. Enter **WORKSTATION1** in the Computer name text box if it hasn't already been filled in for you. Enter **NETPLUSLAB.NET** in the Computer domain text box. Click **Next**. The Domain User Name and Password dialog box opens.

32. In the User name text box, enter **Administrator**. In the Password text box, enter the password for the Administrator account on *SERVER1*. In the Domain text box, enter **NETPLUSLAB.NET**. Click **OK**. The wizard asks if you would like to configure a user account on this computer.

33. Click the **Do not add a user at this time** option button. You will add additional users in later labs. Click **Next**. The Wizard indicates that you have finished.

34. Click **Finish**. The Computer Name Changes dialog box opens, indicating that you must restart the computer before the changes you made will take effect.

35. Click **OK** twice. The System Settings Change dialog box opens, asking if you want to reboot the computer now.

36. Click **Yes**. The computer reboots.

37. After the computer has finished rebooting, press **Ctrl+Alt+Del** to display the Log On to Windows dialog box. Log on as the Administrator. The Windows XP desktop appears. You have now added *WORKSTATION1* to the *netpluslab.net* domain.

38. Log off both computers.

Certification Objectives

Objectives for the Network+ Exam:

➤ Identify the basic capabilities (i.e., client support, interoperability, authentication, file and print services, application support, and security) of the following server operating systems: UNIX/Linux, NetWare, Windows, Macintosh

Review Questions

1. Which of the following services, if stopped, would prevent Active Directory from working properly?

   a. DHCP

   b. XNS

   c. HTTP

   d. DNS

2. You are creating a new Active Directory for a car company. The car company is owned by a holding company that also owns an auto parts company, and both companies need to share some network resources but remain independent of each other. How would you design Active Directory in order to do this?

    a. Put each company in separate forests.

    b. Put each company in separate domains in separate forests.

    c. Put each company in separate domains in the same forest.

    d. Put each company in the same domain.

3. True or False? Active Directory can also be used by computers running Windows Server 2003 that are in a workgroup instead of a domain.

4. A company has offices in four cities on four different continents. In which of the following ways could you organize Active Directory for this company? (Choose all that apply.)

    a. by creating a different forest for each office

    b. by creating a different tree for each office in the same forest

    c. by creating domains for each office in the same forest in the same domain tree

    d. by creating different workgroups for each office in the same domain

5. True or False? Windows Server 2003 requires the NTFS file system in order for many of its security features to operate properly.

6. In this lab you created a domain controller. Which of the following is true about the number of domain controllers you should create for a domain?

    a. One domain controller is sufficient to handle the load.

    b. Create no more than two domain controllers per domain, or client workstations will become confused.

    c. Create at least two domain controllers, so that the domain database will still be available if one domain controller fails.

    d. Create three domain controllers, so that if two domain controllers disagree the third can break the tie.

LAB 8.2 DELEGATING ADMINISTRATIVE RIGHTS

Objectives

One of the advantages of a directory service such as Microsoft's Active Directory or Novell's NetWare Directory Services is that they allow the network administrator granular control over users and network resources. The administrator can make sure that users can access the network resources they need, while at the same time preventing them from accessing network resources they should not be able to access. This also allows the network administrator to delegate specific tasks to certain users without delegating any more authority than is needed.

For instance, in large organizations resetting passwords, creating user accounts, and other relatively straight-forward parts of network administration can take up a lot of time. This prevents the network administrator from concentrating on larger issues of network design and maintenance. In some cases, it's more efficient to have a user in each department reset passwords and create user accounts specifically for that department, and only for that department. The network administrator is then free to spend time on more important issues. A department may also prefer to have control over its own resources. In large organizations, network administration may be divided between two or more groups.

One tool you can use to subdivide a domain is the organizational unit. An organizational unit is a group of users or network resources, such as printers. Organizational units can be used to enforce policies, including the delegation of administrative rights. For instance, a company might have a different organizational unit for each department. Dividing a domain into organizational units is simpler and usually more convenient than dividing a domain into multiple child domains.

Keep in mind that Active Directory can be quite complex, and it is often possible to find multiple ways to solve a particular problem. While the simplest way to solve a problem may not be the best way, keeping your Active Directory installation as simple as possible will make it easier to administer over the long term.

After completing this lab, you will be able to:

➤ Create user accounts in Windows Server 2003

➤ Create organizational units in Windows Server 2003

➤ Delegate network administration roles as needed in Windows Server 2003

Materials Required

This lab will require the following:

➤ The network configured at the end of Lab 8.1

➤ No organizational units named Accounting or Manufacturing in Active Directory

➤ Access to *SERVER1* as the Administrator for the *netpluslab.net* domain

➤ Local logon for all users configured in the Domain Controller Security Policy

Estimated completion time: **40 minutes**

LAB ACTIVITY

ACTIVITY

1. On *SERVER1*, press **Ctrl+Alt+Del** to display the Log On to Windows dialog box. Log onto the computer as the Administrator in the *netpluslab.net* domain. The Windows Server 2003 desktop appears.

2. Click **Start**, point to **Administrative Tools**, and click **Active Directory Users and Computers**. The Active Directory Users and Computers window opens. If necessary, click the **plus sign (+)** next to *netpluslab.net* to expand the tree below it.

3. Right-click **netpluslab.net** in the tree in the left pane. In the pop-up menu, point to **New**, then click **Organizational Unit**. The New Object – Organizational Unit dialog box opens.

4. Type **Accounting** in the Name text box and click **OK**. An Accounting icon appears below netpluslab.net in the tree.

5. Repeat the Steps 3 and 4, creating an organizational unit named **Manufacturing**. Figure 8-2 shows the addition of a new organizational unit.

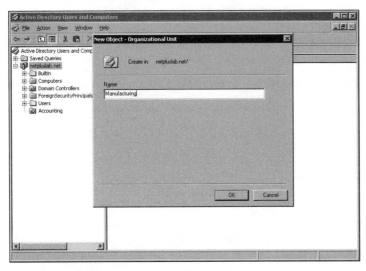

Figure 8-2   Adding an organizational unit

6. Right-click the icon for the **Accounting** object. From the pop-up menu, point to **New**, then click **User**. The New Object – User dialog box opens.

7. In the Full name and User logon name text boxes, enter **accounting-admin**. Click **Next**.

8. In both the Password and the Confirm password text boxes, type a password at least eight characters long that contains at least one number and a mixture of upper- and lower-case letters. Record or memorize this password.

9. Click the **User must change password at next logon** check box to remove the check mark. Click **Next**. The dialog box summarizes the account information.

10. Click **Finish**. The dialog box closes, and an icon for the accounting-admin account appears in the right pane. (If an Active Directory dialog box appears indicating that Windows cannot set the password because it does not meet the minimum password policy requirements, click **OK**. Then click **Back**. Change the password, click **Next**, and then click **Finish**.)

11. Repeat Steps 6 through 10 to create a user named **accountant**. Record the password for this account.

12. Right-click the **Manufacturing** object. On the pop-up menu, point to **New**, then click **User**. The New Object − User dialog box opens. Repeat Steps 7 through 10, creating a user account named **manufacturer**.

13. Right-click the **Accounting** object and select **Delegate Control** from the pop-up menu. The Delegation of Control Wizard opens.

14. Click **Next**. The Wizard offers you the option of selecting users or groups.

15. Click **Add**. The Select Users, Computers, or Groups window opens. In the "Enter the object names to select (examples)" text box, type **accounting-admin** and click **OK**. The name of the user appears in the Selected users and groups box.

16. Click **Next**. The wizard lists a series of tasks you could delegate.

17. Place a check in the **Create, delete, and manage user accounts** check box. Click **Next**. The wizard summarizes the options you have chosen.

18. Click **Finish**. The Wizard closes. You have now delegated control over user accounts in the Accounting Organizational Unit to the accounting-admin user. This user will not have rights over other parts of Active Directory, including the Manufacturing Organizational Unit.

19. Log off *SERVER1*.

20. On *SERVER1*, press **Ctrl+Alt+Del** to display the Log On to Windows dialog box. Log onto the computer as the **accounting-admin** user. The Windows Server 2003 desktop appears.

21. Click **Start**, and then click **Control Panel**. The Control Panel opens.

22. Double-click the **Administrative Tools** icon. The Administrative Tools window opens.

23. Double-click the **Active Directory Users and Computers** icon. The Active Directory Users and Computers window opens.

24. If the tree below *netpluslab.net* (in the tree in the left pane of the window) has not been expanded already, click the **plus sign (+)** next to netpluslab.net. Then click the icon for the **Accounting** object. Icons for user names appear in the right pane of the window.

25. Right-click the **accountant** user icon, and select **Reset Password**. The Reset Password dialog box opens.

26. Enter a new password in the New password and Confirm password text boxes. Click **OK**. A dialog box appears, indicating that the password for the accountant account has been changed.

27. Click **OK**.

28. Repeat Steps 6 through 10 for the Accounting object, creating a user named **bills**. Make sure to record the password.

29. Now you will verify that the accounting-admin account has no rights to other parts of Active Directory. Click the icon for the Manufacturing object. The icon for the manufacturer user appears.

30. Right-click the icon for the **manufacturer** user in the right pane of the window. From the pop-up menu, select **Reset Password**. The Reset Password dialog box opens.

31. Enter the new password in the New password and Confirm password text boxes. Click **OK**. A dialog box appears, indicating that Windows could not complete the password change and that access is denied. Click **OK**.

32. Right-click the **Manufacturing** icon in the left pane of the window. From the pop-up menu, note that you do not have the option to create a new user. Select **Delegate Control**. A dialog box appears, indicating that you do not have permission to write security information for this object.

33. Click **OK**. The dialog box closes.

34. Now you will verify that the user you created works. On *WORKSTATION1*, press **Ctrl+Alt+Del** to display the Log On to Windows dialog box. Log on to the *netpluslab.net* domain as the **bills** user you created in Step 28. The Windows XP desktop appears.

35. Log off both computers.

Certification Objectives

Objectives for the Network+ Exam:

➤ Identify the basic capabilities (i.e., client support, interoperability, authentication, file and print services, application support, and security) of the following server operating systems: UNIX/Linux, NetWare, Windows, Macintosh

Review Questions

1. What is an organizational unit?
   a. a department or division within an organization
   b. a container used to group users with similar permissions and rights
   c. a container used to group similar objects such as users or groups
   d. an organization

2. If a user is assigned "Read" permissions to a folder, what may he do with the folder's contents? (Choose all that apply.)
   a. View the listing of files in the folder.
   b. Launch executable files in the folder.
   c. Delete files in the folder.
   d. View the contents of files in the folder.

3. If a user is assigned "Modify" permissions to a folder, what may she do with the folder's contents? (Choose all that apply.)
   a. View the listing of files in the folder.
   b. Launch executable files in the folder.
   c. Delete files in the folder.
   d. View the contents of files in the folder.

4. Which of the following is a potential advantage of delegating user administration to another user? (Choose all that apply.)
   a. The network administrator can concentrate on more important network maintenance issues.
   b. One or more users in each department can handle user administration for their department.
   c. It allows large network administration departments to delegate tasks.
   d. It allows each user in a department to handle the administration of his or her own account.

5. By default, what permissions do users in the Everyone group have to a newly shared Windows Server 2003 folder?
   a. Read & Execute only
   b. List Folder Contents only
   c. Full Access
   d. By default, users have no rights to newly shared folders.

6. In this lab you grouped users in the same department into organizational units, and then used the organizational units to delegate permissions within those organizational units. What is another approach you could have used to perform the same task?

a. Group each department into separate forests.

b. Group each department into separate domains in the same tree.

c. Create a new forest for each department.

d. Group each department into separate workgroups within the same tree.

LAB 8.3 ADDING A DOMAIN TO A FOREST

Objectives

Active Directory allows you to merge organizations that need to share resources but still remain independent. For instance, a large company may own several smaller companies. These companies may need to share common network resources, while they may be too independent to share the same domain safely. In other cases, employees of a business partner may need access to some of your company's network resources. Since they work for a separate organization, adding them to your organization's tree hardly makes sense.

One way to solve this problem is to create another tree in the same forest. In this situation, Active Directory automatically creates a two-way transitive trust. A trust is a relationship in Active Directory between two domains where one domain accepts authentications from another domain's domain controller. In a two-way transitive trust, both domains accept authentications from the other domain. This means that users in one domain tree can log onto machines for the other domain tree, and vice versa. It is important to keep in mind, however, that users for each domain will still be restricted by Active Directory's security mechanisms.

After completing this lab, you will be able to:

➤ Add a tree to a forest

Materials Required

In this lab, you will need the following:

➤ The network configured at the end of Lab 8.2

➤ A computer running Windows Server 2003 Enterprise Edition named *SERVER2* with an IP address of 192.168.54.2 and a subnet mask of 255.255.255.0 that is *not* configured as a domain controller

➤ *SERVER2* configured to use 192.168.54.1 as its DNS server

➤ Access to *SERVER2* as the Administrator

➤ Each computer connected to a hub with straight-through CAT 5 (or better) cables

➤ The Windows Server 2003 installation CD

Estimated completion time: **40 minutes**

LAB ACTIVITY

ACTIVITY

1. On *SERVER2*, press **Ctrl+Alt+Del** to display the Log On to Windows dialog box. Log on as the Administrator. The Windows Server 2003 desktop appears.

2. Click **Start**, then click **Run**. The Run dialog box opens.

3. Type **dcpromo** and press **Enter**. The Active Directory Installation Wizard opens.

4. Click **Next**. The wizard describes compatibility options for older versions of Windows.

5. Click **Next**. The wizard asks what sort of role you would like to configure for the new domain controller.

6. Make sure the **Domain controller for a new domain** option is selected. Click **Next**. The wizard gives you options for the type of domain you would like to create.

7. Select the **Domain tree in an existing forest** option. Figure 8-3 shows the Active Directory Installation Wizard as you add a new domain tree into an existing forest. Click **Next**.

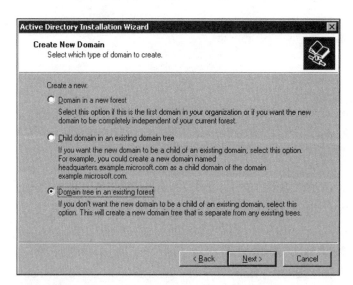

Figure 8-3   The Active Directory Installation Wizard

8. The wizard asks you to supply network credentials. In the User name text box, enter **administrator**. In the Password text box, enter the password of the Administrator for the *netpluslab.net* domain. In the Domain text box, enter **netpluslab.net**. Click **Next**. The wizard asks you for the name of the new domain tree.

9. Type **otherorg.net** in the Full DNS name for new domain text box. Click **Next**. The wizard displays the NetBIOS name for the new domain.

10. Accept the default entry, OTHERORG, by clicking **Next**. The wizard displays the locations of Active Directory database and log files.

11. Click **Next**. The wizard displays the location of the shared system volume.

12. Click **Next**. The wizard shows the results of DNS registration diagnostics, indicating that DNS is configured properly on the server. (Active Directory will not function properly if DNS does not work properly.)

13. Make sure the **Install and Configure the DNS Server on this computer** option is selected. Click **Next**. The wizard shows you default permissions for user and group objects.

14. Click **Next** to accept the defaults. The wizard asks you for the Directory Services Restore Mode Administrator Password.

15. Enter the password **Passw0rd** (or another password selected by your instructor) in the Restore Mode Password and the Confirm password text boxes. Click **Next**. The wizard shows you a summary of the options you have selected.

16. Click **Next**. If prompted, insert the Windows Server 2003 installation CD in the CD-ROM drive, and then click **OK**. An Active Directory Installation Wizard dialog box opens, indicating that the wizard is configuring active directory and that it may take several minutes or longer to complete. The dialog box closes and the computer indicates that you have completed the wizard.

17. Click **Finish**. An Active Directory Installation Wizard dialog box opens, indicating that the computer must be restarted before the changes you made take effect.

18. Click **Restart Now**. The computer reboots.

19. After the computer has rebooted, press **Ctrl+Alt+Del** to display the Log On to Windows dialog box. Log on as the Administrator for the *otherorg.net* domain. The Windows Server 2003 desktop appears.

20. Click **Start**, point to **Administrative Tools**, then click **Active Directory Users and Computers**. The Active Directory Users and Computers window opens.

8

21. Click the **plus sign (+)** next to otherorg.net to expand the tree underneath it. Right-click the icon for the **Users** object in the left pane of the window. From the pop-up menu, point to **New**, then click **User**. The New Object – User window opens.

22. In the Full name and User logon name text boxes, enter **orguser** and then click **Next**.

23. Enter a password in the Password and Confirm password text boxes at least eight letters long, containing at least one upper-case letter and at least one number. Click the **User must change password at next logon** check box to remove the check. Click **Next**. The dialog box summarizes the options you have chosen.

24. Click **Finish**.

25. On *WORKSTATION1*, press **Ctrl+Alt+Del** to display the Log On to Windows dialog box.

26. In the User name text box, enter **orguser**. In the Password text box, enter the password for this account.

27. From the drop-down menu next to Log on to, select **OTHERORG**. Click **OK**. You should now be logged onto *WORKSTATION1* as the orguser user in the *otherorg.net* domain. The Windows XP desktop appears.

28. Log off both computers.

Certification Objectives

Objectives for the Network+ Exam:

➤ Identify the basic capabilities (i.e., client support, interoperability, authentication, file and print services, application support, and security) of the following server operating systems: UNIX/Linux, NetWare, Windows, Macintosh

Review Questions

1. Which of the following best describes a trust?

   a. a relationship between domains in which one domain does all authentication for the other

   b. a relationship between two domains in which one domain does not accept authentication from the other

   c. a relationship between two domains in which one domain accepts authentication from the other

   d. a relationship between two domains in which one domain does not require authentication from the other

2. Which of the following best defines a domain in the context of Windows Server 2003?

   a. a group of users and other resources that reside on the same server

   b. a group of users, servers, and other resources that share a database of account and security information

   c. a group of users, servers, and other resources that are located on the same LAN

   d. a group of users and other resources that are located within the same geographical location

3. On a Windows Server 2003 network, what is the term for a server that does not contain Active Directory information?

   a. member server

   b. domain controller

   c. PDC

   d. BDC

4. If two user accounts belong to the same domain, what else can you assume about them?

   a. They log on to the same server for authentication.

   b. They are located in the same building.

   c. They belong to the same tree.

   d. They belong to the same organizational unit.

5. If Domain A and Domain B are configured to have a two-way transitive trust, which of the following is necessarily true (without assuming anything about user privileges or folder sharing)?

   a. A user from Domain A can access any resources in Domain B, and vice versa.

   b. A user from Domain A can be authenticated by a server in Domain B, and vice versa.

   c. A user from Domain A can launch programs from any server in Domain B, and vice versa.

   d. A user from Domain A can access any resources in Domain B, but the reverse is not necessarily true.

LAB 8.4 SETTING USER PERMISSIONS WITH GROUPS

Objectives

Configuring permissions for network resources on the user level requires a lot of work and maintenance. This is particularly true if you need to give a lot of users access to a specific resource. Instead, you can use groups, which allow you to manage multiple users at one time. By putting many users into a group, you can give them access to additional network resources simply by giving the group access. You can remove access just as easily.

For instance, each manager in a company might need to have access to certain folders containing confidential personnel information. By creating a Managers group, you can add each manager user to this group. Then you can give access to the Managers group to each folder. When the company hires a new manager, you can add them to the Managers group and they will have access to the folders. You can use smaller groups to give more granular permissions. For instance, if the managers in the Safety department need access to confidential safety records, then you can add them to the Safety-Managers group.

Windows Server 2003 uses three major types of groups in order to give access to network resources. Local groups are used on stand-alone servers. Typically you will not want to use these if you have more than one server, since Active Directory will not replicate them. Global groups are replicated by Active Directory, and are compatible with earlier versions of Windows. Universal groups are also replicated by Active Directory, but they are not compatible with versions of Windows prior to Windows 2000.

After completing this lab, you will be able to:Create groupsAdd users to groups

Materials Required

In this lab, you will need the following:The network configured at the end of Lab 8.2No group named Personnel in Active Directory, and no users named hrmanager or employee

Estimated completion time: **30 minutes**

LAB ACTIVITY

ACTIVITY

1. On *SERVER1*, press **Ctrl+Alt+Del** to display the Log On to Windows dialog box. Log on as the Administrator. The Windows Server 2003 desktop appears.

2. Click **Start**, point to **Administrative Tools**, then click **Active Directory Users and Computers**. The Active Directory Users and Computers window opens.

3. If necessary, expand the tree next to netpluslab.net by clicking the **plus sign (+)** next to it.

4. Right-click the icon for the **Users** object. From the pop-up menu, click **New**, then click **Group**. The New Object – Group window opens.

5. In the Group name text box, enter **Personnel**. Make sure that the **Global** and **Security** options are selected, and click **OK**. The window closes.

6. Now you will create a user to put in this group. Right-click the icon for the **Users** object again. From the pop-up menu, click **New**, then click **User**. The New Object – User window opens.

7. In the Full name and User logon name text boxes, enter **hrmanager**. Click **Next**.

8. Enter a password in both the Password and Confirm password text boxes. (Make sure that the password is at least eight characters long, and contains at least one number and a mixture of upper- and lower-case letters.) Click the **User must change password at next logon** check box to remove the check mark from it.

9. Click **Next**. The dialog box summarizes the options you have chosen.

10. Click **Finish**. The New Object – User window closes.

11. Repeat Steps 6 through 10 to create the **employee** user.

12. Click the icon for the **Users** object to select it. In the right pane of the window, a list of the users and groups configured in Active Directory appears. Right-click **hrmanager**. From the pop-up menu, click **Add to a group**. The Select Group window opens.

13. In the box at the bottom of the Select Group window, enter **Personnel**.

14. Click **Check Names**. The computer verifies that it can find the group name you entered in the Active Directory schema and underlines the group name.

15. Click **OK**. An Active Directory dialog box opens, indicating that the group was added successfully.

16. Click **OK**. The dialog box and the Select Group window close.

17. Right-click a blank spot on the Windows Server 2003 desktop. From the pop-up menu, click **New**, then click **Folder**. A folder named New Folder appears on the desktop, with the words "New Folder" highlighted. Type **PersonnelFolder**. The words you type replace the words "New Folder."

18. Right-click the **PersonnelFolder** folder you just created. From the pop-up menu, select **Sharing and Security**. The PersonnelFolder Properties window opens.

19. Select the **Share this folder** option. The computer prints the Share name as "PersonnelFolder."

8

20. Now you will configure sharing permissions. Click **Permissions**. The Permissions for PersonnelFolder window opens.

21. If necessary, in the top pane of the window, click **Everyone** to highlight it. Click **Remove**. The computer removes the Everyone group from the top pane of the window.

22. Click the **Add** button. The Select Users, Computers, or Groups window opens.

23. In the text box at the bottom, enter **Personnel**.

24. Click **Check Names**. The computer verifies that it can find the group name you entered in the Active Directory schema and underlines the group name.

25. Click **OK**. The Select Users, Computers, or Groups window closes.

26. Click the **Full Control** check box under the Allow column. This will give full control over the folder to the Personnel group, but to no users in other groups. Figure 8-4 shows permissions configured for the PersonnelFolder folder. Click **OK**.

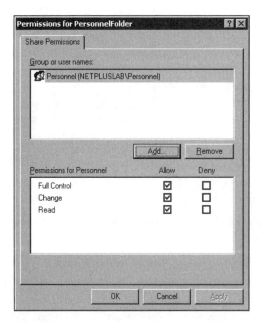

Figure 8-4 Configuration permissions

27. Now you will configure permissions on the file system for the new folder. Click the **Security** tab.

28. Click the **Add** button below "Group or user names" at the top of the Security tab. The Select Users, Computers, or Groups dialog box opens.

29. Repeat Steps 23 through 25.

30. Click **OK** to close the PersonnelFolder Properties window.

31. Double-click the **PersonnelFolder** folder. The folder opens.

32. Right-click a blank spot of the folder. From the pop-up menu, click **New**, then click **Text Document**. A New Text Document icon appears in the folder.

33. Double-click the **Notepad** icon next to the New Text Document icon. Notepad opens the blank document.

34. Write your name in the text document. Click **File**, then click **Save** to save the file.

35. Click **File**, then click **Exit**.

36. On *WORKSTATION1*, press **Ctrl+Alt+Del** to display the Log On to Windows dialog box. Log onto the computer as the **hrmanager** user. The Windows XP desktop appears.

37. Click **Start**, then click **My Computer**. The My Computer window opens.

38. Click **Tools**, then click **Map Network Drive**. The Map Network Drive window opens.

39. Record the drive letter selected in the Drive drop-down menu. In the Folder text box, enter **\\192.168.54.1\PersonnelFolder** and press **Finish**. A dialog box appears briefly, indicating that the computer is attempting to map the network drive. Then the dialog box closes, and an icon for the new mapped drive appears in the My Computer window.

40. Double-click the **PersonnelFolder on '192.168.54.1' (Z:)** icon (where Z is the letter of the drive you recorded in the last step). The folder opens, with the text document you created earlier inside.

41. Double-click the text document. You see your name.

42. Log off *WORKSTATION1*.

43. Repeat Steps 36 through 39 on *WORKSTATION1*, logging on as the **employee** user instead. At the end of Step 39, you see a dialog box indicating that access is denied.

44. Log off both computers.

Certification Objectives

Objectives for the Network+ Exam:

➤ Identify the basic capabilities (i.e., client support, interoperability, authentication, file and print services, application support, and security) of the following server operating systems: UNIX/Linux, NetWare, Windows, Macintosh

Review Questions

1. Which of the following best describes a group?
   a. a collection of users who are authenticated by the same server
   b. a collection of users, groups, or computers that share the same security privileges and restrictions
   c. a collection of users or objects that are located in the same building
   d. a collection of users with some part of their fully distinguished name in common

2. Which of the following is a default group in Windows Server 2003 (in other words, it exists after you install the operating system)?
   a. Guests
   b. Remote_Users
   c. Servers
   d. Printers

3. In the context of Windows Server 2003, what is the difference between a local and a global group?
   a. A local group is used to manage resources within one LAN, while a global group is used to manage resources across several LANs or WANs.
   b. A local group is used to manage resources on a single server, while a global group is used to manage resources on all servers within an organization.
   c. A local group is used to manage resources within a single domain, while a global group is used to manage resources on all domains within a forest.
   d. A local group is used to manage resources on a computer, while a global group is used to manage resources within a domain.

4. What are nested groups?
   a. groups that belong to more than one domain
   b. groups that share the same permissions as other groups in the same domain
   c. groups created within another group
   d. groups that contain objects that are owned by other objects

5. If the user named "JaneY" belongs to the group called "STUDENTS," and the group called "STUDENTS" has been assigned "Full Control" permissions to the folder called "GRADES," which of the following are true? (Choose all that apply.)

    a. JaneY can modify the files in the folder called "GRADES."

    b. JaneY can read, but cannot modify, the files in the folder called "GRADES."

    c. JaneY can delete, but cannot read, the files in the folder called "GRADES."

    d. JaneY can prevent other users who don't belong to the STUDENTS group from reading the files in the folder called "GRADES."

6. What is the term for the database that contains information about Windows Server 2003 objects and their attributes?

    a. NDS

    b. Master Domain

    c. NFS

    d. Active Directory

8

Lab 8.5 Remotely Managing a Computer with Active Directory

Objectives

In addition to controlling users and groups, you can use Active Directory to help you manage remote computers. Through Active Directory, you can perform many of the functions on a remote computer that you can do when directly logged onto that computer. For example, you can start and stop services on the remote computer, look at system information, and browse the Event Viewer. The Event Viewer is where you can view information about error messages and other events that have occurred on the computer. If you need to administer a network with many users and many computers, this can save you significant time.

After completing this lab, you will be able to: Remotely manage Windows computers

Materials Required

This lab will require the following:

➤ The network built at the end of Lab 8.1 or 8.2

Estimated completion time: **40 minutes**

LAB ACTIVITY

ACTIVITY

1. On *SERVER1*, press **Ctrl+Alt+Del** to display the Log On to Windows dialog box. Log onto the server as the Administrator for the *netpluslab.net* domain. The Windows Server 2003 desktop appears.

2. Press **Start**, point to **Administrative Tools**, and click **Computer Management**. The Computer Management window opens.

3. Click the **Disk Management** icon below "Storage." How many hard disks are on the server, how large are they, and what file system have they been configured with?

4. Click the **Event Viewer** in the tree in the left pane of the window. A list of the event logs available appears in the right pane of the window.

5. Double-click the **System** icon. A list of events in the System event log appears in the right pane. Double-click the top event. The Event Properties window opens, showing detailed information about that particular event.

6. Click the down arrow on the upper-right part of the window. The Event Viewer moves to the next event. Repeat a few times in order to see more events.

7. Close the Event Properties window by clicking **OK**.

8. Right-click **Computer Management (Local)** at the top of the tree in the left pane of the window. Select **Connect to another computer** from the pop-up menu. The Select Computer dialog box opens.

9. In the Another computer text box, type **WORKSTATION1** and click **OK**. The icon at the top of the left pane of the window changes to Computer Management (WORKSTATION1).

10. Click the **plus sign** (+) next to System Tools to expand the tree underneath it. Repeat this step with the Services and Applications icon.

11. Repeat Steps 4 through 7 to look at events on *WORKSTATION1*. Does *WORKSTATION1* have as many types of event logs as *SERVER1* does? Figure 8-5 shows the event log on *WORKSTATION1*.

12. On *WORKSTATION1*, press **Ctrl+Alt+Del** to display the Log On to Windows dialog box. Log on as the Administrator of the NETPLUSLAB.NET domain. The Windows XP desktop appears.

13. Click **Start**, then click **Control Panel**. The Control Panel opens.

14. Click the **Performance and Maintenance** category.

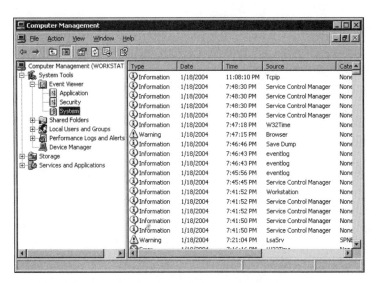

Figure 8-5   Viewing the event log on *WORKSTATION1*

15. Click the **Administrative Tools** icon.

16. Double-click the **Services** icon. The Services window opens.

17. Look for the Automatic Updates icon. Its status is "Started."

18. On *SERVER1*, click the **Services** icon in the left pane of the Computer Management window. A list of the services running on *WORKSTATION1* appears in the right pane of the window.

19. Right-click the **Automatic Updates** icon. From the pop-up menu, select **Stop**. A dialog box appears briefly, indicating that Windows is attempting to stop the service. The status disappears.

20. On *WORKSTATION1*, press **F5** to refresh the Services window. Look at the status of the Automatic Updates icon in the Services window. It is now blank, indicating that the service is not running.

21. Right-click the **Automatic Updates** icon in the Services window. From the pop-up menu, select **Start**. A dialog box appears briefly, indicating that Windows is attempting to start the service. The status changes to "Started."

22. Log off both computers.

Certification Objectives

Objectives for the Network+ Exam:

➤ Identify the basic capabilities (i.e., client support, interoperability, authentication, file and print services, application support, and security) of the following server operating systems: UNIX/Linux, NetWare, Windows, Macintosh

Review Questions

1. Which of the following is a potential advantage of being able to manage computers remotely?

   a. You will not need to log onto each individual computer.

   b. It eliminates the need for authentications.

   c. It uses less CPU time.

   d. It prevents security problems.

2. Which Windows Server 2003 utility would you use to find events that have happened on a particular server?

   a. Device Manager

   b. Disk Defragmenter

   c. Command Prompt

   d. Event Viewer

3. Why are you able to log onto the remote computer without supplying a user name and password?

   a. No user name or password are necessary.

   b. Active Directory handles authentication on the remote computer for you.

   c. Active Directory does not require authentication for remote computers.

   d. Your computer automatically supplies the user name and password without the help of Active Directory.

4. True or False? Management of remote computers can only be performed by the domain administrator.

5. When you select Services from the Administrative Tools menu on a Windows Server 2003 computer, what will you see?

   a. all services currently available on the Windows Server 2003 computer

   b. all services currently running on the Windows Server 2003 computer

   c. all services currently running on the Windows Server 2003 computer and its clients

   d. all services currently running on the Windows Server 2003 computer and other servers in the same domain

NETWORKING WITH UNIX AND LINUX

Labs included in this chapter
➤ Lab 9.1 Starting and Stopping a Linux Server
➤ Lab 9.2 Managing Users, Groups, and File Permissions
➤ Lab 9.3 Connecting a Windows XP Client Using Samba
➤ Lab 9.4 Managing Processes
➤ Lab 9.5 Remotely Managing Linux Servers

Net+ Exam Objectives	
Objective	Lab
Identify the basic capabilities (i.e., client support, interoperability, authentication, file and print services, application support, and security) of the following server operating systems: UNIX/Linux, NetWare, Windows, Macintosh	9.1, 9.2, 9.3, 9.4, 9.5
Identify the basic capabilities (i.e., client connectivity, local security mechanisms, and authentication) of the following clients: UNIX/Linux, Windows, Macintosh	9.3, 9.5

Lab 9.1 Starting and Stopping a Linux Server

Objectives

In this lab, you will stop and start a server running Red Hat Linux Enterprise ES 3.x. While Linux is not identical to UNIX, the two have much in common and managing a Linux server is much like managing a UNIX server. As a result, much of the material in this chapter also applies to UNIX.

While most versions of Linux come with a GUI, it is not always installed. Instead, Linux servers are often managed through a text console. Stopping and restarting the server from a text console is a less intuitive process than it is in Windows. While this makes a Linux server more difficult for a neophyte to administer than a Windows server, the lack of a GUI allows a Linux server to devote its processing power to the task of serving its users.

A Linux server typically has several different text consoles, which you can run at the same time. These consoles are often called virtual consoles, since you can switch back and forth between them. You can always access a console (even from the GUI) through a keyboard shortcut.

In Linux, the init program is the master program which ultimately starts and stops all the programs on the server. It runs as a daemon, or a program that runs and performs its tasks in the background. The init program can also be used to change the runlevel of the computer. A runlevel is a state in which a particular group of software programs are to be run. In most versions of Linux, runlevel 3 is considered the normal state and all programs that should be started at boot are started. Runlevel 0 is used to shut down the computer, while runlevel 6 is used to reboot it. Runlevel 1 puts the computer in single user mode. Single user mode is a special state in which the computer operates with the absolute minimum number of programs running. It is typically used for maintenance. You can change the runlevel directly with the `init` command, or you can use the `halt`, `reboot`, or `shutdown` commands. Each of these commands ultimately calls the `init` command. If you use the `shutdown` command, you can tell the computer to reboot after a certain interval and send a warning message to users. This allows users to save their work and log off the computer before rebooting.

After completing this lab, you will be able to:

➤ Stop and restart a Linux computer

➤ Put a Linux computer into single user mode

➤ Switch back and forth between virtual consoles

Materials Required

This lab will require the following:

➤ A computer running Red Hat Enterprise Linux ES 3.x, named *LINUX1.NETPLUSLAB.NET* and configured with an IP address of 192.168.54.5

➤ The computer configured with a graphical login

➤ The computer configured without firewall software

➤ The computer initially powered off

➤ The root user's password

Estimated completion time: **30 minutes**

9

ACTIVITY

1. Power on the computer. The Welcome to linux1.netpluslab.net page appears.

2. In the Username text box, enter **root**. Press **Enter**. The Password text box appears.

3. Enter the password for the root account in the Password text box. Press **Enter**. The Red Hat desktop appears.

4. Now you will switch to one of the text consoles. Press **Ctrl+Alt+F1**. A text console appears, with the linux1 login prompt.

5. At the linux1 login prompt, type **root**. Press **Enter**. The Password prompt appears.

6. Type the password for the root account and press **Enter**. The computer displays the last login by the root account and displays the prompt.

7. Press **Alt+F2**. The computer switches to another virtual terminal, displaying the linux1 login prompt.

8. Press **Alt+F3**, **Alt+F4**, **Alt+F5**, and then **Alt+F6**. The computer cycles through each of its virtual terminals.

9. Press **Alt+F7**. The computer switches back to the Red Hat desktop.

10. Right-click a blank spot on the desktop. From the pop-up menu, click **New Terminal**. A terminal window named root@linux1:~ opens.

11. Type **init 1** and press **Enter**. The GUI closes, and in a text console the computer displays a message indicating that it is switching to singular user mode. A prompt appears.

12. Type **init 6** and press **Enter**. The computer displays a message indicating that it is switching to runlevel 6, shuts down services, and reboots the computer.

13. Repeat Steps 1 through 3 to log back onto the computer.

14. Right-click a blank spot on the desktop. In the pop-up menu, click **New Terminal**. A terminal window named root@linux1:~ opens.

15. Repeat the previous step to open another terminal window.

16. In either of the terminal windows, type **shutdown -h +2 The computer is shutting down for maintenance** and press **Enter**. The computer prints the text "The computer is shutting down for maintenance" and indicates that the computer is going to halt. Figure 9-1 shows a terminal window after the shutdown command has been run.

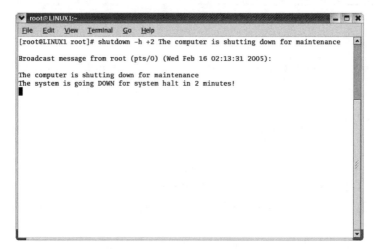

Figure 9-1 Shutting down the computer with the shutdown command

17. Look in the other terminal window. The computer displays the warning message in that window, too. After a minute, the computer displays in both terminals the text "The system is going DOWN for system halt in 1 minute." After another minute, the computer powers itself off.

Certification Objectives

Objectives for the Network+ Exam:

➤ Identify the basic capabilities (i.e., client support, interoperability, authentication, file and print services, application support, and security) of the following server operating systems: UNIX/Linux, NetWare, Windows, Macintosh

Review Questions

1. What is a daemon?

   a. any Linux GUI program that runs in the background

   b. a virus

   c. a Linux program that runs in the background and performs system services

   d. a Linux program that runs in the foreground and runs system services

2. What is the init program used for?

   a. to reboot the computer

   b. to halt the computer

   c. to change the runlevel of the computer

   d. to put the computer into single user mode

3. What is the advantage of running a Linux server without a GUI?

   a. The server can be managed more intuitively without a GUI.

   b. The server can devote more resources to serving users without a GUI.

   c. Server configuration can be performed without the use of a mouse or keyboard.

   d. The server can be rebooted without users logging off.

4. What is the purpose of the kernel?

   a. to change the computer's runlevel

   b. to store information about files and directories

   c. to load files into memory so that they can be accessed quickly

   d. to control access to system resources

5. What is the advantage of using the shutdown command instead of the init command to reboot the computer?

   a. You can announce the reboot with a broadcast message and allow users time to save their files and log off.

   b. You can automatically save the files of any user on the system and log them out.

   c. The shutdown command uses the init program, so there is no advantage.

   d. The shutdown command verifies that all users have logged off before proceeding.

LAB 9.2 MANAGING USERS, GROUPS, AND FILE PERMISSIONS

Objectives

Basic user management in Linux revolves around the user and the group. Each file on a Linux server is configured with read, write, or execute permissions, or some combination of the three. For instance, a user who has only read permissions to a file will be able to read it, but will not be able to either execute it or change it. For each file, these permissions apply to three categories of users: the user who owns the file, the group to which the owner belongs, and all other users.

For instance, suppose a file is owned by the user netplus in the lab group. Its permissions might be set so that the netplus user has the ability only to read, write, and execute the file, users in the lab group have the ability to read the file, and all other users have no access to the file. (Note that the root user has special permissions in Linux and can read any file, or change permissions for any file as needed.) You can view the permissions of a file with the ls -l command (the -l option displays additional information about each file). This command displays the file permissions, the owner and group of the file, its size, the time or date it was created, and its name. For instance, a file might have permissions -rwxr-x---. The first character indicates whether or not the file is a directory (a d indicates that it is a directory, a – that it is not); the next three characters show read, write, and execute permissions for the owner; the next three characters show read, write and execute permissions for the group; and the last three characters show read, write and execute permissions for other users. An r indicates read permission, a w indicates write permission, an x indicates execute permission, and a – indicates no permissions. You can change file permissions with the chmod command.

In order to add a user or group in Linux, you can use the useradd and groupadd commands. After creating a user, you can set its password with the passwd command. These commands create users and groups. You can modify a user account with the usermod command, and groups with the groupmod command. Finally, you can delete user accounts with the userdel command, and groups with the groupdel command. User information is stored in the /etc/passwd file, group information is stored in the /etc/group file, and password information is stored in the /etc/shadow file. Each user is identified by a user ID (UID), and each group by a group ID (GID). Instead of using /etc/shadow, /etc/group and /etc/passwd, a Linux computer can be configured to get account information from a directory service such as Lightweight Directory Access Protocol (LDAP), eDirectory, or Active Directory.

In order to test permissions, you can use the su command to change to another user. The su command is commonly used by a network administrator to change from an ordinary user account to root. You can use the id command to identify which user you are logged in as, and the groups to which that user belongs.

After completing this lab, you will be able to:

➤ Add a new group on a Linux computer using the `groupadd` command

➤ Add a new user on a Linux computer using the `useradd` command

➤ Modify user accounts on a Linux computer with the `usermod` command

➤ Delete user accounts on a Linux computer with the `userdel` command

➤ Modify file permissions with the `chmod` command

Materials Required

This lab will require the following:

➤ A computer running Red Hat Enterprise Linux ES 3.x, configured with an IP address of 192.168.54.5 and with a host name of *LINUX1.NETPLUSLAB.NET*

➤ The root user's password

9

Estimated completion time: **50 minutes**

ACTIVITY

1. Verify that the Welcome to linux1.netpluslab.net page is displayed. In the Username text box, enter **root**. Press **Enter**. The Password text box appears.

2. Enter the password for the root account in the Password text box. Press **Enter**. The Red Hat desktop appears.

3. Right-click a blank spot on the desktop. In the pop-up menu, click **New Terminal**. A terminal window named root@linux1:~ opens.

4. Type **groupadd lab** and press **Enter**. The computer adds the lab group.

5. Type **useradd –m –g lab netplus** and press **Enter**. The computer creates a user named netplus, places it in the lab group, and creates a home directory for this account. See Table 9-1 for a list of common options for the useradd command. Note that the name of the account to be created is always the last argument for this command.

Table 9-1   Command-line options for the `useradd` command

Option	Meaning
`-d home directory`	Specifies the location of the user's home directory
`-e expiration date`	Specifies the account's expiration date
`-g group`	Specifies the user's initial group
`-G group[, ...]`	Specifies one or more additional groups, separated by commas

Table 9-1 Command-line options for the `useradd` command (continued)

Option	Meaning
`-m`	Creates the user's home directory
`-u UID`	Specifies the user's UID
`-D`	Causes the useradd command to set new defaults for users added

6. Type **passwd netplus** and press **Enter**. The computer displays a message indicating that it is changing the password for netplus, and then displays the New password prompt.

7. At the New password prompt, type a password for the netplus account and press **Enter**. (If the password is too short or based on a word commonly found in a dictionary, the computer may print an error message indicating that this is a bad password. If so, simply go on to the next step.)

8. The computer displays the Retype new password prompt. Retype the new password recorded in the previous step and press **Enter**. If the computer prints an error message indicating that the passwords do not match, repeat the previous step and this step. The computer adds the new password for the netplus account.

9. Click the **Red Hat** icon, then click **Log Out**. A dialog box opens, asking if you are sure you want to log out.

10. Select the **Log Out** option button, and click **OK**. The computer logs you out of the Red Hat desktop, and the Welcome to linux1.netpluslab.net page appears.

11. Repeat Steps 1 and 2, logging in as the netplus account and using the password you recorded in Step 7. The Red Hat desktop appears.

12. Right-click a blank spot on the desktop, and click **New Terminal** from the pop-up menu. A terminal window titled netplus@linux1:~ opens. Note that the terminal window prompt ends in a $ character instead of a # character. This indicates that you are using an ordinary user account instead of the root account.

13. Type **more /etc/passwd** and press **Enter**. The computer displays the contents of the /etc/passwd file, which contains information about user accounts. If the computer displays the text "--More--" at the bottom of the terminal window, press the **spacebar** until the prompt returns. The last entry contains the name of the netplus account, its UID and GID, the location of its home directory, and the name of the shell or command interpreter it uses. Figure 9-2 shows the use of the more command.

```
netplus@LINUX1:~
File   Edit   View   Terminal   Go   Help
[netplus@LINUX1 netplus]$ more /etc/passwd
root:x:0:0:root:/root:/bin/bash
bin:x:1:1:bin:/bin:/sbin/nologin
daemon:x:2:2:daemon:/sbin:/sbin/nologin
adm:x:3:4:adm:/var/adm:/sbin/nologin
lp:x:4:7:lp:/var/spool/lpd:/sbin/nologin
sync:x:5:0:sync:/sbin:/bin/sync
shutdown:x:6:0:shutdown:/sbin:/sbin/shutdown
halt:x:7:0:halt:/sbin:/sbin/halt
mail:x:8:12:mail:/var/spool/mail:/sbin/nologin
news:x:9:13:news:/etc/news:
uucp:x:10:14:uucp:/var/spool/uucp:/sbin/nologin
operator:x:11:0:operator:/root:/sbin/nologin
games:x:12:100:games:/usr/games:/sbin/nologin
gopher:x:13:30:gopher:/var/gopher:/sbin/nologin
ftp:x:14:50:FTP User:/var/ftp:/sbin/nologin
nobody:x:99:99:Nobody:/:/sbin/nologin
rpm:x:37:37::/var/lib/rpm:/sbin/nologin
vcsa:x:69:69:virtual console memory owner:/dev:/sbin/nologin
nscd:x:28:28:NSCD Daemon:/:/sbin/nologin
sshd:x:74:74:Privilege-separated SSH:/var/empty/sshd:/sbin/nologin
rpc:x:32:32:Portmapper RPC user:/:/sbin/nologin
rpcuser:x:29:29:RPC Service User:/var/lib/nfs:/sbin/nologin
--More--(54%)
```

Figure 9-2   The MORE command

14. Type **more /etc/group** and press **Enter**. The computer displays the contents of the /etc/group file, which contains information about groups. If the computer displays the text "--More--" at the bottom of the terminal window, press the **spacebar** until the prompt returns. The last entry contains the name of the lab group and its GID. What is the GID of the lab group?

15. Type **more /etc/shadow** and press **Enter**. The computer displays the text "/etc/shadow: Permission denied."

16. Type **ls -l /etc/passwd** and press **Enter**. The computer displays information about the file permissions for the /etc/passwd file. Repeat with the /etc/ group file. Who is the owner of the /etc/passwd and /etc/group files, and what are their permissions?

17. Repeat the previous step with /etc/shadow. How do permissions for /etc/ passwd and /etc/ group differ from permissions for the /etc/shadow file?

18. Type **id** and press **Enter**. The computer displays the UID and user account name for the netplus user, its primary group and GID, and the names and GIDs of all groups it is a member of.

9

19. Now you will create a file. Type **echo TEST >/tmp/test.txt** and press **Enter**. The computer creates a new file named test.txt in the /tmp directory, which contains the text TEST. The > symbol redirects the output of the echo command into the file test.txt.

20. Type **more /tmp/test.txt** and press **Enter**. The computer displays the word "TEST".

21. Now you will change the file permissions so that the netplus user can read and write the file, other users in the lab group only can read it, and no other users or groups can read it. Type **chmod o-rw /tmp/test.txt** and press **Enter**. The computer changes the permissions on the file test.txt by removing read and write permissions for other groups and users.

22. Type **ls -l /tmp/test.txt** and press **Enter**. What are the permissions on the file?

23. Type **su -** and press **Enter**. (The dash tells the su command to act as if the account had just logged into the computer.) The Password prompt appears.

24. Type the password for the root account and press **Enter**. The prompt now ends in a pound symbol (#), indicating that you are logged into the root account. (Note that the users in any other terminal windows would remain unaffected.)

25. Type **id** and press **Enter**. The computer displays the UID and user account name for the root user, its primary group and GID, and the names and GIDs of all groups it is a member of.

26. Type **more /etc/shadow** and press **Enter**. The computer displays the contents of the /etc/shadow file, which contains the passwords for all user accounts on the computer and information about password expiration for each account. If the computer displays the text "--More--" at the bottom of the terminal window, press the **spacebar** until the prompt returns. The last entry contains the password for the netplus account. (Note that the password is encrypted, and so it will not match the password you recorded in Step 7.)

27. Now you will create other user accounts and test their access to the test.txt file. Type **useradd -m -g lab netplus2** and press **Enter**. The computer creates a new user named netplus2.

28. Type **groupadd newgroup** and press **Enter**. The computer creates a new group named newgroup.

29. Type **useradd -m -g newgroup newuser** and press **Enter**. The computer creates a new user named newuser in the newgroup group.

30. Repeat Steps 6 through 8 for **netplus2** and **newuser** to create passwords for the these accounts.

31. Type **su - netplus2** and press **Enter**. The prompt now ends in $. You are logged in as the netplus2 user.

32. Type **more /tmp/test.txt** and press **Enter**. The computer displays the contents of the test.txt file.

33. Type **exit** and press **Enter**. The prompt ends in a pound sign (#), indicating that you are logged in as the root user again.

34. Type **su - newuser** and press **Enter**. The prompt ends in $, indicating that you are logged in as the newuser user.

35. Type **more /tmp/test.txt** and press **Enter**. The computer displays the text "/tmp/test.txt: Permission Denied."

36. Type **exit** and press **Enter**. The prompt ends in a pound sign (#), indicating that you are logged in as the root user again.

37. Now you will move the newuser user into the lab group so that it can access the test.txt file. Type **usermod –g lab newuser** and press **Enter**. The computer changes the primary group for the newuser user.

38. Repeat Steps 34 through 36. This time, the computer displays the contents of the /tmp/test.txt file.

39. Now you will delete the newuser user. Type **userdel newuser** and press **Enter**. The computer deletes the newuser user.

40. Now you will lock the netplus2 user account so that it cannot log into the computer. Type **usermod -L netplus2** and press **Enter**. The computer locks the netplus2 user.

41. Click the **Red Hat** icon, then click **Log Out**. A dialog box opens, asking if you are sure if you want to log out.

42. Click the **Log Out** option button and then click **OK**. The computer logs you out of the Red Hat desktop.

43. Repeat Steps 1 and 2 for the netplus2user, then for the newuser user. You are unable to log in for either user.

44. Log out.

Certification Objectives

Objectives for the Network+ Exam:

➤ Identify the basic capabilities (i.e., client support, interoperability, authentication, file and print services, application support, and security) of the following server operating systems: UNIX/Linux, NetWare, Windows, Macintosh

Review Questions

1. Bob has a Linux user account. He is going on vacation for two weeks. As a Linux system administrator, you need to make sure no one uses his account during his absence. What is the best way to keep his user information intact, while at the same time preventing others from logging in with Bob's user name?

   a. delete Bob's primary group

   b. use the usermod command to change the password for his account

   c. use the usermod command to lock his account

   d. use the finger command to delete his account

2. Which of the following commands would allow you to add a user named "carruthers" on a Linux computer?

   a. usermod -A carruthers

   b. useradd Carruthers

   c. useradd carruthers

   d. add user carruthers

3. Which of the following commands would allow you to add a group named "designers" on a Linux computer?

   a. groupadd designers

   b. useradd -g designers

   c. add group designers

   d. groupmod +G designers

4. On a Linux computer, what command could you use to determine which groups your user account belongs to?

   a. usermod

   b. /etc/groups

   c. id

   d. su

5. What is the purpose of having a new user change his password the first time he logs in to a network?

   a. It allows the user to use a more secure password.

   b. It ensures greater security because no one but the user will know the password.

   c. It allows the user to synchronize all his passwords on all systems.

   d. It allows the user to choose a password that will never expire.

LAB 9.3 CONNECTING A WINDOWS XP CLIENT USING SAMBA

Objectives

In this lab you will connect a Windows XP client to a Linux server using Samba. Samba is a collection of programs that runs the Common Internet File System (CIFS) and NetBIOS on Linux. CIFS is also known as the Server Message Block (SMB) protocol. (The name Samba is an extension of the "SMB" acronym.) Windows clients use CIFS natively, so Samba allows Windows clients to log into Linux servers without the installation of additional client software. Samba also allows Linux clients to connect to Windows servers.

In order to perform this lab, you will use a version of the vi editor. The vi (usually pronounced "vee eye") editor is a text-based editor that can be found in one form or another on virtually all Linux and UNIX computers. While not nearly as intuitive as Notepad or Microsoft Word, it is useful for editing configuration files and programs and contains some powerful features such as searching and text replacement based on pattern matching.

The vi editor has two primary modes, normal mode and insert mode. In normal mode, you can navigate through a document and run commands to delete or change existing text, but you cannot add text. In insert mode, you can add text. You can move the cursor through a document with the arrow keys or with a variety of keyboard shortcuts.

After completing this lab, you will be able to:

➤ Connect a Windows XP Professional client to a Linux server using Samba

➤ Connect a Linux computer to a Windows Server 2003 computer using Samba

➤ Use the vi text editor to edit configuration files

Materials Required

This lab will require the following:

➤ A computer running Red Hat Linux Enterprise Linux ES 3.x named *LINUX1.NETPLUSLAB.NET* and configured with an IP address of 192.168.54.5

➤ Samba installed on *LINUX1.NETPLUSLAB.NET* (this is the default for the server install), and the default /etc/samba/smb.conf file in place

➤ A user named netplus on *LINUX1.NETPLUSLAB.NET* with a known password, and a known password for the root account

➤ A computer running Windows XP Professional named *WORKSTATION1* and configured with an IP address of 192.168.54.3

➤ *WORKSTATION1* configured as part of the NETPLUS workgroup

➤ A computer running Windows Server 2003 Enterprise Edition named *SERVER1* and configured with an IP address of 192.168.54.1

➤ *SERVER1* configured as a domain controller for the netpluslab.net domain, with a user account named linux with a known password and a shared folder named netplus containing one or more files

➤ Access to both *WORKSTATION1* and *SERVER1* as the Administrator

➤ All three computers connected to a hub with CAT 5 (or better) UTP cables

➤ The firewall software not configured on *LINUX1.NETPLUSLAB.NET*

Estimated completion time: **60 minutes**

LAB ACTIVITY

ACTIVITY

1. On *LINUX1.NETPLUSLAB.NET*, type **netplus** in the Username text box on the Welcome to linux1.netpluslab.net screen and press **Enter**. The Password text box appears.

2. Type the password for the netplus account and press **Enter**. The Red Hat desktop appears.

3. Right-click a blank spot on the desktop. In the pop-up menu, click **New Terminal**. A new terminal window named netplus@linux1:~ opens.

4. Type **su –** and press **Enter**. The Password prompt appears.

5. Enter the password for the root account and press **Enter**. The prompt ends in a pound sign (#), indicating that you are logged in as the root user.

6. Type **mkdir /usr/netplus** and press **Enter**. The computer creates a directory named /usr/netplus, which you will share later.

7. Type **chmod a=rwxt /usr/netplus** and press **Enter**. The computer changes the permissions on the directory you just created. The changes in permissions will allow any user to create a file in the new directory, but they will only allow the user who created a file to modify or delete it.

8. Now you will configure Samba in order to share the new directory you created. Type **vi /etc/samba/smb.conf** and press **Enter**. The vi editor opens the file /etc/samba/smb.conf in the terminal window, and displays the name of the file at the bottom of the screen. The cursor blinks in the upper-left corner of the terminal window. Table 9-2 shows some of the most common keyboard commands in the vi editor.

Table 9-2   Keyboard commands in the vi editor

Keyboard shortcut	Meaning
j or ↓	Moves the cursor down
k or ↑	Moves the cursor up
h or ←	Moves the cursor to the left
l or →	Moves the cursor to the right
w	Moves the cursor to the beginning of the next word
i	Puts the vi editor in insert mode at the cursor
a	Puts the vi editor in insert mode after the cursor
A	Puts the vi editor in insert mode at the end of the line
ESC	Takes the vi editor from insert mode to normal mode
/pattern	Searches for *pattern* in the text of the file, where *pattern* is any combination of text or wild-card characters
G	Places the cursor at the end of the file
nG	Places the cursor at line *n*, where *n* is the number of the line
:w	Saves the file
:q	Quits the vi editor
:q!	Quits the vi editor without saving any changes
x	Deletes the character at the cursor
nx	Deletes *n* characters at the cursor, where *n* is the number of characters to be deleted
$	Places the cursor at the end of the line
0	Places the cursor at the beginning of the line
dd	Deletes the current line
dw	Deletes text from the cursor to the end of the word
ndw	Deletes text from the cursor through the next *n* words, where *n* is the number of words to be deleted
d$	Deletes text from the cursor until the end of the line

9. Type **G**. (Take care to type an uppercase "G".) The vi editor places the cursor at the beginning of the last line in the file.

10. Type **i**. The vi editor enters insert mode. "INSERT" appears at the bottom of the terminal window.

11. Type **[netplus]** and press **Enter**. The vi editor inserts the line into the file and moves the curser to the next, blank line. This creates a share called netplus.

12. Type **path = /usr/netplus** and press **Enter**. The vi editor inserts the line into the file and moves the cursor to the next. This makes the directory you created in Step 6 the location of the share named netplus.

13. Press **Esc**. The vi editor goes into normal mode.

14. Type **/workgroup = MYGROUP** and press **Enter**. The vi editor searches for the string "workgroup = MYGROUP" in the text file. If the computer does not find this line, scroll through the file manually looking for a line containing

the text "workgroup =" that does not begin with a #. (The # character is a comment, and any line beginning with a # is not read by Samba.)

15. Press **w** twice. The cursor moves to the beginning of the word MYGROUP.

16. Type **d$**. The computer deletes all text from the cursor to the end of the line.

17. Press **a**. The vi editor goes into insert mode. "INSERT" appears at the bottom of the terminal window.

18. Type **NETPLUS**, then press **Esc**. The vi editor adds the text to the file, then goes back into normal mode. Figure 9-3 shows the use of the vi editor.

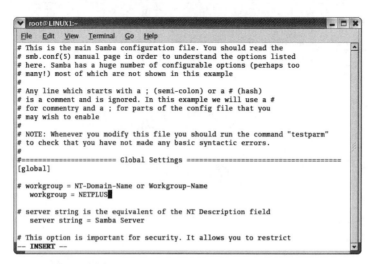

Figure 9-3 Using the vi editor

19. Type **:w** and press **Enter**. The vi editor saves the file.

20. Type **:q** and press **Enter**. The vi editor quits the file.

21. Type **testparm -s** and press **Enter**. This command checks the syntax of the Samba configuration file you just edited for errors. The computer displays the results of the configuration check and then a list of global Samba parameters.

22. Type **/etc/init.d/smb start** and press **Enter**. The computer displays a message indicating that it is starting SMB and NMB services, and that both are OK.

23. Type **cp /etc/samba/smb.conf /usr/netplus** and press **Enter**. This copies the file into the shared directory you created in Step 6.

24. Type **smbpasswd -a netplus** and press **Enter**. The new SMB password prompt appears. Type a password and press **Enter**. The Retype New SMB Password prompt appears. Type the password again and press **Enter**.

25. On *WORKSTATION1*, press **Ctrl+Alt+Del** to display the Log On to Windows window. Log onto the computer as the Administrator. The Windows XP desktop appears.

26. Click **Start**, then click **My Computer**. The My Computer window opens.

27. Click **Tools** on the menu bar, then click **Map Network Drive**. The Map Network Drive window opens.

28. In the Folder text box, enter **\\192.168.54.5\netplus**. From the Drive drop-down menu, select **Z:** if it has not already been selected.

29. Click **Connect using a different user name**. The Connect As dialog box opens.

30. In the User name text box, enter **netplus**. In the Password text box, enter the password for the netplus account that you created in Step 24. Click **OK**. The Connect As dialog box closes.

31. Click **Finish**. The Map Network Drive dialog box appears briefly, and the Z: window opens with the contents of the newly shared folder, including the file smb.conf.

32. Now you will connect to *SERVER1*. On *LINUX1.NETPLUSLAB.NET*, click a blank spot on the desktop and select **New Terminal** from the pop-up menu. A terminal window named netplus@LINUX1:~ opens.

33. In the new terminal window, type smbclient -W netpluslab.net -U Administrator //192.168.54.1/netplus and press **Enter**. The Password prompt appears. Type the password for the Administrator and press **Enter**. The prompt changes to smb: \>. Table 9-3 lists command-line options for the smbclient command. Note that the last option is usually the network resource to be used.

Table 9-3 Options for the smbclient command

Option	Meaning
-W domain/workgroup	The domain or workgroup of the remote computer
-U username	Username on the remote server
-I IP address	IP address of the remote server
-L NetBIOS name	Lists services available on the remote server named name
-n NetBIOS name	Overrides the default NetBIOS name used by Samba

34. Type **ls** and press **Enter**. The computer displays the files in the remote share on *SERVER1*.

35. Log off all computers.

Certification Objectives

Objectives for the Network+ Exam:

➤ Identify the basic capabilities (i.e., client support, interoperability, authentication, file and print services, application support, and security) of the following server operating systems: UNIX/Linux, NetWare, Windows, Macintosh

➤ Identify the basic capabilities (i.e., client connectivity, local security mechanisms, and authentication) of the following clients: UNIX/Linux, Windows, Macintosh

Review Questions

1. You are logged into a Linux computer and you need to access files on a Windows server. What do you need to do to get access to those files?

   a. Start Samba on the Linux server.

   b. Log onto the Windows server with the smbclient program.

   c. Share the files on the Windows server using the Linux File and Print Client.

   d. Use the syntax guide.

2. In what mode of the vi editor can you add text to a document?

   a. text mode

   b. normal mode

   c. insert mode

   d. add mode

3. While editing a text file with the vi editor, what command would allow you to search for the word "password" within that text?

   a. /password

   b. find /password

   c. lookup password

   d. search /password

4. Which of the following is a network protocol used by Samba?

   a. IPX/SPX

   b. NetBIOS

   c. SNA

   d. NetBEUI

5. The chmod command allows you to change the permissions of a file or directory. What command would you use to view the permissions of a file?

   a. id

   b. ls -l

c. vi

d. checkpermissions

Lab 9.4 Managing Processes

Objectives

On a Linux server, the network administrator has a great deal of control over the programs that run on a server. Each program that runs on a Linux server uses at least one numbered process. The kernel allocates resources to and controls access to each process. You can start or stop each process, or change the priority by which the kernel allocates resources to the process. The number assigned to a process by the kernel is called a process ID (PID). If you know the PID of a process, you can use the kill command to send a signal to it. You can also use the kill command to restart processes and perform other tasks.

One scenario in which you might wish to manage processes is when processes on a server are out of control. For instance, a process may be using too many resources, preventing users from accessing any of the server's other resources. You can use the uptime program to find out the system load average over the last one, five, and fifteen minutes. The load average is the number of processes in the kernel's run queue waiting to be executed, and the higher the load average, the busier the computer is. If the load average is high, then you can use the top program to display the PID, percent CPU, and percent memory used by the top processes on the computer (as well as a system summary and much more information about each process). The top program updates this information every three seconds by default. You can then use the kill command and the PIDs to terminate the processes. The kill command can also be used for other purposes, such as restarting a process or sending a signal to a running process.

If you know the names of the processes you would like to stop, you can use the ps command to find their PIDs. The ps command with the -e flag displays information about each process running on the system. However, you must sort through this output to find the PIDs. The Linux command line allows you to string together different commands in order to quickly manipulate the output from a command or text in a file. The pipe symbol, |, allows you to take the output from one command and send it to another command. This would allow you to use the grep command to search for the name of the process in the output of the ps command, and then to use the cut command to remove all text from the output except the PID numbers themselves. You could then use command substitution in order to give the PID numbers to the kill command. Finally, many (but not all) Linux operating systems provide an alternate way to find and terminate processes. The pgrep command searches for processes by name, and the pkill command kills processes by name. Table 9-4 shows the Linux commands that will be used in this lab.

9

Table 9-4   Linux commands used in Lab 9.4

Command	Function
top	Shows the processes running on a Linux computer that are using the most resources, refreshing every three seconds by default
kill *pid*	Sends a signal to PID number *pid*; by default it terminates the process
uptime	Displays the amount of time a computer has been running and its load average
grep *pattern*	Searches through a file for any text that matches the pattern *pattern* and prints the matching text
ps	Displays information about processes running on the computer; displays all processes when used with the −e flag
cut	Removes a section of a line of text
pgrep *pattern*	Displays a list of PIDs for processes whose name matches *pattern*
pkill *pattern*	Sends a signal to each process whose name matches *pattern*; by default, it terminates each process

After completing this lab, you will be able to:

➤ Use the top command to find the processes using the most CPU and memory on a Linux computer

➤ Use the kill and pkill commands to terminate processes

➤ Use the ps and pgrep commands to find processes

➤ Use the pipe symbol | to connect two commands

Materials Required

This lab will require the following:

➤ A computer running Red Hat Enterprise Linux ES 3.x with a name of *LINUX1.NETPLUSLAB.NET* and configured with an IP address of 192.168.54.5

➤ A user account named netplus on *LINUX1.NETPLUSLAB.NET* with a known password

Estimated completion time: **30 minutes**

LAB ACTIVITY

ACTIVITY

1. On *LINUX1.NETPLUSLAB.NET* at the Welcome to linux1.netpluslab.net screen, type **netplus** in the Username text box and press **Enter**. The Password text box appears.

2. Type the password for the netplus account in the Password text box and press **Enter**. The Red Hat desktop appears.

3. Right-click a blank spot on the desktop, and click **New Terminal** in the pop-up menu. A terminal window named netplus@linux1:~ opens.

4. Type **uptime** and press **Enter**. The computer displays a message indicating the amount of time the computer has been running since it last started, and the current load average.

5. Type **top** in the terminal window and press **Enter**. The computer displays a summary of system information at the top of the terminal window, as well as the process ID, the percent of CPU time used by the process, the percent of the computer's memory used by the process, and other information. The terminal window updates every three seconds. Figure 9-4 shows the output of the top command.

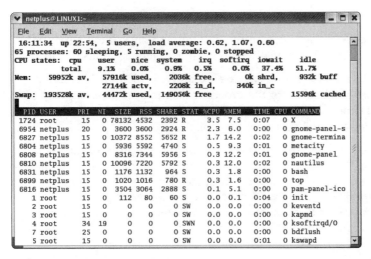

Figure 9-4 The top command

6. Press **Enter**. The computer beeps, and the top program displays "Unknown command."

7. Now you will kill the top command. Watch the top program, and when the name "top" appears in the COMMAND column at the far right, write down its PID (shown in the PID column at the far left). If the name "top" does not appear in the COMMAND column within a minute, repeat Steps 3 and 5 to run the top command in another window. The name "top" should appear shortly in the COMMAND column.

8. Right-click a blank spot on the desktop, and click **New Terminal** in the pop-up menu. A terminal window named netplus@linux1:~ opens.

9. In the terminal window, type **kill** followed by a space and the PID of the top program that you recorded in Step 7, and then press **Enter**. Click the **X** in the upper-right corner of the terminal window to close it. The terminal window closes, showing the terminal window where the top command had been running. The message "terminated" has been printed, and the prompt now appears. (If the terminal window still contains output from the top command, press **Enter** until the output from the top command has scrolled out of sight.)

10. Now you will start some programs in order to kill them by name. Right-click a blank spot on the desktop, and click **New Terminal** in the pop-up menu. A terminal window named netplus@linux1:~ opens.

11. Type **sleep 600** and press **Enter**. The sleep command tells the terminal window to do nothing for 600 seconds. (This command is used in scripts in order to tell the computer to wait while another command performs a task.)

12. Repeat Steps 10 and 11 three times.

13. Right-click a blank spot on the desktop, and click **New Terminal** from the pop-up menu. A terminal window named netplus@linux1:~ opens.

14. In the terminal window, type **ps -e** and press **Enter**. The computer displays information about all of the processes running on the computer, including the PID and the name of the program (sleep) that is currently running. You may need to scroll up to see them all.

15. Now you will use the ps command to find the PIDs of the sleep programs running. Press ↑. The last command appears at the prompt. At the end of the last command, type | **grep sleep** so that the whole command reads **ps -e | grep sleep**. Press **Enter**. The computer displays a list of information about processes that contain the word sleep. This command takes the output of the ps command, and passes it to the grep command. The grep command then looks for each line that contains the word sleep.

16. Now you will display a list of the processes alone. Press ↑. The last command appears at the prompt. At the end of the last command, type | **cut -c 0-6** so that the entire command reads **ps -e | grep sleep | cut -c 0-6** and press **Enter**. The computer displays a list of PIDs. This command takes the output of the previous command, and passes it to the cut program. The cut program cuts all but characters 0 through 6 from each line. What are the PIDs printed by the computer?

17. Now you will kill all the sleep processes. Press ↑. The last command appears at the prompt. At the end of the command, type the backtick (`) character. (On many keyboards, the backtick character is on the same key as the ~ character.) Next, press ← until the cursor is at the beginning of the line. Type **kill `** (so that the entire command reads **kill ` ps -e | grep sleep | cut -c 0-6'**). Press **Enter**. This tells the command interpreter to run the command that's inside the backtick and the apostrophe (i.e., the same command you ran in Step 16), and to give the results to the kill command. You would get the same result if you used the kill command followed by the PIDs that the computer displayed in Step 16.

18. Click the **X** in the upper-right corner of the terminal window to close it. Click one of the netplus@LINUX1:~ icons in the task bar at the bottom of the screen. The computer displays "Terminated." Repeat for the other four netplus@LINUX1:~ icons.

19. Now you will use another method to find PIDs and to kill them. In the open terminal window, type **sleep 600** and press **Enter**.

20. In the task bar at the bottom of the screen, the icon for the current terminal window is a darker grey than the others. Note its location. Click each of the icons for the remaining terminal windows, and repeat Step 19 for each of them.

21. Right-click a blank spot on the desktop, and click **New Terminal** from the pop-up menu. A terminal window named netplus@linux1:~ opens.

22. In the new terminal window, type **pgrep sleep** and press **Enter**. The computer displays a list of PIDs for each process containing the word sleep.

23. Type **pgrep -l sleep** and press **Enter**. The computer displays a list of PIDs for each process containing the word sleep, and the name of the programs.

24. Now you will use the kill command to terminate the sleep programs again. Type **pkill sleep** and press **Enter**.

25. Repeat Step 18 to view the terminated processes.

26. Log out.

Certification Objectives

Objectives for the Network+ Exam:

➤ Identify the basic capabilities (i.e., client support, interoperability, authentication, file and print services, application support, and security) of the following server operating systems: UNIX/Linux, NetWare, Windows, Macintosh

Review Questions

1. Which of the following commands *cannot* be used to find the PID of a process?

    a. top

    b. kill

    c. pgrep

    d. ps

2. What is the purpose of the pipe symbol on the Linux command line?

    a. to chain together two or more commands so that they run consecutively

    b. to chain together two or more commands so that the output of one command is sent to another command

    c. to separate two or more commands

    d. to force two or more commands to run separately

3. You have used the uptime command to determine that the load average on a Linux server is far too high. Which of the following is the most appropriate course of action?

    a. Use the top command to find the processes using the most resources, and then use the pgrep command to stop them.

    b. Use the top command to find the processes using the most resources, and then use the kill command to stop them.

    c. Use the uptime command to find the processes using the most resources, and then use the kill command to stop them.

    d. Use the ps command to find the processes using the most resources, and then use the stop command to stop them.

4. The uptime command tells you the load average of a Linux server. What does "load average" mean?

    a. the average number of processes in the computer's run queue

    b. the average number of users on the computer

    c. the average percentage of CPU in use

    d. the average time that the CPU is in use

5. Which command displays all the processes on a Linux computer, while allowing you to scroll through them?

    a. ps -e | grep process

    b. ps -e | pgrep

    c. ps -e | more

    d. pgrep | more

Lab 9.5 Remotely Managing Linux Servers

Objectives

Linux servers can be managed remotely much as they can be at the console, through a variety of tools. Almost all versions of Linux support telnet servers. A telnet server is a daemon that allows you to open a remote terminal session over a network. The telnet client, usually just called telnet, is available on most modern operating systems. However, the telnet protocol does not use any encryption. As a result, telnet is rapidly being replaced by the Secure Shell Protocol (SSH). The sshd daemon runs an SSH server, and the ssh program allows you to log into a SSH server.

From a remote terminal window opened with the ssh program, you can do nearly anything that you can do on the system console. On a computer running the X-Windows software, you can also run any GUI program on the remote computer. X-Windows software is installed by default on most Linux computers, and can be installed on Windows computers as well. Remote terminal sessions run through either the ssh program or the telnet program have only a few minor differences.

In this lab you will use the Red Hat GUI to configure a virtual NIC. A virtual NIC is treated just like a physical NIC by the operating system. Typically, a virtual NIC is added so that a computer can have an additional IP address; the virtual NIC is therefore referred to as a secondary IP address.

After completing this lab, you will be able to:

➤ Log into a Linux computer remotely using SSH

➤ Configure a NIC on a Linux computer

Materials Required

This lab will require the following:

➤ A computer running Red Hat Enterprise Linux ES 3.x named *LINUX1.NETPLUSLAB.NET*, configured with an IP address of 192.168.54.5

➤ A computer running Red Hat Enterprise Linux ES 3.x named *LINUX2.NETPLUSLAB.NET*, configured with an IP address of 192.168.54.7

➤ Firewall software not configured on *LINUX1.NETPLUSLAB.NET* or LINUX2.NETPLUSLAB.NET

➤ All three computers connected to a hub with straight-through CAT 5 (or better) UTP cables.

➤ Users named netplus and knowledge of the root password on both computers

➤ A computer running Windows XP Professional named *WORKSTATION1* and configured with an IP address of 192.168.54.3

➤ Cygwin (available at *www.cygwin.com*) installed on *WORKSTATION1*, with the OpenSSH and XFree86 packages installed in addition to the default packages

Estimated completion time: **40 minutes**

LAB ACTIVITY

ACTIVITY

1. On *LINUX2.NETPLUSLAB.NET*, at the Welcome to linux2.netpluslab.net screen, type **netplus** in the Username text box and press **Enter**. The Password text box appears.

2. Type the password for the netplus account in the Password text box and press **Enter**. The Red Hat desktop appears.

3. Right-click a blank spot on the desktop, and click **New Terminal** from the pop-up menu. A terminal window named netplus@linux2:~ opens.

4. Type **ssh 192.168.54.5** and press **Enter**. A message may appear indicating that the authenticity of the host cannot be established, followed by the text "Are you sure you want to continue connecting (yes/no)?". If so, type **yes** and press **Enter**. The computer asks for the password for the netplus account.

5. Type the password and press **Enter**. The prompt changes to [netplus@ LINUX1 netplus]$, indicating that you are now logged into *LINUX1. NETPLUSLAB.NET*.

6. Type **su –** and press **Enter**. The Password prompt appears. Type root's password and press **Enter**. The prompt now ends in a pound sign (#), indicating that you are logged in as the root user.

7. Type **ifconfig** and press **Enter**. The computer displays information about the network cards on the computer. In addition to the NIC in the computer (most likely named eth0 or eth1), the computer displays information about the lo NIC, or the loopback. This is a virtual (or software-only) NIC, primarily used for testing. A loopback NIC is configured by default on most devices that use TCP/IP. What are the names and IP addresses of the NICs on the computer?

8. Now you will add a virtual NIC to the computer. A virtual NIC exists in software only, but will be treated like a real NIC by the computer. Type **redhat-config-network-gui** and press **Enter**. The Network Configuration window opens, showing information about the NIC on *LINUX1.NETPLUSLAB.NET* in the Device box at the bottom of the window.

9. Click **New**. The Add New Device Type dialog box opens, showing types of devices that could be used to make a network connection.

10. Click **Ethernet connection**. Click **Forward**. The dialog box asks you to select an Ethernet card.

11. Click the name of the Ethernet card in the computer. Click **Forward**. The dialog box asks you to configure network settings.

12. Click the **Statically set IP addresses** option button. In the Address text box, enter **192.168.54.10**. In the Subnet Mask text box, enter **255.255.255.0**. Click **Forward**. The dialog box summarizes the options you have chosen.

13. Click **Apply**. A new icon for the secondary IP address appears.

14. Click the icon for the new secondary NIC to select it. Make sure that the Profile check box is selected. Click **Activate**. The Question dialog box opens, asking you if you want to make the changes necessary to activate the new virtual NIC.

15. Click **Yes**. The Information dialog box opens, indicating that you may want to restart the network or the computer.

16. Click **OK**. The redhat-config-network dialog box opens briefly, indicating that the computer is activating the virtual NIC.

17. Click **File** on the menu bar, then click **Quit**. The Network Configuration window closes.

18. Type **ifconfig** and press **Enter**. The computer displays information about the NICs on the computer. What is the name of the new interface on the computer?

19. Type **exit** and press **Enter**. Type exit and press **Enter** again to exit from *LINUX1.NETPLUSLAB.NET*. The prompt in the terminal window changes back to indicate that you are on *LINUX2.NETPLUSLAB.NET*.

20. Type **ifconfig** and press **Enter**. The computer indicates that the command cannot be found.

21. Now you will attempt to run the ifconfig command by typing the full path of the command. Type **/sbin/ifconfig** and press **Enter**. The computer displays information about the network cards on the computer.

22. On *WORKSTATION1*, press **Ctrl+Alt+Del** to display the Log On to Windows dialog box. Log onto the computer as the Administrator.

23. Click **Start**, point to **All Programs**, point to **Cygwin**, then click **Cygwin Bash Shell**. A terminal window opens.

24. Type **startxwin.bat** and press **Enter**. This command starts the X-Windows software on *WORKSTATION1*, and opens a new terminal window named X.

9

25. In the terminal window named X, type **ssh –X netplus@192.168.54.5** and press **Enter**. (The –X option tells the ssh program to allow forwarding of GUI programs, while the netplus@ tells the ssh program to use the netplus user when logging into the remote server.) A message may appear indicating that the authenticity of the host cannot be established. If so, type **yes** and press **Enter**. The computer asks for the password for the netplus account.

26. Enter the password for the netplus account and press **Enter**. The prompt indicates that you have logged into *LINUX1.NETPLUSLAB.NET*.

27. Type **su –** and press **Enter**. The Password prompt appears. Type root's password and press **Enter**. The prompt now ends with a pound sign (#), indicating that you are logged in as the root user.

28. Type **redhat-config-network-gui** and press **Enter**. The Network Configuration window opens, as shown in Figure 9-5.

Figure 9-5   The Network Configuration dialog box, as run from *WORKSTATION1*

29. Click **File** on the menu bar, then click **Quit**. The Network Configuration window closes.

30. Type **exit** and press **Enter**. Type exit and press **Enter** again to exit the ssh session on *LINUX1.NETPLUSLAB.NET*.

31. Log off all computers.

Certification Objectives

Objectives for the Network+ Exam:

➤ Identify the basic capabilities (i.e., client support, interoperability, authentication, file and print services, application support, and security) of the following server operating systems: UNIX/Linux, NetWare, Windows, Macintosh

➤ Identify the basic capabilities (i.e., client connectivity, local security mechanisms, and authentication) of the following clients: UNIX/Linux, Windows, Macintosh

Review Questions

1. What is the difference between the SSH protocol and the telnet protocol?

    a. The telnet protocol is encrypted.

    b. The telnet protocol is faster than the SSH protocol.

    c. SSH is encrypted.

    d. SSH can only be used between Linux or UNIX servers.

2. Which of the following commands could you use to display a Linux computer's IP address?

    a. ipconfig

    b. ssh

    c. ipdisplay

    d. ifconfig

3. Why might a virtual NIC be configured on a Linux computer?

    a. because an additional IP address is needed for a Web server

    b. in order for the computer to act as a router between two networks

    c. for redundancy

    d. for load-balancing

4. The ssh command allows you to open a remote terminal window on another computer. What is the major difference between working in an SSH session on a remote computer in another city, and working directly at the console of the remote computer?

    a. You cannot power cycle the remote computer.

    b. You cannot run GUI programs in the SSH session.

    c. You cannot run terminal programs such as top or ps while working in an SSH session.

    d. You cannot log into other remote computers while working in an SSH session.

9

5. In this lab, how could you tell whether a terminal window is for the local computer, or for an SSH session on a remote computer?

   a. The prompt indicates the name of the remote computer.

   b. There is no way to tell.

   c. The prompt indicates the name of the program being run.

   d. The computer beeps when you log into a remote computer.

NetWare-Based Networking

Labs included in this chapter

➤ Lab 10.1 Adding a Client to a NetWare 6.5 Network

➤ Lab 10.2 Starting and Shutting down a NetWare 6.5 Server

➤ Lab 10.3 Delegating Administrative Control with NetWare 6.5

➤ Lab 10.4 Creating Login Scripts

➤ Lab 10.5 Configuring Native File Service on a NetWare Network

---

Net+ Exam Objectives	
Objective	Lab
Identify the basic capabilities (i.e., client support, interoperability, authentication, file and print services, application support, and security) of the following server operating systems: UNIX/Linux, NetWare, Windows, Macintosh	10.1, 10.2, 10.3, 10.4, 10.5
Identify the basic capabilities (i.e., client connectivity, local security mechanisms, and authentication) of the following clients: UNIX/Linux, NetWare, Windows, Macintosh	10.1, 10.3, 10.4, 10.5
Given specific parameters, configure a client to connect to the following servers: UNIX/Linux, NetWare, Windows, Macintosh	10.1, 10.3, 10.4, 10.5

LAB 10.1 ADDING A CLIENT TO A NETWARE 6.5 NETWORK

Objectives

In this lab, you will add a client to a NetWare 6.5 network. While Windows has a built-in NetWare client, the preferred method for connecting to a NetWare network is to use Novell's NetWare client. When configuring a user's client to log into a NetWare server, you will need to find the user's proper context, which is essentially the location of the user object in the eDirectory tree. As in Active Directory, in eDirectory you can create multiple user accounts with the same name in different parts of the tree. When the user logs into eDirectory, the context tells eDirectory which user account is logging in. For instance, suppose that in eDirectory there are user accounts named "netplus" below both the administration and the laboratory organizational units. The context for the user in the administration organizational unit is administration, and the context for the user in the laboratory organizational unit is laboratory. The NetWare client allows you to search for the proper context prior to logging in.

Another issue when connecting clients to a NetWare network is synchronizing local accounts with NetWare accounts. Each user is still required to have a local account on his or her workstation. This gives the user the right to log into the workstation. If a user successfully logs into eDirectory but fails to log into the workstation, then the user will be unable to use the computer. You can eliminate this potential problem by synchronizing the user's account and password on the workstation with their eDirectory user name and password. After this is done, the user will automatically log into the workstation with his or her eDirectory user name and password. (Note that you must remove Novell Modular Authentication Services (NMAS) in order to synchronize the account. NMAS performs sophisticated authentication services, but configuring it is beyond the scope of this lab.)

By default, Windows refers to the most powerful administrative account as the Administrator account. On NetWare networks, however, the most powerful administrative account is known as the admin account. In a Novell network, by default this account is considered to have supervisor rights over the entire eDirectory tree.

After completing this lab, you will be able to:Connect a client to a NetWare networkSynchronize passwords between a NetWare account and a Windows account

Materials Required

This lab will require the following:

➤ A computer named *NETWARE6* with Novell NetWare 6.5 installed as a Basic NetWare File Server

➤ An IP address of 192.168.54.6 and a subnet mask of 255.255.255.0 bound to the NetWare computer's NIC

➤ An eDirectory tree named NETPLUS, with *NETWARE6* and the admin account in the administration context

➤ An organization named laboratory below the *NETPLUS* tree, with a user named netplus

➤ A computer with Windows XP Professional installed named *WORKSTATION1*, with an IP address of 192.168.54.3 and a subnet mask of 255.255.255.0

➤ Access to the Windows XP computer as a user called netplus in the Administrators group

➤ Different passwords for the netplus account on the Windows XP computer and on the NetWare computer, both sufficiently complex to be accepted by Windows XP

➤ A hub and two straight-through CAT5 (or better) UTP cables connecting the NICs of both *NETWARE6* and *WORKSTATION1*

➤ The Novell Client CD-ROM containing NetWare client software, and the Windows XP Professional computer set to automatically run any CD-ROMs inserted (the default)

10

Estimated completion time: **30 minutes**

LAB ACTIVITY

ACTIVITY

1. On *WORKSTATION1*, press **Ctrl+Alt+Del** to bring up the Log On to Windows screen. Log on as the Administrator. The Windows XP desktop appears.

2. Place the CD-ROM with the NetWare client software in the CD-ROM drive. The WinSetup – Novell Clients window opens.

3. Click **Novell Client 4.9 for Windows NT/2000/XP**. The next window of the installation program asks you to select a language.

4. Click **English**. The Software License Agreement dialog box opens.

5. Read the agreement and click **Yes**. The Software License Agreement dialog box closes and the Novell Client Installation window opens, as shown in Figure 10-1.

6. Make sure the **Typical Installation** option button is selected and click **Install**. The Novell Client Installation window indicates that it is installing the Novell Client for Windows, and the Copying Files dialog box opens. The computer copies the files, and the Copying Files dialog box closes. The Installation Complete window opens.

7. Click **Reboot**. The computer reboots.

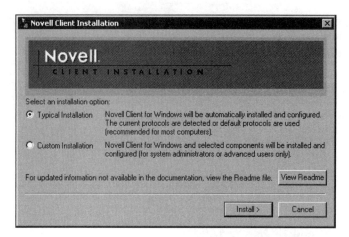

Figure 10-1   Novell Client Installation window

8. Press **Ctrl+Alt+Del** to display the Novell Login window. Click **Advanced**. The Novell Login window expands, showing more options.

9. Enter **netplus** in the User Name text box, and the password for this account in the NETPLUS eDirectory tree in the Password text box.

10. In the bottom half of the window, click **Trees**. The NetWare client attempts to find any available eDirectory trees. The Tree window opens, with an icon for the NETPLUS tree highlighted.

11. Click **OK**. The Tree window closes.

12. Click **Contexts**. The NETPLUS window opens again, showing a list of the eDirectory contexts in which you could log in.

13. Click **laboratory** to highlight it. Click **OK**. The NETPLUS window closes.

14. Click the **Windows** tab. The Windows tab opens with additional options. This tab controls how the NetWare client will log onto Windows.

15. In the Local username text box, enter **netplus**. Select **WORKSTATION1** from the From drop-down menu.

16. Click **OK**. The Windows Workstation dialog box opens.

17. If the Name text box does not already contain the name of the netplus account, add it. In the Password text box, enter the password of the netplus account on the Windows XP computer. Click **OK**. Note that the "Change your Windows password to match your NetWare password after a successful login" check box is unavailable. The Login Script dialog box appears briefly, then disappears as the Windows XP desktop opens.

18. Now you will configure the NetWare client so that it will synchronize your password. Click **Start**, then click **Control Panel**. The Control Panel opens.

19. Click **Add or Remove Programs**. The Add or Remove Programs window opens.

20. Click **NMAS Client Components (2.2.0)** to highlight it. Note that the version number may be different on your computer. Click **Change/Remove**. The NMAS Client Components dialog box opens, asking if you wish to proceed.

21. Click **Yes**. The computer removes the NMAS Client Components software from the computer. The NMAS Client Components dialog box opens, indicating that the software has been removed from the computer.

22. Click **OK** to close the NMAS Client Components dialog box, and then click **Close** to close the Add or Remove Programs window.

23. Click **Start**, then click **Log Off**. The Log Off Windows dialog box opens.

24. Click **Log Off**. The computer logs off.

25. Press **Ctrl+Alt+Del** to display the Novell Login window. Repeat Steps 9 through 16 to log into the computer. (Note that most of the information should already be filled in.)

26. In the Windows Workstation dialog box, click the **Change your Windows password to match your NetWare password after a successful login** check box. Enter the password for the netplus account in the Password text box.

27. The computer logs you into the computer, and synchronizes the passwords for the Novell account and the Windows account.

28. Log off *WORKSTATION1*.

Certification Objectives

Objectives for the Network+ Exam:

➤ Identify the basic capabilities (i.e., client support, interoperability, authentication, file and print services, application support, and security) of the following server operating systems: UNIX/Linux, NetWare, Windows, Macintosh

➤ Identify the basic capabilities (i.e., client connectivity, local security mechanisms, and authentication) of the following clients: UNIX/Linux, NetWare, Windows, Macintosh

➤ Given specific parameters, configure a client to connect to the following servers: UNIX/Linux, NetWare, Windows, Macintosh

10

Review Questions

1. What is the difference between a local Windows account and a NetWare account?

   a. The local Windows account must be authenticated against a Windows Server 2003 domain controller, and the NetWare account must be authenticated against the local machine.

   b. The local Windows account must be authenticated against a Windows Server 2003 domain controller, and the NetWare account must be authenticated against eDirectory.

   c. The local Windows account must be authenticated against the local machine, and the NetWare account must be authenticated against a Windows Server 2003 domain controller.

   d. The local Windows account must be authenticated against the local machine, and the NetWare account must be authenticated against eDirectory.

2. Instead of TCP/IP, what protocol suite was used by NetWare prior to NetWare 4.11?

   a. IPX/SPX

   b. SNA

   c. DEC

   d. VINES

3. Which of the following is a disadvantage of the Windows and NetWare passwords not being synchronized?

   a. Users must create their own local Windows accounts.

   b. Users must remember two passwords.

   c. Local user names and passwords are not administrated by the network administrator.

   d. The network administrator cannot change the Windows password if a user locks themselves out of their account.

4. On a Novell NetWare network, a user's context is:

   a. the user's location in the Active Directory tree, specified by the user name, followed by each organizational unit and the organization (each separated by a period)

   b. the user's location in the eDirectory tree, specified by the user name and the eDirectory tree name (separated by periods)

    c. the user's location in the eDirectory tree, specified by the user name and the domain, followed by each organizational unit and the organization (separated by periods)

    d. the user's location in the eDirectory tree, specified by the user name, followed by each organizational unit and the organization (separated by periods)

5. What can you do if a user's context is too long for the user to remember?

    a. Configure the user's workstation so that it logs in automatically.

    b. Configure the user's workstation so that the proper context is chosen automatically.

    c. Configure the user's workstation to log into the nearest NetWare server instead.

    d. Configure the user's workstation to log into the nearest domain controller instead.

10

Lab 10.2 Starting and Shutting down a NetWare 6.5 Server

Objectives

In this lab, you will learn how to start and stop a Novell NetWare 6.5 server. (Stopping a NetWare server is called "downing the server".) You will often have to restart a server because of software updates, and you will often have to down a server before powering it off to make hardware changes. You are probably aware that simply powering down a computer without shutting down the operating system can cause problems. Doing so on a server is especially dangerous. The computer will not have the opportunity to close files that are open, and these files may become damaged. For instance, shutting down a database server improperly might result in the corruption of the database.

When a computer running NetWare starts, it first boots into DOS. Then the autoexec.bat file, which runs whenever DOS starts, loads NetWare. Stopping NetWare returns the computer to DOS. Keep in mind that, once the computer is running DOS, the server cannot be restarted over the network. When you restart the server, the server is automatically downed and then restarted. Resetting the server reboots it.

You can stop or restart a NetWare server in more than one way. First, you may stop it using the NetWare console. Like a Unix server, you can run a GUI on top of the Novell console. However, it is not required like it is in Windows. Running a NetWare server without a GUI will save system resources that can be better spent serving your users. As with the Linux server in Chapter 9, you can switch around between various programs by pressing different combinations of keys. The console may also be run remotely. Second, you can use NetWare Remote Manager from a Web browser on a client workstation. In addition to stopping and restarting the server, NetWare Remote Manager allows you to partition disks, configure TCP/IP parameters, manage eDirectory and much more.

After completing this lab, you will be able to:

➤ Start up a Novell NetWare 6.5 server

➤ Shut down a Novell NetWare 6.5 server

Materials Required

This lab will require the following:

➤ A computer named *NETWARE6* with Novell NetWare 6.5 installed as a Basic NetWare File Server

➤ An IP address of 192.168.54.6 and a subnet mask of 255.255.255.0 bound to the NetWare computer's NIC

➤ An eDirectory tree named NETPLUS, with *NETWARE6* and the admin account in the administration context

➤ A computer with Windows XP Professional named *WORKSTATION1* configured with an IP address of 192.168.54.3 and a subnet mask of 255.255.255.0

➤ Novell Client 4.9 for Windows NT/2000/XP installed on *WORKSTATION1*

➤ The password for the netplus account in the laboratory context synchronized with the password for the local Windows XP netplus account

➤ A hub connecting the NICs of *NETWARE6* and *WORKSTATION1* with two straight-through CAT 5 (or better) UTP cables

Estimated completion time: **25 minutes**

LAB ACTIVITY

ACTIVITY

1. First you will use NetWare Remote Manager to restart the server. On *WORKSTATION1*, press **Ctrl+Alt+Del** to display the Novell Login window. Log into the computer as the netplus user. The Windows XP desktop appears.

2. Click **Start**, then click **Internet Explorer**. Internet Explorer opens.

3. In the Address bar, type **https://192.168.54.6:8009** and press **Enter**. The Security Alert dialog box may open, indicating that you are about to view pages over a secure connection. If so, click **OK**. The Security Alert dialog box opens, indicating that there is a problem with the site's security certificate.

4. Click **Yes**. The NetWare Remote Manager Web page opens, as in Figure 10-2.

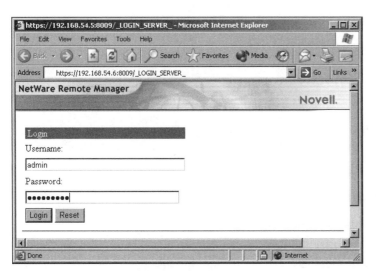

Figure 10-2   NetWare Remote Manager Web page window

5. In the Username text box, enter **admin**. In the Password text box, enter the password for the admin account. Click **Login**. The computer logs you into the NetWare Remote Manager.

6. On the menu on the left side of the screen, click **Down / Restart**.

7. Click **Restart**. The Microsoft Internet Explorer dialog box opens, asking if you're sure you want to down the server.

8. Click **OK**. The Web page indicates that Server NETWARE6 is going down, and that this might take a few minutes. *NETWARE6* reboots, showing the NetWare Graphical Console.

9. On *NETWARE6*, press **Alt+Esc**. The server displays another window. Repeat this step by pressing **Alt+Esc** until you see the NetWare Graphical Console again.

10. Now press **Ctrl+Esc**. The Current Screens window is displayed. This window allows you to select from any of the screens currently running on the NetWare server.

11. Now you will choose the System Console. Type **1** (or the number for the System Console, if different) and press **Enter**. The System Console opens, displaying the NETWARE6 prompt.

12. Type **down** and press **Enter**. The computer downs the server and returns to DOS and the C:\NWSERVER> prompt. (Note that if you down the server remotely, someone else must be present to restart it from DOS.) If the computer powers itself off, power it back on and go to Step 14.

13. Type **server** and press **Enter**. The NetWare server restarts.

14. Log off *WORKSTATION1*.

Certification Objectives

Objectives for the Network+ Exam:

➤ Identify the basic capabilities (i.e., client support, interoperability, authentication, file and print services, application support, and security) of the following server operating systems: UNIX/Linux, NetWare, Windows, Macintosh

Review Questions

1. What is the purpose of the NetWare 6.5 kernel?

    a. to organize the server's file system

    b. to arbitrate task priority in multiprocessing

    c. to oversee all critical server functions

    d. to act as a gateway with other network operating systems

2. What command starts the NetWare network operating system?

    a. kernel

    b. nos

    c. server

    d. start

3. What DOS file automatically starts a Novell server?

    a. autoexec.exe

    b. config.exe

    c. start.exe

    d. autoexec.bat

4. What does "NLM" stand for?

    a. Novell Layered Management

    b. NetWare Loadable Module

    c. Novell Licensed Memory

    d. NetWare Logical Master

5. From which of the following is it *not* possible to restart a NetWare 6.5 server?

    a. from the system console

    b. through NetWare Remote Manager

    c. from DOS

    d. through iManager

LAB 10.3 DELEGATING ADMINISTRATIVE CONTROL WITH NETWARE 6.5

Objectives

Like Active Directory, eDirectory allows a network administrator a great deal of flexibility in managing the network. eDirectory treats each user, computer, printer, and every other type of network resource as an eDirectory object. Each object belongs to a particular class. For instance, users belong to the user class, and printers belong to the printers class. eDirectory stores information about all these objects and their attributes and properties in a database, which is usually distributed across multiple NetWare servers for fault tolerance.

eDirectory is particularly useful in large organizations. You can use eDirectory to delegate administrative control of part of the eDirectory tree to another administrator. For instance, you might delegate control of the Manufacturing organizational unit to a network administrator who works more closely with the Manufacturing department. You do this by delegating administrative functions to a trustee. The trustee user may be able to add and delete user accounts in the Manufacturing organizational unit. However, this user will be unable to add and delete user accounts in other parts of the eDirectory tree. (Note that the trustee does not have to be a member of the group for which it is a trustee.)

After completing this lab, you will be able to:

➤ Use ConsoleOne to create users

➤ Create organizational units in eDirectory

➤ Delegate administrative control of an organizational unit to a trustee

Materials Required

This lab will require the following:

➤ A computer named *NETWARE6* with Novell NetWare 6.5 installed, as a Basic NetWare File Server

➤ An IP address of 192.168.54.6 and a subnet mask of 255.255.255.0 bound to the NetWare computer's NIC

➤ An eDirectory tree named NETPLUS, with *NETWARE6* and the admin account in the administration context

➤ A computer with Windows XP Professional named *WORKSTATION1* configured with an IP address of 192.168.54.3 and a subnet mask of 255.255.255.0

➤ Novell Client 4.9 for Windows NT/2000/XP installed on WORKSTATION1

➤ ConsoleOne installed on the Windows XP computer

➤ The password for the netplus account in the laboratory context synchronized with the password for the local Windows XP netplus account

10

➤ A hub connecting the NICs of *NETWARE6* and *WORKSTATION1* with two straight-through CAT 5 (or better) UTP cables

➤ An icon for ConsoleOne on the desktop; this should be installed by default, but if not an icon pointing to C:\novell\consoleone\1.2\bin\consoleone.exe should be created

Estimated completion time: **30 minutes**

ACTIVITY

1. On *WORKSTATION1*, press **Ctrl+Alt+Del** to display the Novell Login window. Log into the computer as the admin user. The Windows XP desktop appears.

2. Double-click the **ConsoleOne** icon on the Windows XP desktop. ConsoleOne opens.

3. In the left pane of the window, click the **plus sign (+)** next to NDS. The NETPLUS tree unfolds below NDS.

4. Click the **plus sign (+)** next to NETPLUS. The tree expands below NETPLUS, showing the administration, laboratory, and Security objects.

5. Right-click the **NETPLUS** icon. From the pop-up menu, click **New**, then click **Object**. The New Object dialog box opens. Figure 10-3 shows the ConsoleOne window as a new object is created.

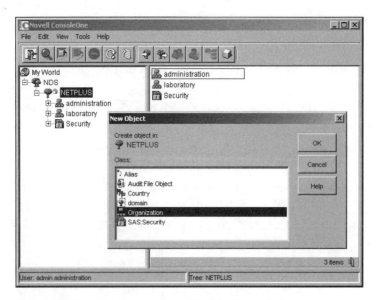

Figure 10-3   Creating a new object in ConsoleOne

6. Click **Organization** to select it and then click **OK**. The New Organization window opens.

7. In the Name text box, enter **Sales**. Click **OK**. The New Organization window closes.

8. Press **F5** to refresh the ConsoleOne window. The Sales object appears in the tree below NETPLUS.

9. Right-click the **Sales** object. From the pop-up menu, click **New**, then click **User**. The New User dialog box opens.

10. In the Name text box, enter **salestrustee**. In the Surname text box, enter **Trustee**. The Unique ID text box displays the name entered in the Name text box, salestrustee. Click **OK**. The Set Password dialog box opens.

11. Enter a password in the New Password text box. Enter the same password in the Retype password text box. Record or remember the password. Click **Set Password**. The Set Password and New User dialog boxes close, returning to the Novell ConsoleOne window.

12. Right-click the **Sales** object in the left pane of the window. From the pop-up menu, click **Trustees of this Object**. The Properties of Sales window opens.

13. Click **Add Trustee**. The Select Objects window opens.

14. Click the **salestrustee** icon to select it. Click **OK**. The Select Objects window closes, and the Rights assigned to selected objects window opens.

15. Click the **Create** and **Delete** check boxes to place a check in them. Click **OK**. An icon for the salestrustee.Sales object appears in the Properties of Sales window as an assigned trustee. Click **OK** to close the Properties of Sales window. Close ConsoleOne.

16. Right-click the red **N** (for Novell) icon in the system tray. From the pop-up menu, select **NetWare Login**. The Novell Login window opens.

17. Click **Advanced**. Additional options appear at the bottom of the Novell Login window.

18. In the Context text box, enter **Sales**. In the username text box, enter **salestrustee**. Enter the password you created for the salestrustee account in Step 11 in the Password box. Click **OK**. The Confirm dialog box opens, asking if you want to log in as .salestrustee.Sales. (This is one way that NetWare describes user contexts—stating the most specific part of the eDirectory tree first, followed by a dot and the container for the first object, and so on.)

19. Click **Yes**. The computer logs the salestrustee account into the NETPLUS tree.

20. Double-click the **ConsoleOne** icon on the desktop. The Novell ConsoleOne window opens.

10

21. Click the **plus sign (+)** next to NETPLUS. The tree expands below NETPLUS.

22. Right-click the **Sales** object. From the pop-up menu, click **New**, then click **User**. The New User dialog box opens.

23. Repeat Steps 10 through 11 to create a new user with the name and unique ID of **person1**, and a surname of **Last**.

24. Now you will attempt to create a user account in another organizational unit while still logged in as the trustee of the Sales organizational unit. Right-click the **laboratory** object in the tree below NETPLUS. From the pop-up menu, click **New**, then click **User**. The Create Object window opens, indicating that you are unable to create the object and that add rights are required to create at this location.

25. Click **OK**. The Create Object window closes.

26. Log off *WORKSTATION1*.

Certification Objectives

Objectives for the Network+ Exam:

➤ Identify the basic capabilities (i.e., client support, interoperability, authentication, file and print services, application support, and security) of the following server operating systems: UNIX/Linux, NetWare, Windows, Macintosh

➤ Identify the basic capabilities (i.e., client connectivity, local security mechanisms, and authentication) of the following clients: UNIX/Linux, NetWare, Windows, Macintosh

➤ Given specific parameters, configure a client to connect to the following servers: UNIX/Linux, NetWare, Windows, Macintosh

Review Questions

1. What do you call the account to which you delegate administrative control of part of the eDirectory?
   a. the trustee
   b. the designee
   c. the admin account
   d. the Administrator account

2. What is the purpose of an organizational unit?
   a. to represent an organization's hierarchy in the schema
   b. to group files with similar permissions
   c. to group objects with similar security requirements
   d. to facilitate faster e-mail gateway operation

3. Which of the following are examples of leaf objects? (Choose all that apply.)

   a. user

   b. printer

   c. organizational unit

   d. container

4. What is the uppermost level of the eDirectory tree called?

   a. leaf

   b. branch

   c. twig

   d. root

5. What is the difference between a group member and a group trustee?

   a. A member belongs to a group, while a trustee can modify the properties of that group.

   b. A member belongs to a group and can modify the properties of that group, while a trustee can modify the properties of the group, but does not necessarily belong to the group.

   c. A member belongs to a group all the time, while a trustee belongs to that group only according to certain time restrictions.

   d. A member can be any object (such as user or printer) that belongs to a group, while a trustee is only a user object that belongs to a group.

10

LAB 10.4 CREATING LOGIN SCRIPTS

Objectives

In this lab, you will create a simple login script on a NetWare server. A login script allows the administrator to set up parameters and perform actions for each user as they log in. Often login scripts will set up drive mappings for users. Drive mappings allow a user with a Windows client to reach a volume on the NetWare server with a drive letter just as if the volume were on a hard disk on their computer. For instance, you might have the ACCOUNTING volume on a NetWare server mapped to the drive letter U:. This allows all the people who need to access the files on the ACCOUNTING volume to access them through the drive letter U:.

A drive mapping might also refer to a subdirectory on a NetWare volume. For instance, you could map the SALES directory on the DATA volume to the drive letter V: so that the sales staff could access their files more conveniently. A network administrator might write login scripts that map different drives for different users on the network. This is useful in situations in which you want to grant all users access to a common network drive, and some users access to a network drive that only they need.

Login scripts can do many other things. You might, for example, run a batch file in each user's login script that notifies the network administrator that the user has logged in. However, it is important to keep in mind that login scripts are not mandatory. For instance, the Novell client allows users to skip the login script (which may be necessary in order to troubleshoot a problem).

After completing this lab, you will be able to:

➤ Create a login script for a user

➤ Create a drive mapping for a user

Materials Required

This lab will require the following:

➤ A computer named *NETWARE6* with Novell NetWare 6.5 installed as a Basic NetWare File Server

➤ An IP address of 192.168.54.6 and a subnet mask of 255.255.255.0 bound to the NetWare computer's NIC

➤ An eDirectory tree named NETPLUS, with *NETWARE6* and the admin account in the administration context

➤ An organizational unit named laboratory below the NETPLUS tree, with a user named netplus

➤ A computer with Windows XP Professional installed named *WORKSTATION1*, with an IP address of 192.168.54.3 and a subnet mask of 255.255.255.0

➤ ConsoleOne installed on WORKSTATION1

➤ Novell Client 4.9 for Windows NT/2000/XP installed on *WORKSTATION1*

➤ Access to the Windows XP computer as a user called netplus in the Administrators group

➤ Different passwords for the netplus account on the Windows XP computer and on the NetWare computer, both sufficiently complex to be accepted by Windows XP

➤ A hub and two straight-through CAT 5 (or better) UTP cables connecting the NICs of both *NETWARE6* and *WORKSTATION1*

Estimated completion time: **25 minutes**

LAB ACTIVITY

ACTIVITY

1. On *WORKSTATION1*, press **Ctrl+Alt+Del** to display the Novell Login window. Log into eDirectory as the admin user.

2. The Windows Workstation dialog box opens. Enter the password for the Administrator account on *WORKSTATION1* and click **OK**. The Windows XP desktop appears.

3. Click **Start**, then click **My Computer**. The My Computer window opens.

4. Double-click the **Public on 'Netware6\Sys' (Z:)** folder. The folder opens.

5. Right-click a blank area in the right pane of the window. From the pop-up menu, click **New**, then click **Folder**. A new folder appears, with the words "New Folder" highlighted.

6. Type **Home** and press **Enter** to rename the folder. The folder is renamed "Home".

7. Double-click the **Home** folder. The Home folder opens.

8. Repeat Steps 5 and 6 to create a new folder named **netplus**.

9. Right-click the **netplus** folder. From the pop-up menu that appears, click **Properties**. The netplus Properties window opens.

10. Click the **NetWare Rights** tab. The NetWare Rights tab of the netplus Properties window opens.

11. In the box in the middle of the netplus Properties window, there is a tree containing the laboratory object. Click the **plus sign (+)** next to the laboratory object. Click the **netplus** user to highlight it.

12. Click **Add**. In the Trustees pane of the window, a line for netplus. laboratory appears, listing the rights this user has to the file.

13. Click the **W**, **E**, **C**, **M**, and **A** check boxes to place check marks in each of them. This will assign all rights possible for this user. Note that the S check box (for supervisor) remains grayed out.

14. Click **OK**. The netplus Properties window closes.

15. Double-click the ConsoleOne icon on the desktop. The Novell ConsoleOne window opens.

16. Click the **plus sign (+)** next to the NETPLUS icon in the tree in the left pane of the window. The tree expands below it.

17. Click the **laboratory** icon in the tree. A list of objects in the laboratory context appears in the right pane, including the netplus user object.

18. Right-click the **netplus** user object. From the pop-up menu, click **Properties**. The Properties of netplus dialog box opens.

19. Click the arrow next to General. From the drop-down menu that appears, click **Environment**. Options related to the environment for the netplus user appear.

10

20. In the Volume text box, enter **NETWARE6_SYS.administration**. In the Path text box, enter **PUBLIC/Home/netplus**. Figure 10-4 shows the Properties of netplus dialog box.

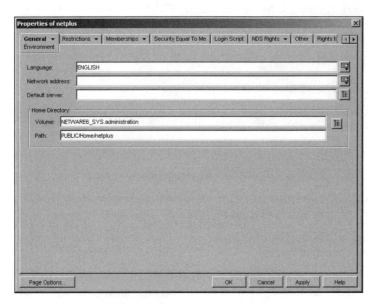

Figure 10-4   The Properties of netplus dialog box

21. Click the **Login Script** tab. The computer displays options related to the login script for the netplus user.

22. In the Login Script text box, enter **map X:=NETWARE6\SYS: PUBLIC\Home\%LOGIN_NAME**. Click **OK**. The text %LOGIN_ NAME is a variable which stands for the user's login name. By using the variable name instead of netplus, you can use the same login script for all users without having to retype the user login name in each login script.

23. Click **Start**, then click **Log Off**. The Log Off Windows dialog box opens.

24. Click **Log Off**. The computer logs off.

25. Press **Ctrl+Alt+Del** to display the Novell Login window. Click the **Advanced** tab. Additional options appear at the bottom of the Novell Login window.

26. In the Username text box, enter **netplus**. In the Password text box, enter the password for this account. If necessary, enter **laboratory** in the Context text box. Click the **Script** tab. Options related to the login script appear.

27. Click the **Close automatically** check box to remove the check mark from it, and make sure that the **Run scripts** and **Display results window** check boxes contain check marks. Click **OK**. The Windows XP desktop appears, along with the Results dialog box displaying information about the netplus login and the login script.

28. Click **Close** to close the Results dialog box.

29. Click **Start**, then click **My Computer**. The My Computer window opens.

30. Double-click the **Netplus on 'Netware6\Sys\Public\Home' (X:)** folder. The folder on the server opens.

31. Log off *WORKSTATION1*.

Certification Objectives

Objectives for the Network+ Exam:

➤ Identify the basic capabilities (i.e., client support, interoperability, authentication, file and print services, application support, and security) of the following server operating systems: UNIX/Linux, NetWare, Windows, Macintosh

➤ Identify the basic capabilities (i.e., client connectivity, local security mechanisms, and authentication) of the following clients: UNIX/Linux, NetWare, Windows, Macintosh

➤ Given specific parameters, configure a client to connect to the following servers: UNIX/Linux, NetWare, Windows, Macintosh

Review Questions

1. What is the purpose of the map command?
   a. to display a graphical representation of a NetWare server's directory
   b. to load a portion of the NetWare kernel on a client workstation
   c. to format a subdirectory according to a different file system than its parent directory
   d. to associate a NetWare directory with a drive letter for easier client access

2. On a Windows XP Professional client, how would a user find his or her drive mappings?
   a. Click Start, point to Control Panel, then click Drive Maps options.
   b. Click Start, point to Network and Dial-up Connections, then click LAN Connection.
   c. Click Start, point to My Computer, then click My Network Places.
   d. Click Start, then click My Computer.

10

3. What is one advantage to establishing drive mappings through the login script on a NetWare server?

    a. prevents users from being able to create their own drive mappings

    b. simplifies the process of mapping drives according to users and groups

    c. enables more drive letters to be used for mapping

    d. prevents the mapping of secured data directories

4. What is the advantage of using login variables such as %LOGIN_NAME instead of user names in a login script?

    a. Users can skip the login script altogether.

    b. Users do not need to type their user name an additional time.

    c. Network administrators do not need to type the user's login name in each login script.

    d. Network administrators do not need to type the user's login name when adding their account to eDirectory.

5. You suspect that a user on your network has been abusing network resources. In order to monitor the user's actions on the network, you have added a batch file to their login script that notifies you when they log into the network. What is one potential problem with this?

    a. Login scripts will not run batch files.

    b. Login scripts are only run when the user logs off.

    c. Login scripts may be skipped by the user.

    d. Login scripts may be skipped if the user is accessing the network through ConsoleOne.

Lab 10.5 Configuring Native File Service on a NetWare Network

Objectives

In addition to the NetWare client, you may configure other methods of accessing files on a NetWare server. For instance, NetWare servers offer native access to files. This means that clients can use whatever built-in methods they normally use in order to access the files. Unix computers can use Network File System (NFS), Apple computers can use Apple File Protocol (AFP), and Windows computers can use Common Internet File Structure (CIFS). This can be useful when you wish users to access files on a NetWare server, but do not wish to install and configure the NetWare client on their laptops or workstations. For instance, you may want to give visiting users access to files on your file server, but want to avoid installing and configuring the Novell client on their laptops, which would be inconvenient and time-consuming. Use of CIFS allows these Windows users access to files with relatively minimal configuration.

In order for Windows clients to access files through CIFS, two steps must be taken. First, the CIFS protocol must be enabled on the server using iManager, and shares must be set up on the NetWare server. Second, because the clients do not have direct access to the eDirectory tree, you must set up user authentication so that users can use CIFS to access the shares on the NetWare server. One approach is to configure each user with an account in eDirectory, and then with a simple password for that account. The simple password is used only for access to files through CIFS, and is not used for regular access to the eDirectory tree.

After completing this lab, you will be able to:

➤ Configure CIFS access to a NetWare 6.5 server

Materials Required

This lab will require the following:

➤ A computer named *NETWARE6* with Novell NetWare 6.5 installed as a Basic NetWare File Server

➤ An IP address of 192.168.54.6 and a subnet mask of 255.255.255.0 bound to the NetWare computer's NIC

➤ An eDirectory tree named NETPLUS, with *NETWARE6* and the admin account in the administration context

➤ An organizational unit named laboratory below the *NETPLUS* tree, with a user named netplus

➤ A computer with Windows XP Professional installed named *WORKSTATION1*, with an IP address of 192.168.54.3 and a subnet mask of 255.255.255.0

➤ Novell Client 4.9 for Windows NT/2000/XP installed on *WORKSTATION1*

➤ Access to the Windows XP computer as a user called netplus in the Administrators group

➤ A computer running Windows XP Professional named *WORKSTATION2*, configured with an IP address of 192.168.54.4 and a subnet mask of 255.255.255.0

➤ Access as an ordinary user to *WORKSTATION2*

➤ *WORKSTATION2* configured in the WORKGROUP workgroup without the Novell client

➤ A hub and two straight-through CAT 5 (or better) UTP cables connecting the NICs of both computers

➤ iManager installed on *NETWARE6*

10

Estimated completion time: **30 minutes**

ACTIVITY

1. On WORKSTATION1, press **Ctrl+Alt+Del** to display the Novell Login window. Log into the computer as the netplus user. The Windows XP desktop appears.

2. Click **Start**, then click **Internet Explorer**. Internet Explorer opens.

3. In the Address bar, type **http://192.168.54.6/nps/iManager.html** and press **Enter**. The Security Alert dialog box opens, indicating that there is a problem with the site's security certificate.

4. Click **Yes**. Another Security Alert dialog box may open, indicating that you are about to view pages over a secure connection. If not, go to Step 6.

5. Click **Yes**. The Novell iManager page loads.

6. In the Username text box, enter **admin**. In the Password text box, enter the password for the admin account. Click **Login**. The computer logs you into iManager.

7. Underneath Roles and Tasks, click the **plus sign (+)** sign next to File Protocols. The tree expands below it.

8. Click **CIFS / AFP**. The CFS / AFP Management window opens in Internet Explorer's right pane. Figure 10-5 shows iManager.

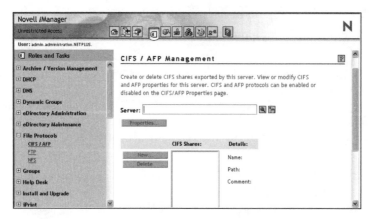

Figure 10-5   iManager

9. In the Server text box, enter **NETWARE6.administration**. Click **Properties**. The CIFS / AFP Properties page opens in the right pane of Internet Explorer.

10. Make sure that both the **CIFS** and the **AFP** check boxes have check marks in them. Click **OK**.

11. Click **New**. A Novell iManager – Microsoft Internet Explorer window opens.

12. In the Name text box, enter **PUBLIC**. In the Path text box, enter **SYS:Public**. In the Comment text box, enter **Public shares**. Click **Finish**. The window closes, and the PUBLIC share is displayed below CIFS Shares. Details about the share are shown below the heading "Details."

13. In the left pane of the iManager window, click the **plus sign (+)** next to Users. The tree expands below Users.

14. Click **Modify User**. The Modify User page opens in the right pane of Internet Explorer.

15. In the Username text box, enter **netplus.laboratory**. Click **OK**. User information for the netplus account appears.

16. Click the **Restrictions** tab. Configuration options related to passwords appear.

10

17. Click the **Set Password** link. The Novell iManager – Microsoft Internet Explorer window opens.

18. Click the **Set simple password** check box. Text boxes for setting a simple password appear.

19. In the Simple password text box, enter a password. This does not need to be the same as the existing password for the netplus account. Enter the password again in the Retype simple password text box. Record the password you entered for later use. Click **OK**. The General Message – Microsoft Internet Explorer page opens, indicating that the Set Password request succeeded.

20. Click **OK**. The General Message window closes.

21. On *WORKSTATION2*, press **Ctrl+Alt+Del** to display the Log On to Windows dialog box. Log on. The Windows XP desktop appears.

22. Click **Start**, then click **My Computer**. The My Computer window opens.

23. Click **Tools** on the menu bar, then click **Map Network Drive**. The Map Network Drive window opens.

24. In the Folder text box, enter **\\192.168.154.51\public**. Click **Connect using a different name**. The Connect As dialog box opens. In the Username text box, enter **Netplus**. In the Password textbox, enter the simple password you configured for this account in Step 19. Click **OK**. The Connect As dialog box closes.

25. Click **Finish**. The My Network Drive dialog box closes, and an icon for public on 'netware6_w (192.168.54.6)' (Z:) appears.

26. Double-click the icon for the newly mapped network drive. You have successfully accessed these files through CIFS.

27. Log off both computers.

Certification Objectives

Objectives for the Network+ Exam:

➤ Identify the basic capabilities (i.e., client support, interoperability, authentication, file and print services, application support, and security) of the following server operating systems: UNIX/Linux, NetWare, Windows, Macintosh

➤ Identify the basic capabilities (i.e., client connectivity, local security mechanisms, and authentication) of the following clients: UNIX/Linux, NetWare, Windows, Macintosh

➤ Given specific parameters, configure a client to connect to the following servers: UNIX/Linux, NetWare, Windows, Macintosh

Review Questions

1. What does "native file access" refer to?
   a. file sharing through the Novell client
   b. file sharing through IPX/SPX
   c. file sharing through methods of network access built into the computer
   d. file sharing through TCP/IP

2. True or False? If a NetWare server is configured to share files through CIFS, users accessing the files are not required to have a user account in eDirectory.

3. Which of the following sets of tasks must be completed in order to share files on a NetWare server through CIFS?
   a. CIFS must be activated on the server, a share must be created, and users must be configured to access the share.
   b. CIFS must be activated on the server and users must be configured to access the share.
   c. CIFS must be activated on the server, and users need not be configured to access the share.
   d. A CIFS share must be created, and users must be configured to access the share.

4. Why must a simple password be configured for users accessing files on a Net-Ware server through CIFS?

   a. Users do not have access to a Windows Server 2003 domain.

   b. Users do not have access to the eDirectory tree.

   c. CIFS requires different authentication methods.

   d. Users must authenticate against the local Windows workstation.

5. Which of the following are possible ways a Unix client could access files on a NetWare server? Choose all that apply.

   a. through the use of the `smbclient` program onto a CIFS volume

   b. through the use of NetWare client software onto a NetWare volume

   c. through the use of NFS client software onto an NFS volume

   d. through the use of IPX/SPX client software onto a NetWare volume

10

NETWORKING WITH TCP/IP
AND THE INTERNET

Labs included in this chapter

➤ Lab 11.1 Understanding the Purpose of the Default Gateway

➤ Lab 11.2 Understanding the TCP/IP Hosts File

➤ Lab 11.3 Configuring Domain Name System (DNS) Properties

➤ Lab 11.4 Using FTP

➤ Lab 11.5 Understanding Port Numbers

➤ Lab 11.6 Configuring a Mail Server

Net+ Exam Objectives	
Objective	**Lab**
Identify the purpose, features, and functions of the following network components: hubs, switches, bridges, routers, gateways, CSU/DSU, Network Interface Cards/ISDN adapters/system area network cards, wireless access points, modems	11.1
Identify the purpose of subnetting and default gateways	11.1
Given a network configuration, select the appropriate NIC and network configuration settings (DHCP, DNS, WINS, protocols, NetBIOS/host name, etc.)	11.1, 11.2, 11.3
Identify the purpose of the following network services: DHCP/bootp, DNS, NAT/ICS, WINS, and SNMP	11.2
Given output from a diagnostic utility (e.g., Tracert, Ping, Ipconfig, etc.), identify the utility and interpret the output	11.1, 11.2, 11.3
Given a scenario, predict the impact of modifying, adding, or removing network services (e.g., DHCP, DNS, WINS, etc.) on network resources and users	11.2, 11.3
Given a troubleshooting scenario, select the appropriate TCP/IP utility from among the following: Tracert, Ping, Arp, Netstat, Nbtstat, Ipconfig/Ifconfig, Winipcfg, Nslookup	11.1, 11.3
Identify the basic capabilities (i.e., client support, interoperability, authentication, file and print services, application support, and security) of the following server operating systems: UNIX/Linux, NetWare, Windows, Macintosh	11.3, 11.4, 11.5, 11.6
Define the purpose, function, and/or use of the following protocols within TCP/IP: IP, TCP, UDP, FTP, TFTP, SMTP, HTTP, HTTPS, POP3/IMAP4, Telnet, ICMP, Arp, NTP	11.4, 11.5, 11.6
Define the function of TCP/UDP ports; identify well-known ports	11.5

Lab 11.1 Understanding the Purpose of the Default Gateway

Objectives

To ensure that a computer knows where to send packets outside of its own network, you can configure a default gateway. The default gateway is a computer or router that knows where to send packets so that they will reach their destination. Often the default gateway appears in a computer's routing table as a route to 0.0.0.0 with a subnet mask of 0.0.0.0. The IP address 0.0.0.0 is a generic way to refer to all possible IP addresses.

For instance, suppose a small network has a single router that is attached to the Internet. Suppose also that each computer on the network has this Internet router configured as its default gateway. Each computer has a route in its routing table for the local network, so that it can send packets bound for local network resources to the appropriate computer. If the address of a network resource is not on the local network, then each computer sends the packet to the Internet router. The Internet router knows where to send the packet so that it will reach its destination.

Often the Internet router's routing table will specify just a few local routes and a default route to an ISP router. It will send any packet with a destination address that is not in its routing table to the ISP router. The ISP router will usually have a large routing table containing information about destination networks on the Internet.

After completing this lab, you will be able to:

➤ Identify the purpose of a default gateway

➤ Configure a default gateway

Materials Required

This lab will require the following:

➤ A computer running Windows XP Professional named *WORKSTATION1* and configured with an IP address of 192.168.54.3, a subnet mask of 255.255.255.0, and no default gateway

➤ A computer running Windows XP Professional named *WORKSTATION2* and configured with an IP address of 192.168.54.4, a subnet mask of 255.255.255.0, and no default gateway

➤ Administrator access to both computers

➤ Both computers connected to an Ethernet hub with straight-through CAT 5 (or better) UTP cables

Estimated completion time: **30 minutes**

ACTIVITY

1. On *WORKSTATION1*, press **Ctrl+Alt+Del** to display the Log On to Windows dialog box. Log on as the Administrator. The Windows XP desktop appears.

2. Click **Start**, point to **All Programs**, point to **Accessories**, and then click **Command Prompt**. A command prompt window appears.

3. At the command prompt, type **ping 192.168.54.4** and press **Enter**. On the screen, the computer indicates that it has received four replies from the remote computer.

4. Repeat Steps 1 through 3 on *WORKSTATION2*. However, ping the address **192.168.54.3** instead.

5. Now you will add a secondary IP address to one of the computers. On *WORKSTATION1*, click **Start**, point to **All Programs**, point to **Accessories**, point to **Communications**, then click **Network Connections**. The Network Connections window opens.

6. Right-click **Local Area Connection**, and then click **Properties** from the pop-up menu. The Local Area Connection Properties window appears.

7. Double-click **Internet Protocol (TCP/IP)**. The Internet Protocol (TCP/IP) Properties window appears.

8. Click **Advanced**. The Advanced TCP/IP Settings window appears.

9. Below the IP Address text box, click **Add**. The TCP/IP Address window appears. In the IP address text box, type **172.16.1.1**. In the Subnet mask text box, type **255.255.255.0**.

10. Click **Add**. Click **OK** three times to finish configuring the secondary IP address.

11. In the command prompt window on *WORKSTATION2*, type **ping 172.16.1.1** and press **Enter**. The computer indicates that it is unable to reach the remote computer. *WORKSTATION2* does not know where to send packets destined for 172.16.1.1.

12. Type **netstat -r** and press **Enter** to display the routing table on *WORKSTATION2*. Below, record the destination addresses listed in the routing table. Figure 11-1 shows typical output of the netstat -r command.

13. You will now add a default gateway to *WORKSTATION2*. Repeat Steps 5 through 7 on *WORKSTATION2* to open the Internet Protocol (TCP/IP) Properties window.

11

Figure 11-1   Output of the `netstat -r` command

14. In the Default gateway text box, type **192.168.54.3**. This tells *WORKSTATION2* to send packets to 192.168.54.3 whenever it does not have another route for them. Click **OK** twice to exit.

15. At the command prompt on *WORKSTATION2*, type **ping 172.16.1.1**. The computer indicates that it has received four replies from *WORKSTATION1*.

16. Type **netstat -r** and press **Enter** to show the routing table again on *WORKSTATION2*. Compare this routing table to the one you saw in Step 12. What are the new destination addresses? Record them below.

17. Log off both computers.

Certification Objectives

Objectives for the Network+ Exam:

➤ Identify the purpose, features, and functions of the following network components: hubs, switches, bridges, routers, gateways, CSU/DSU, Network Interface Cards/ ISDN adapters/system area network cards, wireless access points, modems

➤ Identify the purpose of subnetting and default gateways

➤ Given a network configuration, select the appropriate NIC and network configuration settings (DHCP, DNS, WINS, protocols, NetBIOS/host name, etc.)

➤ Given output from a diagnostic utility (e.g., Tracert, Ping, Ipconfig, etc.), identify the utility and interpret the output

➤ Given a troubleshooting scenario, select the appropriate TCP/IP utility from among the following: Tracert, Ping, Arp, Netstat, Nbtstat, Ipconfig/Ifconfig, Winipcfg, Nslookup

Review Questions

1. What is the purpose of the default gateway?

    a. to assign IP addresses to clients as soon as they log on to the network

    b. to ensure that no two nodes on the same subnet have identical TCP/IP addresses

    c. to accept and relay packets from nodes on one network destined for nodes on another network

    d. to advertise the best, current routing paths between networks from one router to another

2. Which of the following is most likely to act as a default gateway?

    a. modem

    b. hub

    c. switch

    d. router

3. What type of information would the `netstat -r` command yield, when typed at the command prompt of a networked client?

    a. a list of all routers to which that client might connect

    b. a list of the client's NIC adapter IP addresses

    c. the client's routing table

    d. the client's TCP/IP settings

4. What is the default subnet mask for a Class B network in the IP version 4 addressing scheme?

    a. 255.255.0.0

    b. 255.255.255.0

    c. 255.255.255.255

    d. 0.0.0.0

5. Which of the following utilities can show the route a packet traverses between its source node and destination node on a network?

    a. Ping

    b. Nbtstat

    c. Netstat

    d. Tracert

11

LAB 11.2 UNDERSTANDING THE TCP/IP HOSTS FILE

Objectives

To use host names instead of IP addresses to reach remote computers, a computer must have some way to find the IP address that corresponds to each remote computer. One of the simplest ways to do this is to use the hosts file. The hosts file is a file that contains a list of IP addresses and the names of the computers at those addresses. When the computer recognizes the name of another computer in its hosts file, it will use the associated IP address when it tries to communicate with that computer.

Because it would be impossible to distribute hosts files to all the computers on the Internet, computers typically use the Domain Name System (DNS) to associate host names with IP addresses rather than using a copy of the hosts file. However, the hosts file is often useful as a temporary measure or when you cannot make a DNS entry. The hosts file can be useful, for example, when you wish to make a DNS entry in a domain you do not control, or when you are using Network Address Translation (NAT). An IP address translated by NAT may not match the actual IP address of a computer, but a hosts entry will force the computer to use the appropriate IP address.

After completing this lab, you will be able to:

➤ Identify the purpose of the hosts file

➤ Modify a computer's hosts file

➤ Connect to another computer using its host name

Materials Required

This lab will require the following:

➤ A computer running Windows XP Professional named *WORKSTATION1* with an IP address of 192.168.54.3 and a subnet mask of 255.255.255.0

➤ Access as the Administrator to the Windows XP computer

➤ A computer running Red Hat Enterprise Linux ES 3.x named *LINUX1.NETPLUSLAB.NET* with an IP address of 192.168.54.5 and a subnet mask of 255.255.255.0

➤ A user named netplus on *LINUX1.NETPLUSLAB.NET*, and the root password for *LINUX1.NETPLUSLAB.NET*

➤ Each computer connected to a hub with straight-through CAT 5 (or better) UTP cables

Estimated completion time: **25 minutes**

ACTIVITY

1. On *WORKSTATION1*, press **Ctrl+Alt+Del** to display the Log On to Windows dialog box. Log on to *WORKSTATION1* as the Administrator. The Windows XP desktop appears.

2. Click **Start**, point to **All Programs**, point to **Accessories**, and then click **Command Prompt**. A command prompt window opens.

3. In the command prompt window, type **cd C:\windows\system32\drivers\etc** and press **Enter**. On a Windows XP computer, this directory contains the hosts file.

4. To modify the hosts file, type **notepad hosts** and then press **Enter**. Notepad opens with the text of the hosts file. Note that many lines begin with a pound sign (#). These lines are comments, and are ignored by the computer when it uses the hosts file.

5. At the bottom of the file, on a line by itself, type **192.168.54.5 linux1. netpluslab.net. Click File on the menu bar, and then click Save. Figure 11-2 shows the Windows XP hosts file.**

Figure 11-2   Windows XP hosts file

6. Click **File** on the menu bar, then click **Exit**. Notepad closes.

7. At the command prompt, type **ping linux1.netpluslab.net**, and then press **Enter**. The computer indicates that it has received four replies from *LINUX1.NETPLUSLAB.NET*.

8. On *LINUX1.NETPLUSLAB.NET* at the Welcome to linux1.netpluslab.net screen, enter **netplus** in the Username text box and press **Enter**. The Password text box appears.

9. In the Password text box, type the password for the netplus user and press **Enter**. The Red Hat desktop appears.

10. Right-click a blank spot on the desktop. From the pop-up menu, click **New Terminal**. A terminal window opens.

11. At the prompt in the terminal window, type **su –** and press **Enter**. The Password prompt appears.

12. Type the root password for *LINUX1.NETPLUSLAB.NET* and press **Enter**. The prompt changes to end in #, indicating that you are now logged on as the root user.

13. Type **cd /etc** and press **Enter**.

14. Type **echo "192.168.54.3 workstation1.netpluslab.net" >> hosts** and press **Enter**. The computer appends the IP address and the host name between the parentheses into the hosts file.

15. To see what the hosts file contains, type **cat hosts** and press **Enter**. The computer displays the contents of the hosts file.

16. Type **ping workstation1.netpluslab.net** and press **Enter**. The computer indicates that it is receiving replies from *WORKSTATION1*. Press **Ctrl+C** to stop the ping utility.

17. Log off both computers.

Certification Objectives

Objectives for the Network+ Exam:

➤ Given a network configuration, select the appropriate NIC and network configuration settings (DHCP, DNS, WINS, protocols, NetBIOS/host name, etc.)

➤ Identify the purpose of the following network services: DHCP/bootp, DNS, NAT/ICS, WINS, and SNMP

➤ Given output from a diagnostic utility (e.g., Tracert, Ping, Ipconfig, etc.), identify the utility and interpret the output

➤ Given a scenario, predict the impact of modifying, adding, or removing network services (e.g., DHCP, DNS, WINS, etc.) on network resources and users

Review Questions

1. What is the purpose of a host name?

    a. to uniquely identify a node on a network

    b. to associate a node with a particular domain

    c. to indicate which domain a node belongs to

    d. to identify the IP address of a host

2. What is the purpose of a hosts file?

    a. to help determine the best route for packets between gateways

    b. to make it easier for network administrators to remember a computer's IP address

    c. to map IP addresses to host names

    d. to indicate which hosts on a network are available to a client

3. What file on a Linux system holds information about host names and their IP addresses?

    a. /etc/hosts

    b. /bin/hosts

    c. /lib/users/hostfile

    d. /root/hostfile

4. Which of the following symbols indicates a comment in the hosts file?

    a. >

    b. >>

    c. :

    d. #

5. What is the alias of the computer whose host name is "C2" in the following hosts file?

    ```
    160.12.122.13    C1C2.gameco.com     canasta
    156.11.21.145    Comp2.gameco.com    chess
    123.14.11.214    C2.gameco.com       checkers
    44.112.133.15    CIC2.gameco.com     backgammon
    ```

    a. canasta

    b. chess

    c. checkers

    d. backgammon

11

LAB 11.3 CONFIGURING DOMAIN NAME SYSTEM (DNS) PROPERTIES

Objectives

As explained in Lab 11.2, the Domain Name System (DNS) is a method of associating an IP address with a host name. It is an alternative to the hosts file, and is much easier to manage and maintain over many servers. For that reason, DNS is used throughout the Internet. When you open a Web browser and attempt to connect to *www.comptia.com*, for example, the Web browser first queries a DNS server to find the IP address of the Web site. If the DNS server your computer is configured to use does not know the IP address associated with *www.comptia.com*, it queries the authoritative nameserver for the comptia.com domain (or zone). The authoritative nameserver is the DNS server with the definitive DNS information for that domain. When the authoritative DNS server responds with the IP address to your DNS server, your DNS server sends that information to your computer. The Web browser on your computer then uses that IP address to connect to the Web site.

In addition to finding the IP address belonging to a particular host name (a process known as a forward DNS lookup), DNS is also used to find the host name belonging to a particular IP address. This process is known as a reverse DNS lookup. A computer can use a reverse DNS lookup to determine the name of a computer attempting to access its network resources. However, reverse DNS lookups are not a reliable way of determining this information.

One tool you can use to find DNS information directly is the nslookup command. This command allows you to find out the IP address associated with a particular host name and other information.

Keep in mind that beginning with Windows 2000 Server, DNS has become tightly integrated with Active Directory. Before Windows 2000 Server, making a mistake when configuring DNS might prevent you from accessing a server by name. Now, making a mistake configuring DNS can prevent Active Directory from working properly. Keeping DNS working properly is very important in networks that use Windows Server 2003.

After completing this lab, you will be able to:

➤ Add a DNS server to DNS

➤ Add a DNS zone

➤ Add a DNS host

➤ Configure a computer to refer to the DNS server

➤ Access a computer using its DNS name

Materials Required

This lab will require the following:

➤ A computer running Windows Server 2003 Enterprise Edition named *SERVER1* configured with an IP address of 192.168.54.1 and a subnet mask of 255.255.255.0

➤ The Windows 2003 Server computer configured as a domain controller for the netpluslab.net domain with the DNS server installed

➤ A reverse lookup zone configured for the 192.168.54.x subnet

➤ A computer running Windows XP Professional named *WORKSTATION1* configured with an IP address of 192.168.54.3 and a subnet mask of 255.255.255.0, but without a DNS server configured

➤ Access as the Administrator to both computers

➤ A computer running Red Hat Enterprise Linux ES 3.x named *LINUX1.NETPLUSLAB.NET* and configured with an IP address of 192.168.54.5 and a subnet mask of 255.255.255.0

➤ Each computer connected to a hub with straight-through CAT 5 (or better) UTP cables

11

Estimated completion time: **30 minutes**

ACTIVITY

1. On *SERVER1*, press **Ctrl+Alt+Del** to display the Log On to Windows dialog box. Log on as the Administrator. The Windows Server 2003 desktop appears.

2. Click **Start**, point to **Administrative Tools**, and then click **DNS**. The dnsmgmt window opens.

3. In the left pane of the window, right-click the name of the server. Click **New Zone**. The New Zone Wizard appears.

4. Click **Next**. The next window in the wizard asks you to select the type of zone you wish to configure.

5. Make sure that the **Primary zone** option button is selected and click **Next**. The next window in the wizard asks you to choose how DNS data will be replicated through your network.

6. Click **Next** to select the default option. The next window in the wizard asks you to choose whether you wish to create a forward or reverse lookup zone.

7. Make sure that the **Forward lookup zone** option is selected and click **Next**. The wizard now asks you to choose a name for the zone.

8. In the Zone name text box, type **otherorg.net**, and then click **Next**. The next window in the wizard asks you to select the type of DNS updates to be used.

9. Click **Next** to select the default option. The next window in the wizard summarizes the options that you have chosen and indicates that you have finished.

10. Click **Finish**. The New Zone Wizard closes.

11. In the left pane of the dnsmgmt window, click the **plus sign (+)** next to the Forward Lookup Zones folder. The tree expands, showing a list of domains for which this DNS server is authoritative, including the new otherorg.net domain.

12. In the left pane, click the **otherorg.net** folder to select it. Right-click the **otherorg.net** folder, and click **New Host (A)** from the pop-up menu. The New Host dialog box opens.

13. In the Name text box, type **workstation1**. In the IP address text box, type **192.168.54.3**. Place a check in the **Create associated pointer (PTR) record** check box. Figure 11-3 shows the dnsmgmt and the New Host dialog boxes.

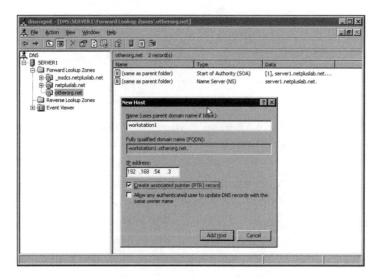

Figure 11-3   The dnsmgmt and New Host dialog boxes

14. Click the **Add Host** button. The DNS dialog box opens, indicating that the host record workstation1.otherorg.net was successfully created.

15. Click **OK**. The DNS dialog box closes.

16. Click **Done**. The New Host dialog box closes.

17. Right-click the **netpluslab.net** folder, and click **New Host (A)** from the pop-up menu. The New Host dialog box opens.

18. In the New Host dialog box, repeat Steps 13 through 15, creating the domain name **workstation1.netpluslab.net** with an IP address of **192.168.54.3**.

19. Repeat Steps 13 through 15 again, creating the domain name **linux1.netpluslab.net** with an IP address of **192.168.54.5**.

20. Click **Done**.

21. On *WORKSTATION1*, press **Ctrl+Alt+Del** to display the Log On to Windows dialog box. Log on to the client computer as an Administrator. The Window XP desktop appears.

22. Click **Start**, point to **All Programs**, point to **Accessories**, point to **Communications**, and then click **Network Connections**. The Network Connections window opens.

23. Right-click **Local Area Connection** and click **Properties** from the pop-up menu. The Local Area Connection Properties window appears.

24. Double-click **Internet Protocol (TCP/IP)**. The Internet Protocol (TCP/IP) Properties window opens.

25. Click the **Use the following DNS server addresses** option button, if necessary. In the Preferred DNS server text box, type **192.168.54.1**.

26. Click **OK** twice to exit the Local Area Connection Properties window.

27. Click **Start**, point to **All Programs**, point to **Accessories**, and click **Command Prompt**. A command prompt window appears.

28. In the command prompt window, type **nslookup workstation1. netpluslab.net** and press **Enter**. The computer displays the name *workstation1.netpluslab.net* and its IP address, as well as the IP address of the DNS server answering the request.

29. Type **ping workstation1.otherorg.net** and press **Enter**. The computer indicates that it has received four replies from the remote computer, and displays its IP address.

30. Repeat the previous step twice, pinging **workstation1.netpluslab.net** and **linux1.netpluslab.net**.

31. Now you will configure a DNS server on a Linux computer. On *LINUX1.NETPLUSLAB.NET* at the Welcome to linux1.netpluslab.net screen, enter **netplus** in the Username text box and press **Enter**. The Password text box appears.

32. In the Password text box, type the password for the netplus user and press **Enter**. The Red Hat desktop appears.

33. Right-click a blank spot on the desktop. In the pop-up menu, click **New Terminal**. A terminal window opens.

34. At the prompt in the terminal window, type **su** – and press **Enter**. The Password prompt appears.

11

35. Type the root password and press **Enter**. The prompt now ends in a pound sign (#), indicating that you are now logged on as the root user.

36. Type `echo "nameserver 192.168.54.1" >/etc/named.conf` and press **Enter**. This overwrites the file /etc/named.conf so that it contains the text "nameserver 192.168.54.1." The computer will now use 192.168.54.1 as its DNS server.

37. Type `nslookup workstation1.otherorg.net` and press **Enter**. The computer displays the IP address of *WORKSTATION1.OTHERORG.NET*. If the computer displays an error message instead, wait 15 seconds and try again. Repeat this step until the computer displays the IP address of *WORKSTATION1.OTHERORG.NET*.

38. Type `ping workstation1.otherorg.net` and press **Enter**. The computer indicates that it is receiving replies from the remote computer, displaying its name and IP address. Press **Ctrl+C** to stop the ping utility.

39. Repeat Steps 37 and 38 twice, using **workstation1.netpluslab.net** and **linux1.netpluslab.net**.

40. Log off all three computers.

Certification Objectives

Objectives for the Network+ Exam:

➤ Given a network configuration, select the appropriate NIC and network configuration settings (DHCP, DNS, WINS, protocols, NetBIOS/host name, etc.)

➤ Given output from a diagnostic utility (e.g., Tracert, Ping, Ipconfig, etc.), identify the utility and interpret the output

➤ Given a scenario, predict the impact of modifying, adding, or removing network services (e.g., DHCP, DNS, WINS, etc.) on network resources and users

➤ Given a troubleshooting scenario, select the appropriate TCP/IP utility from among the following: Tracert, Ping, Arp, Netstat, Nbtstat, Ipconfig/Ifconfig, Winipcfg, Nslookup

➤ Identify the basic capabilities (i.e., client support, interoperability, authentication, file and print services, application support, and security) of the following server operating systems: UNIX/Linux, NetWare, Windows, Macintosh

Review Questions

1. What is the purpose of a nameserver?
   a. to maintain the DNS database for an entire zone
   b. to supply clients with IP address resolution for requested hosts
   c. to track and record all TCP/IP host name information for a network
   d. to track and record all NetBIOS naming information for a network

2. What is the term for the group of devices that a nameserver manages?

   a. hierarchy

   b. tree

   c. zone

   d. directory

3. Which of the following are examples of top-level domains? (Choose all that apply.)

   a. .net

   b. .com

   c. .uk

   d. .aut

4. When a DNS server retrieves the host name associated with an IP address, what type of lookup is it accomplishing?

   a. forward

   b. adjacent

   c. backward

   d. reverse

5. What is one advantage of using DNS instead of hosts files?

   a. DNS does not require manual updating of files on multiple networked nodes.

   b. DNS is more compatible with Linux systems.

   c. DNS will map both NetBIOS and TCP/IP host names to IP addresses, while hosts files will map only TCP/IP host names to IP addresses.

   d. Using DNS is more secure than using hosts files.

LAB 11.4 USING FTP

Objective

In this lab, you will connect to a File Transfer Protocol (FTP) server on a remote host. FTP is used throughout the Internet to make files available for downloading. If a network administrator would like to make files available to the general public, he may create an anonymous FTP server. Users can log on to an anonymous FTP server by using a special account named "anonymous" without knowing the password.

FTP servers are available on nearly all platforms. If you run an anonymous FTP server, you should be careful when allowing anonymous users to upload files (that is, transfer files to the server) because malicious users could fill up your server's disk drive with their files. Another potential problem with FTP is that it sends passwords in unencrypted text, so they could be captured by a malicious user.

A variety of FTP clients are available for almost all modern operating systems. Command-line FTP clients are built into most modern operating systems, including Linux and Windows, but various GUI clients are also available. A GUI client will automate the FTP process for you, and may include additional features such as the ability to resume interrupted downloads.

After completing this lab, you will be able to:

➤ Log on to an FTP site

➤ Download files from an FTP site

➤ Copy files to an FTP site

➤ Define security policies for an FTP site

Materials Required

This lab will require the following:

➤ A computer running Windows Server 2003 Enterprise Edition named *SERVER1*, configured as a domain controller for the netpluslab.net domain with an IP address of 192.168.54.1 and a subnet mask of 255.255.255.0

➤ Internet Information Services (IIS) installed and running on *SERVER1* with the File Transfer Protocol (FTP) Service installed, with a root of C:\inetpub and with the default configuration and sample files in place

➤ The folder C:\inetpub\ftproot configured so that users in the Domain Users group have Read, Write, and Execute permissions

➤ Access to *SERVER1* as the Administrator

➤ A user account named netplus in the Domain Users group in the netpluslab.net domain

➤ A computer running Windows XP Professional named *WORKSTATION1*, configured with an IP address of 192.168.54.3 and a subnet mask of 255.255.255.0

➤ Both computers connected to a hub with CAT 5 (or better) UTP cables

Estimated completion time: **35 minutes**

LAB ACTIVITY

ACTIVITY

1. On *SERVER1*, press **Ctrl+Alt+Del** to display the Log On to Windows dialog box. Log on as the Administrator. The Windows Server 2003 desktop appears.

2. Click **Start**, point to **All Programs**, point to **Accessories**, and then click **Command Prompt**. A command prompt window opens.

3. In the command prompt window, type **echo "**your name**" > C:\ inetpub\ftproot\netplus.txt** and press **Enter**. (Substitute your name for "*your name*.") This creates a file named netplus.txt containing your name in the C:\inetpub\ftproot directory.

4. At the command prompt, type **copy C:\inetpub\wwwroot\pagerror. gif C:\inetpub\ftproot** and press **Enter**. The computer copies the file from one directory to the other. This image file now will be available on the FTP site configured on this computer.

5. On *WORKSTATION1*, press **Ctrl+Alt+Del** to display the Log On to Windows dialog box. Log on as the netplus user. The Windows XP desktop appears.

6. Click **Start**, point to **All Programs**, point to **Accessories**, and then click **Command Prompt**. A command prompt window opens.

7. In the command prompt window, type **ftp 192.168.54.1** and press **Enter**. The computer indicates that you have connected to 192.168.54.1, and that the remote computer is running the Microsoft FTP Service. The prompt changes to User (192.168.54.1:(none)):.

8. At the User (192.168.54.1:(none)): prompt, type **anonymous** and press **Enter**. The computer indicates that anonymous access is allowed and asks you to type an e-mail address or other form of identity as a password. The Password prompt also appears. At the Password prompt, type an e-mail address or a brief phrase, and then press **Enter**. The computer indicates that you have logged on successfully, and the prompt changes to ftp>. Figure 11-4 shows a user logging onto an FTP server.

9. Type **dir** and press **Enter**. A list of the files found on the remote computer, including pagerror.gif and netplus.txt, is displayed.

10. Type **ls** and press **Enter**. A list of the files found on the remote computer is displayed.

11

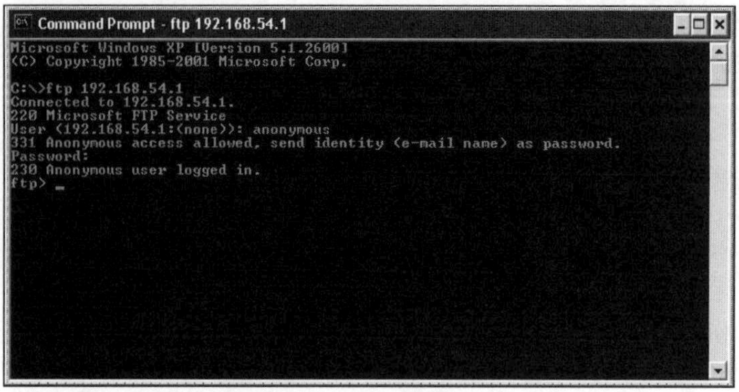

```
Command Prompt - ftp 192.168.54.1                              _ □ ×
Microsoft Windows XP [Version 5.1.2600]
(C) Copyright 1985-2001 Microsoft Corp.

C:\>ftp 192.168.54.1
Connected to 192.168.54.1.
220 Microsoft FTP Service
User (192.168.54.1:(none)): anonymous
331 Anonymous access allowed, send identity (e-mail name) as password.
Password:
230 Anonymous user logged in.
ftp> _
```

Figure 11-4 Logging onto an FTP server

11. At the prompt, type **get netplus.txt** and press **Enter**. The computer indicates that it is opening an ASCII mode data connection. ASCII mode allows FTP to transfer plain text files more quickly, and ensures that a plain text file is readable by the computer that downloads it. An ASCII mode transfer will corrupt files that are not in plain text, such as image or program files. (It will also corrupt many word processor files, such as Microsoft Word documents, since these are not stored as plain text files by the word processor.)

12. To transfer the image file, type **binary** at the prompt, and then press **Enter**. The computer now transfers the file using binary mode. In a binary mode transfer, an exact copy of the file is transferred from the server.

13. Type **get pagerror.gif** at the prompt, and then press **Enter**. The computer indicates that the file is being transferred in binary mode. The ftp> prompt returns when the transfer is complete.

14. Type **!copy netplus.txt upload.txt** and press **Enter**. The computer displays the message "1 file(s) copied". The exclamation mark (!) tells the FTP program that you wish to run a command on *WORKSTATION1* that copies the file netplus.txt to upload.txt in the directory you are working in on *WORKSTATION1*.

15. To try to upload a file onto the remote server, type **put upload.txt** and press **Enter**. The computer indicates that access is denied.

16. Type **quit** and press **Enter** to exit the FTP site.

17. Now you will remove anonymous FTP access to the server, and allow users to upload files. On *SERVER1*, click **Start**, point to **Administrative Tools**, and then click **Internet Information Services (IIS) Manager**. The Internet Information Services (IIS) Manager window opens.

18. Click the **SERVER1 (local computer)** icon in the left pane. Icons for services run by IIS appear in the right pane, including an icon for FTP Sites.

19. Double-click the **FTP Sites** icon in the right pane. An icon for Default FTP Site appears.

20. Right-click **Default FTP Site** and click **Properties**. The Default FTP Site Properties window opens.

21. Click the **Security Accounts** tab. Uncheck the **Allow anonymous connections** check box. The IIS Manager dialog box opens, indicating that the authentication option you have selected will result in unencrypted passwords being transmitted over the network.

22. Click **Yes** to close the IIS Manager dialog box.

23. Click the **Home Directory** tab. Select the **Write** check box. At this point, you are ready to upload files. Click **OK**.

24. Right-click **SERVER1 (local computer)** in the left pane, point to **All Tasks**, and click **Restart IIS**. The Stop/Start/Restart dialog box opens.

25. Make sure that **Restart Internet Services on SERVER1** is selected in the "What do you want IIS to do?" drop-down menu and click **OK**. The Shutting Down dialog box opens briefly, indicating that the computer is shutting down IIS. An hourglass appears while Internet services are restarted, and then the Internet Information Services dialog box reappears.

26. In the command prompt window on WORKSTATION1, type **ftp 192.168.54.1** and then press **Enter**. The logon prompt appears. Type **anonymous** and then press **Enter**. Type a password and then press **Enter**. The ftp prompt indicates that User anonymous cannot log on and that the logon failed.

27. Type **quit** and press **Enter**.

28. Type **ftp 192.168.54.1**, and then press **Enter**. The logon prompt appears. Type **netplus** and press **Enter**. At the Password prompt, type the password for the netplus account and press **Enter**. You are now logged on to the remote server.

29. Type **put upload.txt** and press **Enter**. The computer indicates that the file is being uploaded onto the remote computer in ASCII mode data connection.

30. Type **quit**, and then press **Enter**.

31. On *SERVER1*, click **Start** and then click **My Computer**. The My Computer window opens.

32. Double-click the **Local Disk (C:)** icon. Double-click the **Inetpub** folder. Double-click the **ftproot** folder. The C:\Inetpub\ftproot folder opens, showing the upload.txt text file and the other files on the FTP server.

33. Log off both computers.

11

Certification Objectives

Objectives for the Network+ Exam:

➤ Identify the basic capabilities (i.e., client support, interoperability, authentication, file and print services, application support, and security) of the following server operating systems: UNIX/Linux, NetWare, Windows, Macintosh

➤ Define the purpose, function, and/or use of the following protocols within TCP/IP: IP, TCP, UDP, FTP, TFTP, SMTP, HTTP, HTTPS, POP3/IMAP4, Telnet, ICMP, ARP, NTP

Review Questions

1. Which of the following commands would you type at the ftp> prompt to copy a file named "textfile.doc" from your C:\ directory to an FTP server?

   a. `copy "textfile.doc"`

   b. `put C:\textfile.doc`

   c. `get C:\textfile.doc`

   d. `move C:\textfile.doc`

2. On what Transport layer protocol does FTP rely?

   a. TCP

   b. UDP

   c. ICMP

   d. NTP

3. What is the term for an FTP site that allows any user to access its directories?

   a. anonymous

   b. restricted

   c. private

   d. unlimited

4. What command allows you to list the contents of a directory on an FTP server?

   a. `list`

   b. `lf`

   c. `ls`

   d. `la`

5. What would you type at the ftp> prompt to view a list of available FTP commands? (Choose all that apply.)

    a. `list`

    b. `?`

    c. `help`

    d. `commands`

6. What two file types can you specify when transferring files via FTP?

    a. ascii and binary

    b. alphabetical and numeric

    c. program and data

    d. dynamic and static

Lab 11.5 Understanding Port Numbers

11

Objectives

In TCP/IP, servers use port numbers to identify processes associated with different services. For instance, a server might run several different services over TCP, including HTTP and FTP. Based only on the IP address, there is no way to distinguish between the two services. However, requests from client computers can connect to different port numbers. The default port number for the HTTP service, for example, is 80, while the default port number for the FTP control service is 21.

Most client software is designed to look for the default port number when connecting to a service. For example, by default, Web browsers attempt to find Web servers at port 80. However, you can usually configure a service to run on another port and configure the client software to look for that service on the new port.

You can tell a Web browser to look for a Web server at a non-default port by adding a colon and the port number after the Web site name or IP address in the URL. For instance, to go to the Microsoft Web site using the default port (80), you would use the URL *www.microsoft.com*. To look for a Web server at the same site on port 7777, you would use the URL *www.microsoft.com:7777* instead. Port numbers in UDP work the same way as port numbers in TCP.

After completing this lab, you will be able to:

➤ Identify default port numbers for several services

➤ Modify a service's default port numbers

➤ Connect to a service using a non-default port number

Materials Required

This lab will require the following:

➤ A computer running Windows Server 2003 Enterprise Edition named *SERVER1*, configured as a domain controller for the netpluslab.net domain with an IP address of 192.168.54.1 and a subnet mask of 255.255.255.0

➤ Internet Information Services (IIS) installed and running on *SERVER1* with the default configuration; to ensure that the default configuration is enabled you can remove and reinstall the software

➤ A text file in *SERVER1*'s Web root (C:\inetpub\wwwroot) named default.htm and containing the text "This is a test page"

➤ Access as the Administrator to *SERVER1*

➤ A computer running Windows XP Professional named *WORKSTATION1*, configured with an IP address of 192.168.54.3 and a subnet mask of 255.255.255.0

➤ Access with an ordinary user account to the client computer

➤ Both computers connected to a hub with straight-through CAT 5 (or better) cables

---

Estimated completion time: **20 minutes**

LAB ACTIVITY

ACTIVITY

1. On *WORKSTATION1*, press **Ctrl+Alt+Del** to display the Log On to Windows dialog box. Log on with an ordinary user account. The Windows XP desktop appears.

2. Click **Start**, then click **Internet Explorer**. Internet Explorer opens.

3. In the Address bar, type **http://192.168.54.1** and press **Enter**. A Web page opens, containing the text "This is a test page."

4. On *SERVER1*, press **Ctrl+Alt+Del** to display the Log On to Windows dialog box. Log on as the Administrator. The Windows Server 2003 desktop appears.

5. Click **Start**, point to **Administrative Tools**, and then click **Internet Information Services (IIS) Manager**. The Internet Information Services (IIS) Manager window opens.

6. In the left pane of the window, click **SERVER1 (local computer)**. Icons for services controlled by the IIS Manager appear in the right pane.

7. In the right pane, double-click the **Web Sites** icon. The Default Web Site icon appears in the right pane.

8. Right-click the **Default Web Site** icon in the right pane of the window, and then click **Properties**. The Default Web Site Properties window opens.

9. In the TCP port text box, change the number from 80 to **8880**. This will tell IIS to run the Web server on port 8880 instead of on port 80. Figure 11-5 shows the Default Web Site Properties dialog box. Click **OK**.

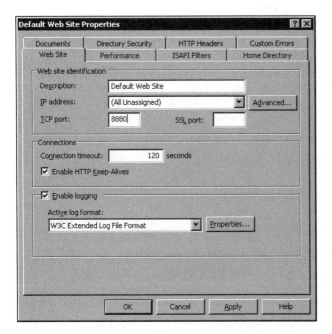

Figure 11-5 The Default Web Site Properties window

10. In the left pane of the Default Web Site Properties dialog box, right-click **SERVER1 (local computer)**. In the pop-up menu, point to **All Tasks**, then click **Restart IIS**. The Stop/Start/Restart dialog box opens.

11. Make sure that **Restart Internet Services on SERVER1** is selected in the "What do you want IIS to do?" drop-down menu. Click **OK**. The Shutting Down dialog box opens, indicating that the computer is attempting to shut down IIS, and then closes. An hourglass appears briefly, and then the computer restarts IIS.

12. On the menu bar, click **File**, then click **Exit** to close the Internet Services Manager.

13. On *WORKSTATION1*, close Internet Explorer. This will ensure that Internet Explorer does not use its disk cache of the Web page when you try to load the Web page again.

14. Click **Start**, point to **All Programs**, and then click **Internet Explorer**. Internet Explorer opens.

11

15. In the Address bar, type **http://192.168.54.1**, and then press **Enter**. An error message appears indicating that the page cannot be displayed.

16. In the Address bar, type **http://192.168.54.1:8880**, and then press **Enter**. A Web page displays the text "This is a test page."

17. Log off both computers.

Certification Objectives

Objectives for the Network+ Exam:

➤ Identify the basic capabilities (i.e., client support, interoperability, authentication, file and print services, application support, and security) of the following server operating systems: UNIX/Linux, NetWare, Windows, Macintosh

➤ Define the purpose, function, and/or use of the following protocols within TCP/IP: IP, TCP, UDP, FTP, TFTP, SMTP, HTTP, HTTPS, POP3/IMAP4, Telnet, ICMP, ARP, NTP

➤ Define the function of TCP/UDP ports; identify well-known ports.

Review Questions

1. What symbol is used to separate the computer name from the port number in a URL (assuming that IP version 4 is in use)?
   a. ;
   b. :
   c. #
   d. .

2. What is the default port number for the Telnet service?
   a. 20
   b. 21
   c. 22
   d. 23

3. What is the default port number for the HTTP service?
   a. 40
   b. 44
   c. 60
   d. 80

4. What range of port numbers comprises the well-known port numbers?
   a. 0 to 64
   b. 0 to 128

     c. 0 to 1023

     d. 0 to 8800

  5. What is a socket?

     a. a virtual connector that associates a URL with its IP address

     b. a method of identifying the IP addresses belonging to clients as they connect to servers

     c. a logical address assigned to a specific process running on a computer

     d. a discreet unit of data

  6. Which of the following addresses could represent the SMTP service using its default port on a mail server?

     a. 188.65.79.80:25

     b. 188.65.79.80...24

     c. 188.65.79.80$24

     d. 188.65.79.80;25

11

Lab 11.6 Configuring a Mail Server

Objectives

E-mail is one of the most important applications on the majority of business networks. E-mail is sent from a user's computer to its destination using the Simple Mail Transport Protocol (SMTP). A wide variety of programs run SMTP. In this lab, you will configure one such program, Sendmail. Sendmail is used primarily on Linux and UNIX computers.

A computer running SMTP looks at the domain name in the e-mail address, and performs a DNS lookup to find the mail exchanger, or MX, record for the domain. The MX record is the domain name of the e-mail server where e-mail for that domain must be sent. For instance, the netpluslab.net domain might have an MX record of linux1.netpluslab.net. This tells other computers running SMTP that any e-mail sent to e-mail addresses in the netpluslab.net domain (such as netplus@netpluslab .net) should be sent to the server linux1.netpluslab.net. As you might expect, DNS must be properly configured in order for SMTP to work correctly and for e-mail to be delivered. A domain may have multiple MX records with different priorities, which allows for load balancing or for a backup server to collect e-mail in case the primary server fails.

After an e-mail has been delivered to its final destination, the user must collect it. E-mail programs employ a variety of methods to collect e-mail. Some popular protocols used for collecting e-mail include the POP3 and IMAP protocols. In this lab you will configure the Outlook Express program to use POP3 to collect e-mail. Typically, settings for receiving mail are given to users by their network administrators.

After completing this lab, you will be able to:

➤ Configure an e-mail server

Materials Required

This lab will require the following:

➤ A computer running Windows Server 2003 Enterprise Edition named *SERVER1*, configured as a domain controller for the netpluslab.net domain and with an IP address of 192.168.54.1 and a subnet mask of 255.255.255.0

➤ A user named netplus configured in the netpluslab.net domain

➤ A computer running Windows XP Professional named *WORKSTATION1* configured with an IP address of 192.168.54.3 and a subnet mask of 255.255.255.0

➤ A computer running Red Hat Enterprise Linux ES 3.x named *LINUX1.NETPLUSLAB.NET* configured with an IP address of 192.168.54.5 and a subnet mask of 255.255.255.0

➤ A user named netplus configured on *LINUX1.NETPLUSLAB.NET*

➤ The sendmail-cf and imap-2002d-2 packages installed on *LINUX1.NETPLUSLAB.NET* (both are available on the third disk of the Red Hat Enterprise Linux ES 3.x installation CD-ROMs)

➤ *LINUX1.NETPLUSLAB.NET* configured to use 192.168.54.1 as its DNS server; the file /etc/resolv.conf should contain the line "nameserver 192.168.54.1"

➤ The DNS server on *SERVER1* configured and running, with a domain named netpluslab.net

➤ Forward and reverse DNS entries for *LINUX1.NETPLUSLAB.NET* at 192.168.54.5 and for *WORKSTATION1.NETPLUSLAB.NET* at 192.168.54.3

➤ All three computers configured to use 192.168.54.1 for DNS resolution

➤ A line in the /etc/hosts file on *LINUX1.NETPLUSLAB.NET* for 192.168.54.5 containing the text "192.168.54.5 linux1.netpluslab.net"

➤ The default /etc/sendmail.mc file on *LINUX1.NETPLUSLAB.NET*

➤ No e-mail accounts configured in Outlook Express on WORKSTATION1

Estimated completion time: **90-120 minutes**

ACTIVITY

1. On *LINUX1.NETPLUSLAB.NET* at the Welcome to linux1.netpluslab.net screen, enter **netplus** in the Username text box and press **Enter**. The Password text box appears.

2. In the Password text box, type the password for the netplus user and press **Enter**. The Red Hat desktop appears.

3. Right-click a blank spot on the desktop. In the pop-up menu, click **New Terminal**. A terminal window opens.

4. At the prompt in the terminal window type **su –** and press **Enter**. The Password prompt appears. Type the root password and press **Enter**. The prompt now ends in a pound sign (#), indicating that you are logged on as the root user.

5. Next, you will configure the xinetd daemon to allow users to check for e-mail from this computer. The xinetd daemon controls access to a variety of network programs on some Linux machines. Type **vi /etc/xinetd.d/ ipop3** and press **Enter**. The vi editor opens the file /etc/xinetd.d/ipop3 in normal mode.

6. If the next-to-last line of the file does not read disable = yes, skip to Step 11. If it does, press **G**. Press ↑ once to go up one line, and then press → until the cursor is positioned to the left of the "y" in "yes."

7. Type **d$** and press **Enter**. The vi editor deletes all text between the cursor and the end of the line, including the entire word "yes."

8. Press **a**. The vi editor goes into insert mode, and displays – INSERT – at the bottom of the terminal window.

9. Type **no** and press **Esc**. The vi editor returns to normal mode.

10. Type **:w** and press **Enter**. The vi editor saves the file.

11. Type **:q** and press **Enter**. The computer exits the file.

12. Type **cat /var/run/xinetd.pid** and press **Enter**. The computer displays the PID used by the xinetd daemon. Record the PID number below.

13. Type **kill -HUP** followed by the PID number you recorded in Step 12, and then press **Enter**. (For instance, if the PID recorded in Step 12 was 1563, you would type kill -HUP 1563.) This command sends the HUP (or HangUP) signal to PID 1563, which tells it to restart. The computer restarts the xinetd daemon.

11

14. Now you will configure the Sendmail program so that this computer can be used to send e-mail. Type **vi /etc/mail/sendmail.mc** and press **Enter**. The /etc/mail/sendmail.mc file opens.

15. Type **/DAEMON_OPTIONS** and press **Enter**. The computer places the cursor at the beginning of the text "DAEMON OPTIONS."

16. Type **/LOCAL_DOMAIN** and press **Enter**. The cursor moves to the start of a line containing the text LOCAL_DOMAIN.

17. Press **w** twice. The cursor moves to the beginning of the word "localhost. localdomain."

18. Type **d3w**. The computer deletes the text "localhost.localdomain."

19. Press **i**. The vi editor goes into insert mode. Type **netpluslab.net** and press **Esc**.

20. Type **:wq** and press **Enter**. The vi editor saves the file and then closes.

21. Type **cd /etc/mail** and press **Enter**. The computer changes your current working directory to /etc/mail.

22. Type **m4 sendmail.mc >sendmail.cf** and press **Enter**. The m4 program processes the sendmail.mc file and puts it into a form that allows the Sendmail program to use it more easily.

23. Type **cat /var/run/sendmail.pid** and press **Enter**. The computer displays the PID number of the currently running sendmail process, as well as the command line options used to start it. Record the PID below.

24. Type **kill -HUP** followed by the PID number you recorded in Step 23, and then press **Enter**. The computer restarts the sendmail daemon.

25. Now you will configure DNS so that each computer on the network knows where to send e-mail. On *SERVER1*, press **Ctrl+Alt+Del** to display the Log On to Windows dialog box. Log on as the Administrator. The Windows Server 2003 desktop appears.

26. Press **Start**, point to **Administrative Tools**, then click **DNS**. The dnsmgmt window opens.

27. In the left pane of the window, click **SERVER1**. Icons appear in the right pane.

28. Double-click the **Forward Lookup Zones** icon in the right pane of the window. A list of domains appears. Double-click the **netpluslab.net** icon in the right pane.

29. Right-click **netpluslab.net** in the left pane, and click **New Mail Exchanger (MX)**. The New Resource Record dialog box appears.

30. In the "Fully qualified domain name (FQDN) of mail server" text box, enter **linux1.netpluslab.net**. See Figure 11-6.

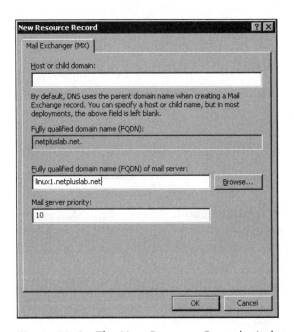

Figure 11-6 The New Resource Record window

31. Click **OK**. The New Resource Record dialog box closes. Right-click the **netpluslab.net** icon, and click **Reload**. The DNS dialog box appears, asking if you want to reload the domain.

32. Click **Yes**. The computer reloads the netpluslab.net domain.

33. On *WORKSTATION1*, press **Ctrl+Alt+Del** to display the Log On to Windows dialog box. Log on as the netplus user. The Windows XP desktop appears.

34. Click **Start**, then click **Outlook Express**. The Outlook Express window opens. If the Internet Connection Wizard does not open, click **Tools** on the menu bar, then click **Accounts**. The Internet Accounts window opens. Click **Add**, then click **Mail**.

35. In the Display name text box, enter **Net+ Lab**. Click **Next**. The next wizard window asks for an e-mail address.

36. In the E-mail address text box, enter **netplus@netpluslab.net**. Click **Next**. The next wizard window asks for information about the e-mail servers you will use.

37. In the Incoming mail (POP3, IMAP or HTTP) server text box, enter **linux1. netpluslab.net**. In the Outgoing mail (SMTP) server text box, enter **linux1. netpluslab.net**. Click **Next**. Now the wizard asks you for information about the account you will use.

38. In the Account name text box, enter **netplus**. In the Password text box, enter the password for the netplus account on *LINUX1.NETPLUSLAB.NET*. If necessary, uncheck the **Log on using Secure Password Authentication (SPA)** checkbox. Click **Next**. The next wizard window indicates that you have finished.

39. Click **Finish**. The Internet Connection Wizard closes.

40. In the Outlook Express window, click **Create Mail**. The New Message dialog box opens.

41. In the To text box, enter **netplus@netpluslab.net**. In the Subject text box, enter **Test Message**. In the bottom window, enter your name. Click **Send**. Outlook Express sends the message.

42. Click **Send/Recv**. The Outlook Express dialog box appears briefly as the program checks for e-mail.

43. In the tree in the left pane, click **Inbox**. In the top right pane, a message with the subject Test Message appears.

44. Double-click the message with the subject Test Message. The message opens in the Test Message dialog box.

45. Click **File** on the menu bar, then click **Close** to close the Test Message dialog box.

46. Click **File** on the menu bar, and then click **Exit**. Outlook Express closes.

47. Log off all three computers.

Certification Objectives

Objectives for the Network+ Exam:

➤ Identify the basic capabilities (i.e., client support, interoperability, authentication, file and print services, application support, and security) of the following server operating systems: UNIX/Linux, NetWare, Windows, Macintosh

➤ Define the purpose, function, and/or use of the following protocols within TCP/IP: IP, TCP, UDP, FTP, TFTP, SMTP, HTTP, HTTPS, POP3/IMAP4, Telnet, ICMP, Arp, NTP

Review Questions

1. Which of the following protocols is used to send e-mail?

   a. POP3

   b. SMTP

   c. IMAP

   d. SNMP

2. You are sending e-mail to your friend Bob, whose e-mail address is bob@otherdomain.com. What information does your SMTP server need in order to deliver this e-mail to Bob?

   a. It needs to look up the IP address of otherdomain.com.

   b. It needs to look up the IP address of the otherdomain.com POP3 server.

   c. It needs to use the MX record for the otherdomain.com domain to find the IP address of the appropriate IMAP server.

   d. It needs to use the MX record for the otherdomain.com domain to find the IP address of the appropriate SMTP server.

3. The DNS server on your network is not functioning properly. Which of the following is *not* a possible consequence of this?

   a. User e-mail programs inside your network are unable to find the IP address of your SMTP server.

   b. SMTP servers outside your network are unable to make TCP connections to your mail server.

   c. Your SMTP server is unable to find the IP addresses of remote mail servers.

   d. User e-mail programs inside your network are unable to find the IP address of your IMAP server.

11

4. Why is it important to secure and configure a mail server properly?

   a. A misconfigured or improperly secured mail server may not be able to deliver e-mail.

   b. A misconfigured or improperly secured mail server may be hijacked in order to send large amounts of unsolicited commercial e-mail.

   c. A misconfigured or improperly secured mail server may not be able to run SMTP.

   d. A misconfigured or improperly secured mail server may not allow clients to download their e-mail.

5. A user has been given an e-mail address of sally@otherorg.net. How is this user most likely to determine the settings she needs in order to receive e-mail?

   a. from the MX record for the otherorg.net domain

   b. by finding the IP address of the otherorg.net domain

   c. from their network administrator

   d. from other SMTP servers on the Internet

TROUBLESHOOTING NETWORK PROBLEMS

Labs included in this chapter

➤ Lab 12.1 Using the Ping Utility to Troubleshoot a TCP/IP Network

➤ Lab 12.2 Using the Traceroute utility to Troubleshoot a TCP/IP Network

➤ Lab 12.3 Troubleshooting Client Logon Problems

➤ Lab 12.4 Troubleshooting Web Client Problems

Net+ Exam Objectives	
Objective	**Lab**
Given a troubleshooting scenario, select the appropriate TCP/IP utility from among the following: Tracert, Ping, Arp, Netstat, Nbtstat, Ipconfig/Ifconfig, Winipcfg, Nslookup	12.1, 12.2, 12.3, 12.4
Given output from a diagnostic utility (e.g., Tracert, Ping, Ipconfig, etc.), identify the utility and interpret the output	12.1, 12.2, 12.3, 12.4
Given a network problem scenario, select an appropriate course of action based on a general troubleshooting strategy. This strategy includes the following steps: 1. Establish the symptoms, 2. Identify the affected area, 3. Establish what has changed, 4. Select the most probable cause, 5. Implement a solution, 6. Test the result, 7. Recognize the potential effects of the solution, 8. Document the solution	12.1, 12.2, 12.3, 12.4
Given a network troubleshooting scenario involving a wiring/infrastructure problem, identify the cause of the problem (e.g., bad media, interference, network hardware)	12.1, 12.2, 12.3, 12.4
Given a scenario, predict the impact of modifying, adding, or removing network services (e.g., DHCP, DNS, WINS, etc.) on network resources and users	12.3, 12.4
Given a network scenario, interpret visual indicators (e.g., link lights, collision lights, etc.) to determine the nature of the problem	12.3, 12.4
Given a network troubleshooting scenario involving a client connectivity problem (e.g., incorrect protocol/client software/authentication configuration, or insufficient rights/permissions), identify the cause of the problem	12.3, 12.4

LAB 12.1 USING THE PING UTILITY TO TROUBLESHOOT A TCP/IP NETWORK

Objectives

The Ping utility (also know as the `ping` command) is one of the basic tools used to check network connectivity in a TCP/IP network. Every operating system that supports TCP/IP also supports the Ping utility.

The `ping` command works by sending an ICMP message to the target asking for a reply. If the message reaches the target, it sends an ICMP reply. This indicates that you have network connectivity between the computer where you used the `ping` command and the computer you are trying to reach. Keep in mind, however, that the Ping utility does not tell you anything about network services running on the remote computer, nor does the Ping utility tell you anything about the type or number of hops that the ICMP messages took to reach a host.

When you use the `ping` command to troubleshoot a connectivity problem, you should first verify that TCP/IP is working properly by pinging the loopback address (127.0.0.1) and the computer's own IP address. Then you should ping each stop along the way to the remote host that you cannot reach to verify that you can reach each stop. For instance, if you cannot ping a router along the way to a remote host, this may indicate that the router is down and explain why you cannot reach the remote host. (Note that some routers may block ICMP packets and prevent the Ping utility from working properly.)

After completing this lab, you will be able to:

➤ Use the `ping` command to determine the source of problems in a TCP/IP network

➤ Isolate a problem by following a logical methodology

Materials Required

This lab will require the following:

➤ A computer running Windows Server 2003 Enterprise Edition named *SERVER1* with two NICs

➤ One NIC configured with an IP address of 192.168.54.1 and a subnet mask of 255.255.255.0, and the other NIC configured with an IP address of 172.16.1.1 and a subnet mask of 255.255.255.0

➤ Routing and Remote Access configured on *SERVER1* so that it acts as a router

➤ A hub named *HUB1* connected (with a straight-through CAT 5 or better UTP cable) to the NIC on *SERVER1* that was configured with an IP address of 192.168.54.1

➤ A hub named *HUB2* connected (with a straight-through CAT 5 or better UTP cable) to the NIC on SERVER1 that was configured with an IP address of 172.16.1.1

➤ A computer running Windows XP Professional named *WORKSTATION1* configured with an IP address of 192.168.54.2 and a subnet mask of 255.255.255.0, connected to *HUB1* with a straight-through CAT 5 (or better) UTP cable

➤ A computer running Windows XP Professional named *WORKSTATION2* configured with an IP address of 172.16.1.2 and a subnet mask of 255.255.255.0, connected to *HUB2* with a straight-through CAT 5 (or better) UTP cable

➤ Access to all three computers as the Administrator

Estimated completion time: **45 minutes**

ACTIVITY

1. Review the layout and IP addresses of the network in Figure 12-1.

12

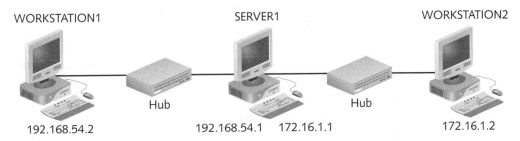

Figure 12-1 Network layout of Lab 12.1

2. Now you can determine if *WORKSTATION2* (which has an IP address of 172.16.1.2) is up and running. Review the following problem-isolation methodology. (Do not perform the steps yet; simply review them so that you have an overall view of how you will go about troubleshooting the network.)

- Log on to the *WORKSTATION1* computer. Ping the local computer's local loopback address, 127.0.0.1, to ensure that TCP/IP is installed.

- Ping the local computer's IP address to ensure that the local computer's NIC is addressed and functioning properly.

- Ping the near side of the router to ensure that the connection between 192.168.54.2 and 192.168.54.1 is operating properly. The term "near side" refers to the router's NIC with an IP address on the same network as the local computer.

- Ping the far side of the router to ensure that the connection through the router is operating properly; specifically, this test ensures that the connection between 192.168.54.2 and 172.16.1.1 is functional. The term "far side" refers to the router's NIC that is on the path to a destination host with an IP address on a different network than the local computer.

- Ping a computer on the network segment on the far side of the router; in this situation, the computer on the far side of the router is the *WORKSTATION2* computer. This ensures connectivity all the way from *WORKSTATION1* at 192.168.54.2 to *WORKSTATION2* at 172.16.1.2.

The following steps walk you through the procedure outlined in Step 2. For each ping test, the `ping` command will issue a message indicating either success or failure. If the `ping` command returns an error at any step, you can assume that the problem lies with the connection at the particular step that produced the error.

3. On *WORKSTATION1*, press **Ctrl+Alt+Del** to display the Log On to Windows dialog box. Log on as the Administrator. The Windows XP desktop appears.

4. Click **Start**, point to **All Programs**, point to **Accessories**, and then click **Command Prompt**. A command prompt window appears.

5. To determine if the local computer's NIC is operating correctly, type **ping 127.0.0.1**, and then press **Enter**. Was the `ping` command successful?

6. To determine if TCP/IP is operating properly, type **ping 192.168.54.2**, and then press **Enter**. Was the `ping` command successful?

7. To determine if the connection to the near side of the router is operating properly, type **ping 192.168.54.1**, and then press **Enter**. Was the `ping` command successful?

8. To determine if the router is operating properly, type **ping 172.16.1.1**, and then press **Enter**. Was the `ping` command successful?

9. To determine if a computer on the network segment on the far side of the router is operating properly, type **ping 172.16.1.2**, and then press **Enter**. Was the `ping` command successful?

10. Cover the link lights on each hub with a piece of paper or another obstruction. If the link lights on each computer's NICs are visible, place a box or another obstruction in front of each NIC.

11. Have your instructor or lab partner unplug one of the cables from one of the NICs in the back of the router. This should be done so that you cannot identify which cable has been removed.

12. Without looking at the link lights on the NICs or the hubs, repeat Steps 7 through 9. Record the step that failed, and record the cable you think failed.

13. Remove the obstructions added in Step 10 and examine the link lights on the hubs and on the NICs. Which cable was unplugged?

14. Plug in the cable that was unplugged in Step 11.

15. If you have a lab partner, repeat Steps 10 through 14 with your lab partner.

16. Log off *WORKSTATION1*.

Certification Objectives

Objectives for the Network+ Exam:

➤ Given a troubleshooting scenario, select the appropriate TCP/IP utility from among the following: Tracert, Ping, Arp, Netstat, Nbtstat, Ipconfig/Ifconfig, Winipcfg, Nslookup

➤ Given output from a diagnostic utility (e.g., Tracert, Ping, Ipconfig, etc.), identify the utility and interpret the output

➤ Given a network problem scenario, select an appropriate course of action based on a general troubleshooting strategy. This strategy includes the following steps: 1. Establish the symptoms, 2. Identify the affected area, 3. Establish what has changed, 4. Select the most probable cause, 5. Implement a solution, 6. Test the result, 7. Recognize the potential effects of the solution, 8. Document the solution

➤ Given a network troubleshooting scenario involving a wiring/infrastructure problem, identify the cause of the problem (e.g., bad media, interference, network hardware)

12

Review Questions

1. What would you ping to determine whether TCP/IP on your computer was functioning properly?

   a. the gateway address

   b. the near side of the router

   c. the loopback address

   d. the far side of the router

2. Which of the following responses to a `ping` command issued on a Windows-based computer indicates that the ping test was successful?

   a. Packets: Sent = 4, Received = 4, Loss = 0 (0%)

   b. Packets: Sent = 0, Received = 0, Loss = 0 (0%)

   c. Packets: Sent = 0, Received = 0, Loss = 4 (100%)

   d. Packets: Sent = 4, Received = 4, Loss = 4 (100%)

3. When you issue a `ping` command, what Application layer protocol sends a message to the destination host?

   a. Arp

   b. RARP

   c. SNMP

   d. ICMP

4. Suppose you were troubleshooting a network connectivity problem between a workstation on a private LAN and a server on the Internet. As part of a logical troubleshooting methodology, what address would you ping after determining that the TCP/IP stack on the workstation was functioning properly?

   a. the workstation's loopback address

   b. the workstation's default gateway

   c. the private LAN's Internet nameserver

   d. the Internet server you're trying to reach

5. In the scenario described in Question 4, as part of a logical troubleshooting methodology, what address would you ping second?

   a. the workstation's loopback address

   b. the workstation's default gateway

   c. the private LAN's Internet nameserver

   d. the Internet server

6. Which of the following is the loopback address in IP version 4 addressing?

   a. 127.0.0.1

   b. 1.1.1.1

   c. 127.0.0.0

   d. 10.0.0.0

7. What type of message would you receive if you were trying to ping *www.comptia.org* from a Windows XP computer and misspelled the host's name as *wwv.comptia.org* in the `ping` command syntax?

   a. Host wwv.comptia.org not responding

   b. Ping request could not find host wwv.comptia.org. Please check the name and try again.

   c. Reply from wwv.comptia.org: bytes= 0

   d. unknown host wwv.comptia.org

LAB 12.2 USING THE TRACEROUTE UTILITY TO TROUBLESHOOT A TCP/IP NETWORK

Objectives

Another useful troubleshooting command in a TCP/IP network is the `traceroute` command. The `traceroute` command traces the path that a packet travels as it goes over the network from a source to a destination node. This is particularly useful on large networks (including the Internet), as it can indicate at which hop along the route between two computers a problem exists. In smaller networks where you already know the network path, you can use the `ping` command instead. Note that on the Internet, firewalls and packet filtering can restrict the usefulness of the `traceroute` and `tracert` commands (as well as the `ping` command).

On Windows machines, the `traceroute` command is known as `tracert`. Both the `traceroute` command and the `tracert` command begin by sending a packet to the destination host with a TTL (Time to Live) value of one. When the packet reaches the first router along the way, the TTL expires and the router sends an ICMP message back to the computer running the command. The command uses this ICMP message to identify the first router along the path. The computer increases the TTL value by one and sends another packet to the destination host. When the packet reaches the next router, the TTL expires and the next router sends an ICMP message. The command continues to increase the value of the TTL value until it either reaches the destination, or until a maximum number of routers have been tested (usually 30 by default). While each program uses the same basic technique, the implementation varies slightly. The Unix `traceroute` command sends UDP packets as their test packets, while the Windows `tracert` command sends ICMP packets.

After completing this lab, you will be able to:

➤ Use the `traceroute` and `tracert` commands to trace the path to a destination

➤ Interpret both successful and unsuccessful `traceroute` responses

Materials Required

This lab will require the following:

➤ The lab setup built for Lab 12.1

➤ A computer running Red Hat Enterprise Linux ES 3.x named *LINUX1.NETPLUSLAB.NET*, configured with an IP address of 192.168.54.5 and a subnet mask of 255.255.255.0, connected to *HUB1* with a straight-through CAT 5 (or better) UTP cable

➤ Access to *LINUX1.NETPLUSLAB.NET* as the netplus user

➤ A computer running Windows XP Professional or Windows Server 2003 that is connected to the Internet

12

Estimated completion time: **35 minutes**

LAB ACTIVITY

ACTIVITY

1. On *WORKSTATION1*, press **Ctrl+Alt+Del** to display the Log On to Windows dialog box. Log on as the Administrator. The Windows XP desktop appears.

2. Click **Start**, point to **All Programs**, point to **Accessories**, and then click **Command Prompt**. A command prompt window appears.

3. At the command prompt, type **tracert 172.16.1.2**, and press **Enter**. The tracert command traces the path from *WORKSTATION1* to *WORKSTATION2*, showing the number of each hop, three round-trip response times, and the name or IP address for each hop. (Note that you can also use a domain name, such as microsoft.com.) Figure 12-2 shows an example of the output of the tracert command.

```
Command Prompt                                                    _ □ ×
Microsoft Windows XP [Version 5.1.2600]
(C) Copyright 1985-2001 Microsoft Corp.

C:\Documents and Settings\Administrator>tracert 172.16.1.2

Tracing route to 172.16.1.2 over a maximum of 30 hops

  1    <1 ms    <1 ms    <1 ms  server1.netpluslab.net [192.168.54.1]
  2    <1 ms    <1 ms    <1 ms  172.16.1.2

Trace complete.

C:\Documents and Settings\Administrator>
```

Figure 12-2   Output of the tracert command

4. Remove the cable from the NIC attached to *WORKSTATION2*.

5. Type **tracert 172.16.1.2**, and press **Enter**. Instead of recording two hops and stopping, the tracert command continues. However, after the first hop, the response times are replaced by asterisks and the IP address is replaced by "Request timed out". This indicates that the tracert command could not determine the path to the destination address after the first hop.

6. Replace the cable you removed from *WORKSTATION2* in Step 4.

7. Remove the cable from the NIC on *SERVER1* attached to *HUB1*.

8. Repeat Step 3. This time the tracert command exits with the message "Destination host unreachable."

9. Replace the cable you removed in Step 7.

10. On *LINUX1.NETPLUSLAB.NET* at the Welcome to linux1.netpluslab.net screen, type **netplus** in the Username text box and press **Enter**. The Password text box appears.

11. Enter the password for the netplus account in the Password text box and press **Enter**. The Red Hat desktop appears.

12. Right-click a blank spot on the desktop and click **New Terminal** in the pop-up menu that opens. A terminal window opens.

13. Type **traceroute 172.16.1.2** and press **Enter**. The traceroute command traces the path to *WORKSTATION2,* showing the number of each hop, three response times, and the name or IP address for each hop.

14. Remove the cable from the NIC attached to *WORKSTATION2*.

15. Repeat Step 13. How do the results differ from those in Step 13?

16. Replace the cable you removed in Step 14, and log off both computers.

17. On the Windows XP Professional or Windows Server 2003 computer connected to the Internet, repeat Steps 1 through 3. However, substitute the name of a Web site such as *www.cisco.com* or *www.yahoo.com* for the IP address in Step 3. Note that firewalls and other security measures between this computer and the Web site, as well as the security configuration of the Web site itself, may prevent the tracert command from working as expected. Repeat with several different Web sites.

Certification Objectives

Objectives for the Network+ Exam:

➤ Given a troubleshooting scenario, select the appropriate TCP/IP utility from among the following: Tracert, Ping, Arp, Netstat, Nbtstat, Ipconfig/Ifconfig, Winipcfg, Nslookup

➤ Given output from a diagnostic utility (e.g., Tracert, Ping, Ipconfig, etc.), identify the utility and interpret the output

➤ Given a network problem scenario, select an appropriate course of action based on a general troubleshooting strategy. This strategy includes the following steps: 1. Establish the symptoms, 2. Identify the affected area, 3. Establish what has changed, 4. Select the most probable cause, 5. Implement a solution, 6. Test the result, 7. Recognize the potential effects of the solution, 8. Document the solution

➤ Given a network troubleshooting scenario involving a wiring/infrastructure problem, identify the cause of the problem (e.g., bad media, interference, network hardware)

Review Questions

1. Which of the following commands can reveal the number of hops a packet takes between a source and target node?

   a. `ipconfig`

   b. `ping`

   c. `tracert`

   d. `ifconfig`

2. Which of the following commands can indicate whether a host is unreachable? (Choose all that apply.)

   a. `ping`

   b. `ipconfig`

   c. `ifconfig`

   d. `winipcfg`

3. Which of the following commands would you use to determine the relative location of network congestion between your Windows XP Professional workstation and an Internet host?

   a. `netstat`

   b. `nbtstat`

   c. `tracert`

   d. `ipconfig`

4. If you attempted the `tracert` command on an Internet host, and that host was not connected to the network, which of the following would the `tracert` command's response contain?

   a. Destination host unreachable.

   b. Unknown host.

   c. Host not responding.

   d. Request timed out.

5. What does a hop represent in the context of a `traceroute` command?

   a. an Internet client

   b. a modem, hub, switch, or router

   c. a router

   d. a carrier's POP

LAB **12.3** TROUBLESHOOTING CLIENT LOGON PROBLEMS

Objectives

In this lab, you will troubleshoot a scenario in which a user cannot log on to the server. From a user's perspective, when he cannot log on to the server, the network is unavailable, no matter what the reason. However, the ultimate cause of the problem may be anything from a hardware failure on the server to an expired password.

When troubleshooting problems, you should attempt to be as methodical as possible. You can start by determining the scope of the problem. Is only one user affected, or are all users affected? Then determine if the user's computer (or the users' computers, if multiple users are affected) and the server have physical connectivity. Do all the NICs seem to be working properly? Is the hub functioning and is the network cabled properly? After establishing that physical connectivity is not the problem, determine if the user's computer has network connectivity. Can you ping the server from the user's computer? After you have determined that network connectivity is not the problem, try to determine if the application is functioning properly.

Keep in mind that being able to log onto a computer does not necessarily indicate that the network is functioning properly. Windows computers cache passwords for user names, so that a user can still log onto a computer during a network outage.

In this lab, you will first verify that the network, the client computers, and the server are all functioning properly by logging on to two client computers. Then your instructor or another set of lab partners will do something to prevent at least one of the computers from logging on to the server. Your mission will be to identify and solve the problem.

After completing this lab, you will be able to:

➤ Follow a logical troubleshooting methodology to determine the nature of client connectivity problems

➤ Identify a network problem by interpreting the results of diagnostic utilities such as Ping and Ipconfig

Materials Required

This lab will require the following:

➤ A computer named *SERVER1* running Windows Server 2003 Enterprise Edition, configured as a domain controller for the netpluslab.net domain with an IP address of 192.168.54.1 and a subnet mask of 255.255.255.0

➤ The DHCP server running on *SERVER1* and configured to assign DHCP addresses in the range from 192.168.54.50 to 192.168.54.100, with subnet masks of 255.255.255.0

12

➤ A shared folder named NETPLUS on *SERVER1*

➤ Access as the Administrator to the netpluslab.net domain, and user accounts named client1 and client2 in the Domain Users group

➤ Two computers running Windows XP Professional named *WORKSTATION1* and *WORKSTATION2*, each configured to receive DHCP addresses

➤ Both *WORKSTATION1* and *WORKSTATION2* configured as members of the netpluslab.net domain

➤ All three computers configured to use *SERVER1* as their DNS server

➤ No network protocols besides TCP/IP configured on any of the computers

➤ Each computer connected to a hub with straight-through CAT 5 (or better) UTP cables, as shown in Figure 12-3

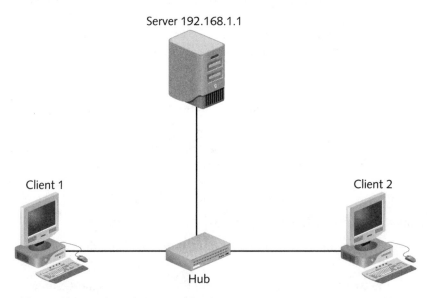

Figure 12-3   Network layout of Lab 12.3

➤ A faulty straight-through cable that is the same color of at least one of the working CAT 5 cables; a crossover cable may be substituted

➤ An instructor or classmate assigned to cause a problem in the network

Estimated completion time: **60–90 minutes**

LAB ACTIVITY

ACTIVITY

1. On *WORKSTATION1*, press **Ctrl+Alt+Del** to display the Log On to Windows dialog box. Log on as client1. The Windows XP desktop appears.

2. Click **Start**, then click **My Computer**. The My Computer window opens.

3. Click **Tools** on the menu bar, then click **Map Network Drive**. The Map Network Drive dialog box appears.

4. Accept the default setting for the Drive drop-down menu, Z:. In the Folder text box, type **\\192.168.54.1\netplus** and click **Finish**. The computer maps the NETPLUS shared folder.

5. Click the **up arrow** below the menu bar to return to My Computer. The netplus on '192.168.54.1' (Z:) icon now appears below the heading "Network Drives".

6. Repeat Steps 1 through 5 on *WORKSTATION2*, logging on as the client2 user. You have now verified that you can log on to *SERVER1* with both client computers.

7. Leave the room while your instructor or classmate causes a network problem by performing one of the actions listed in Table 12-1. After performing one of the actions, your instructor or classmate should log off all three computers.

Table 12-1 Possible actions to be performed by classmate or instructor

Action	Instruction
Install faulty cable on WORKSTATION1	Replace the network cable connecting *WORKSTATION1* to the hub with the faulty network cable.
Install faulty cable on server	Replace the network cable connecting the Windows Server 2003 computer to the hub with the faulty network cable.
Disrupt cable connection	Pull the cable far enough out of *WORKSTATION1*'s NIC so that the link light turns off but not so far that it falls completely out of the NIC.

12

Table 12-1 Possible actions to be performed by classmate or instructor (continued)

Action	Instruction
Reconfigure the IP address on *WORKSTATION1*	a Log off *WORKSTATION1*, then press **Ctrl+Alt+Del** to display the Log On to Windows screen. Log on as the Administrator. The Windows XP desktop appears. b Click **Start**, point to **All Programs**, point to **Accessories**, point to **Communications**, and then click **Network Connections**. The Network Connections dialog box appears. c Right-click **Local Area Connection** and click **Properties**. The Local Area Connection Properties window opens. d Double-click **Internet Protocol (TCP/IP)**. The Internet Protocol (TCP/IP) Properties window opens. e Click the **Use the following IP address** option button. In the IP address text box, type **192.168.154.50**. In the Subnet mask text box, type **255.255.255.0**. f Click **OK** twice, then close all open dialog boxes.
Reconfigure the IP address on *SERVER1*	a Log off *SERVER1*. Then press **Ctrl+Alt+Del** to display the Log On to Windows screen. Log on as the Administrator. The Windows Server 2003 desktop appears. b Click **Start**, point to **Control Panel**, point to **Network Connections**, and then click **Local Area Connection**. The Local Area Connection Status window appears. c Click **Properties**. The Local Area Connection Properties window opens. d Double-click **Internet Protocol (TCP/IP)**. The Internet Protocol (TCP/IP) Properties window opens. e Click the **Use the following IP address** option button. In the IP address text box, type **192.168.54.11**. In the Subnet mask text box, type **255.255.255.0**. f Click **OK** twice, then close all open dialog boxes or windows.

Table 12-1   Possible actions to be performed by classmate or instructor (continued)

Action	Instruction
Reconfigure the IP address and subnet mask on *WORKSTATION2*	a Log off *WORKSTATION2*. Then press **Ctrl+Alt+Del** to display the Log On to Windows screen. Log on as the Administrator. The Windows XP desktop appears. b Click **Start**, point to **All Programs**, point to **Accessories**, point to **Communications**, and then click **Network Connections**. The Network Connections dialog box appears. c Right-click **Local Area Connection** and click **Properties**. The Local Area Connection Properties window opens. d Double-click **Internet Protocol (TCP/IP)**. The Internet Protocol (TCP/IP) Properties window opens. e Click the **Use the following IP address** option button. In the IP address text box, type **192.168.154.50**. In the Subnet mask text box, type **255.255.255.248**. f Click **OK** twice, then close all open dialog boxes.

7. When you return to the room, reboot both client computers.

8. Attempt to repeat Steps 1 through 5 on *WORKSTATION1*. You should be unable to browse to the NETPLUS folder. You will now attempt to solve the problem using the following steps. If you identify the problem before completing all the steps, proceed to Step 16.

9. Begin to determine the scope of the problem by attempting to log on to *WORKSTATION2*. Repeat Steps 1 through 5. If you are able to log on and browse the NETPLUS folder, the problem is local to the *WORKSTATION1* computer and you may concentrate on potential problems that affect only *WORKSTATION1*. Otherwise, the problem is common to all clients and you should concentrate on potential problems that affect all clients.

10. To determine the state of physical connectivity in the network, check the status of the link lights on the hub and in the NICs for each computer.

11. To determine the state of network connectivity in the network, on *WORKSTATION1*, click **Start**, point to **All Programs**, point to **Accessories**, and click **Command Prompt**. A command prompt window appears. Type **ping 127.0.0.1** and then press **Enter**. Success indicates that the TCP/IP stack on *WORKSTATION1* is working. Depending on the scope of the problem, repeat this step for *WORKSTATION2*.

12. At the command prompt on *WORKSTATION1*, type **ping 192.168.54.1** and then press **Enter**. If the output indicates success, then network connectivity exists between *WORKSTATION1* and the server. Depending on the scope of the problem, repeat this step for *WORKSTATION2*.

13. If there is no network connectivity, at the command prompt on *WORKSTATION1*, type **ipconfig** and then press **Enter**. IP addressing information displays on the computer. If this is correct, then there may be a problem with the network configuration on the server. Depending on the scope of the problem, repeat for *WORKSTATION2*.

14. On *SERVER1*, repeat Steps 12 through 14. However, in Step 13 ping the IP addresses of the client computers.

15. By this time, you should have identified the problem. Fix it, and repeat Steps 7 through 15, asking your instructor or classmate to perform another action listed in Table 12-1.

Certification Objectives

Objectives for the Network+ Exam:

➤ Given a troubleshooting scenario, select the appropriate TCP/IP utility from among the following: Tracert, Ping, Arp, Netstat, Nbtstat, Ipconfig/Ifconfig, Winipcfg, Nslookup

➤ Given output from a diagnostic utility (e.g., Tracert, Ping, Ipconfig, etc.), identify the utility and interpret the output

➤ Given a network problem scenario, select an appropriate course of action based on a general troubleshooting strategy. This strategy includes the following steps: 1. Establish the symptoms, 2. Identify the affected area, 3. Establish what has changed, 4. Select the most probable cause, 5. Implement a solution, 6. Test the result, 7. Recognize the potential effects of the solution, 8. Document the solution

➤ Given a network troubleshooting scenario involving a wiring/infrastructure problem, identify the cause of the problem (e.g., bad media, interference, network hardware)

➤ Given a scenario, predict the impact of modifying, adding, or removing network services (e.g., DHCP, DNS, WINS, etc.) on network resources and users

➤ Given a network scenario, interpret visual indicators (e.g., link lights, collision lights, etc.) to determine the nature of the problem

➤ Given a network troubleshooting scenario involving a client connectivity problem (e.g., incorrect protocol/client software/authentication configuration, or insufficient rights/permissions), identify the cause of the problem

Review Questions

1. Which of the following comes first in the series of steps recommended for a logical approach to network troubleshooting?

   a. Establish what has changed on the network.

   b. Implement a solution.

   c. Establish the symptoms.

   d. Identify the affected area.

2. If a client workstation has been assigned the wrong IP address, which of the following will be true?

   a. The client will be able to connect to other nodes on the LAN, but will not be able to connect through its default gateway to the Internet.

   b. The client will be able to ping the loopback address successfully, but will not be able to connect to other nodes on the LAN.

   c. The client will not be able to ping the loopback address successfully, nor will it be able to connect to other nodes on the LAN.

   d. The client will be able to connect to other nodes on its LAN segment, but will not be able to connect to nodes on other segments.

3. Which of the following commands will reveal TCP/IP addressing information on a Windows Server 2003 computer?

   a. `ipconfig`

   b. `winipcfg`

   c. `ifconfig`

   d. `netipcfg`

4. If the LED on a workstation's NIC is blinking green, which of the following is true?

   a. The workstation is connected to the network and successfully exchanging data over its connection.

   b. The workstation is connected to the network, but is not currently exchanging data over its connection.

   c. The workstation is connected to the network, but is experiencing errors when attempting to exchange data over the network.

   d. The workstation is not successfully connected to the network.

12

5. Of the troubleshooting actions listed below, which one would come first in a logical troubleshooting methodology?

    a. Replace a faulty memory chip on a server.

    b. Determine whether a problem is limited to a segment or the whole network.

    c. Summarize your solution in a troubleshooting database.

    d. Determine whether your solution will result in any other problems.

LAB 12.4 TROUBLESHOOTING WEB CLIENT PROBLEMS

Objectives

In this lab, you will troubleshoot a problem with a Web client. Because the connection between a client and a host on the Internet usually relies on a great number and type of connections, problems are common. They may also be difficult to identify and fix. Even if the nature of the problem is clear, you may not have any control over the network resources that are causing the problem. Coordination with other network administrators and other organizations is often essential to solving problems on the Internet.

In addition to basic physical and logical network connectivity, you must also make sure that DNS is working properly. Issues involving DNS are a common source of problems with Web servers and Web browsers. If the Web server is operating correctly but the client is unable to use DNS to find its address, the client will be unable to reach the Web server. The effect is the same as if the Web server were not functioning properly. However, the Web server will typically be reachable through its IP address (if its IP address is known at all). DNS problems can occur for a variety of reasons, including incorrect DNS entries, misconfigured DNS servers, or even failure to pay domain name registration fees.

After completing this lab, you will be able to:

➤ Use a methodical troubleshooting approach to identify and solve a problem involving a Web client

➤ Investigate potential problems caused by DNS errors

Materials Required

This lab will require the following:

➤ A computer running Windows Server 2003 named *SERVER1* with two NICs

➤ One NIC configured with an IP address of 192.168.54.1 and a subnet mask of 255.255.255.0, and the other NIC configured with an IP address of 172.16.1.1 and a subnet mask of 255.255.255.0

➤ Routing and Remote Access configured on *SERVER1* so that it acts as a router

➤ A hub named *HUB1* connected to the NIC on *SERVER1* that was configured with an IP address of 192.168.54.1 with a straight-through CAT 5 (or better) UTP cable

➤ A hub named *HUB2* connected to the NIC on *SERVER1* that was configured with an IP address of 172.16.1.1 with a straight-through CAT 5 (or better) UTP cable as shown in Figure 12-4

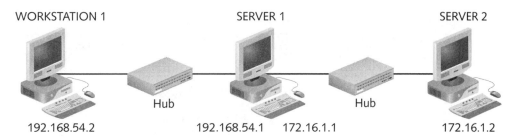

WORKSTATION 1   SERVER 1   SERVER 2

Hub   Hub

192.168.54.2   192.168.54.1   172.16.1.1   172.16.1.2

Figure 12-4   Network layout of Lab 12.4

➤ A computer running Windows XP Professional named *WORKSTATION1* configured with an IP address of 192.168.54.2 and a subnet mask of 255.255.255.0, connected to *HUB1* with a straight-through CAT 5 (or better) UTP cable

➤ A computer running Windows Server 2003 Enterprise Edition named *SERVER2* configured with an IP address of 172.16.1.2 and a subnet mask of 255.255.255.0, connected to *HUB2* with a straight-through CAT 5 (or better) UTP cable

➤ IIS installed and running on *SERVER2*, with a file named default.htm containing the text "This is a test page" in C:\inetpub\wwwroot

➤ The DNS server running on *SERVER1*, with an entry for *www.netpluslab.net* pointing to 172.16.1.2

➤ *WORKSTATION1* configured to use *SERVER1* as its DNS server

➤ Access to all three computers as the Administrator

➤ A faulty network cable that is the same color as the network cables used elsewhere

➤ An instructor or classmate assigned to cause a problem in the network

Estimated completion time: **60–90 minutes**

ACTIVITY

1. On **WORKSTATION1**, press **Ctrl+Alt+Del** to display the Log On to Windows screen. Log on as the Administrator. The Windows XP desktop appears.

2. Click **Start**, then click **Internet Explorer**. Internet Explorer opens.

3. In the Address bar, type **www.netpluslab.net**, and then press **Enter**. A Web page opens with the text "This is a test page."

4. Close Internet Explorer.

5. Leave the room and ask your instructor or classmate to cause a network problem by performing one of the actions listed in Table 12-2.

Table 12-2 Possible actions to be performed by instructor or classmate

Action	Instruction
Install faulty cable on server	Replace the network cable connecting the Web server to the hub with the faulty network cable.
Reconfigure the IP address on the Web server	a On *SERVER2*, press **Ctrl+Alt+Del** to display the Log On to Windows screen. Log on as the Administrator. The Windows Server 2003 desktop appears.
	b Click **Start**, point to **Control Panel**, point to **Network Connections**, and then click **Local Area Connection**. The Local Area Connection Status window appears.
	c Click **Properties**. The Local Area Connection Properties window opens.
	d Double-click **Internet Protocol (TCP/IP)**. The Internet Protocol (TCP/IP) Properties window opens.
	e Click the **Use the following IP address** option button. In the IP address text box, type **172.16.1.5**. In the Subnet mask text box, type **255.255.255.0**.
	f Click **OK** twice, then close any open dialog boxes or windows.

Table 12-2   Possible actions to be performed by instructor or classmate (continued)

Action	Instruction
Change the DNS server on *WORKSTATION1*	a On *WORKSTATION1*, click **Start**, point to **All Programs**, point to **Accessories**, point to **Communications**, and then click **Network Connections.** The Network Connections dialog box appears. b Right-click **Local Area Connection** and click **Properties**. The Local Area Connection Properties window opens. c Double-click **Internet Protocol (TCP/IP).** The Internet Protocol (TCP/IP) Properties window opens. d Click the **Use the following DNS server addresses** option button. In the Preferred DNS server text box, type **192.168.154.1**. e Click **OK** twice, then close all open dialog boxes.
Change the DNS entry for *www.netpluslab.net*	a On *SERVER1*, press **Ctrl+Alt+Del** to display the Log On to Windows screen. Log on as the Administrator. The Windows Server 2003 desktop appears. b Click **Start**, point to **Administrative Tools**, and then click **DNS**. The dnsmgmt window appears. c In the tree in the left pane of the window, click the **plus sign (+)** next to *SERVER1* to expand the tree underneath it. Click **Forward Lookup Zones** in the tree in the left pane. Icons for the forward lookup zones appear in the right pane. d In the right pane, double-click **netpluslab.net**. More icons appear, including an icon for www. e Right-click the **www** icon, and then click **Properties**. The www Properties window opens. f Type **172.16.1.200** in the IP address text box, and then click **OK**. g Close the DNS window.

12

6. After you return to the room, attempt to repeat Steps 1 through 3 on *WORKSTATION1*. You are unable to open the Web page. Attempt to solve the problem using the following steps. If you solve the problem before completing all the steps, proceed to Step 17.

7. Attempt to determine the state of physical connectivity in the network. Check the status of the link lights on both hubs and the NICs in *WORKSTATION1*, the router, and the Web server.

8. Attempt to determine the state of network connectivity. On *WORKSTATION1*, click **Start**, point to **All Programs**, point to **Accessories**, and then click **Command Prompt**. A command prompt window opens. Type **ping 127.0.0.1** and then press **Enter**. Success indicates that the TCP/IP stack on *WORKSTATION1* is working.

9. At the command prompt on *WORKSTATION1*, type **ping 192.168.54.1**, and then press **Enter**. Success indicates that you can connect to the near NIC on the router.

10. Type **ping 172.16.1.1** and then press **Enter**. Success indicates that you can connect to the far NIC on the router.

11. Type **ping 172.16.1.2** and then press **Enter**. Success indicates that you can connect to the Web server.

12. If there is no network connectivity, at the command prompt on *WORKSTATION1*, type **ipconfig**, and then press **Enter**. IP addressing information displays. Verify that the IP address is correct.

13. If you cannot find a problem with the IP addressing information on *WORKSTATION1*, repeat the previous step on *SERVER1* and *SERVER2*.

14. If you have verified network connectivity between *WORKSTATION1* and the Web server, on *WORKSTATION1* type **http://172.16.1.2** in the Address bar in Internet Explorer, and then press **Enter**. If you can open the Web page, this indicates that there is a problem with DNS.

15. At the command prompt on *WORKSTATION1*, type **ipconfig /all**, and then press **Enter**. Look through the IP addressing information to verify that *WORKSTATION1* is configured to use *SERVER1* (at 192.168.54.1) as its DNS server.

16. If *WORKSTATION1* is using the correct DNS server, type **nslookup www.netpluslab.net**, and then press **Enter**. The IP address for www.netpluslab.net displays. Check to see if this matches the IP address of the Web server (172.16.1.2).

17. By this time, you should have been able to identify the problem. Fix it, and repeat Steps 5 through 16, asking your instructor or classmate to perform a different action listed in Table 12-2.

Certification Objectives

Objectives for the Network+ Exam:

➤ Given a troubleshooting scenario, select the appropriate TCP/IP utility from among the following: Tracert, Ping, Arp, Netstat, Nbtstat, Ipconfig/Ifconfig, Winipcfg, Nslookup

➤ Given output from a diagnostic utility (e.g., Tracert, Ping, Ipconfig, etc.), identify the utility and interpret the output

➤ Given a network problem scenario, select an appropriate course of action based on a general troubleshooting strategy. This strategy includes the following steps: 1. Establish the symptoms, 2. Identify the affected area, 3. Establish what has changed, 4. Select the most probable cause, 5. Implement a solution, 6. Test the result, 7. Recognize the potential effects of the solution, 8. Document the solution

➤ Given a network troubleshooting scenario involving a wiring/infrastructure problem, identify the cause of the problem (e.g., bad media, interference, network hardware)

➤ Given a scenario, predict the impact of modifying, adding, or removing network services (e.g., DHCP, DNS, WINS, etc.) on network resources and users

➤ Given a network scenario, interpret visual indicators (e.g., link lights, collision lights, etc.) to determine the nature of the problem

➤ Given a network troubleshooting scenario involving a client connectivity problem (e.g., incorrect protocol/client software/authentication configuration, or insufficient rights/permissions), identify the cause of the problem

12

Review Questions

1. What does the `nslookup` command reveal?

   a. a client's current connections

   b. a client's routing table entries

   c. the IP address of a given host name or vice versa

   d. the NetBIOS name based on a computer's IP address

2. If the link light on a hub port is not lit, what can you assume about the client connected to that hub's port?

   a. There are no connectivity problems with the client.

   b. The client cannot exchange data with the network.

   c. The client can exchange data only with other nodes on its segment.

   d. The client can exchange Network layer, but not Transport layer data.

3. If a client does not have the correct DNS server address specified in its TCP/IP properties, which of the following will occur?

    a. The client cannot log on to or exchange data with the network.

    b. The client can exchange data with nodes on its local network, but not with nodes on other networks.

    c. The client can exchange data with nodes on local and external networks, but not by name.

    d. The client can exchange data with most, but not all, nodes on both its local and external networks by name.

4. What would happen if you assigned your Web server a new IP address that didn't match its DNS entry?

    a. It would be unavailable to clients.

    b. It would be available only to local clients, but not to clients accessing it over the Internet.

    c. It would be available to clients accessing it over the Internet, but not to local clients.

    d. It would still be available to all clients.

5. Which of the following tools will issue a simple pass/fail indication for a CAT 5 UTP cable?

    a. cable checker

    b. time domain reflectometer

    c. multimeter

    d. tone generator

6. True or False? Suppose you ping the IP address of a known Web server, and the response to your command indicates that the Web server is responding. It then follows that the Web server would successfully respond to HTTP requests from clients.

ENSURING INTEGRITY AND AVAILABILITY

Labs included in this chapter

➤ Lab 13.1 Viruses

➤ Lab 13.2 Uninterruptible Power Supplies (UPSs)

➤ Lab 13.3 Configuring RAID

➤ Lab 13.4 Backing up a Windows Server 2003 Computer

➤ Lab 13.5 Backing up a Linux Computer

Net+ Exam Objectives	
Objective	**Lab**
Identify the purpose and characteristics of fault tolerance	13.2, 13.3, 13.4, 13.5
Identify the basic capabilities (i.e., client support, interoperability, authentication, file and print services, application support, and security) of the following server operating systems: UNIX/Linux, NetWare, Windows, Macintosh	13.1, 13.3, 13.4, 13.5
Identify the purpose and characteristics of disaster recovery	13.4

Lab 13.1 Viruses

Objectives

Viruses can infect computers from a variety of sources. For instance, you can infect a client (or a server) with a virus by running an infected executable file, by previewing e-mail with an e-mail client that has not been upgraded with the latest patches, by browsing the Web with a Web browser that has not been upgraded with the latest patches, or even by running certain services on the Internet. Keeping a file server free of viruses can be even more challenging, as your users may try to store infected files on its shared drives. Sometimes users will save infected files to a shared drive, have their computers cleared of viruses, and then re-infect their computers from the files on the shared drive.

Virus scanners will not be helpful if you do not keep them up to date. Many virus scanners require that you periodically update the virus definition files they use to search for viruses. If you do not, the virus scanner will be unable to find newer viruses.

After completing this lab, you will be able to:Describe different types of virusesUse virus scanning software

Materials Required

This lab will require the following:

➤ A computer running Windows XP Professional named *WORKSTATION1* with an Internet connection

➤ Norton AntiVirus 2004 (full or evaluation version)

Estimated completion time: **30 minutes**

Activity

1. On *WORKSTATION1*, press **Ctrl+Alt+Del** to display the Log On to Windows dialog box. Log on as the Administrator. The Windows XP desktop appears. Connect to the Internet.

2. Click **Start**, point to **All Programs**, point to **Norton AntiVirus**, and then click **LiveUpdate – Norton AntiVirus**. The LiveUpdate dialog box opens.

3. Click **Next**. LiveUpdate checks for updates, and displays any updates found. Figure 13-1 shows LiveUpdate after it has found updates. If no updates are found, proceed to Step 5.

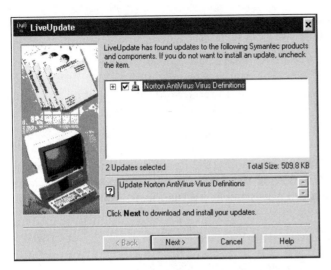

Figure 13-1 LiveUpdate after finding an update

4. Click **Next**. LiveUpdate downloads and installs the updates.

5. Click **Finish**. LiveUpdate closes.

6. Click **Start**, point to **All Programs**, point to **Norton AntiVirus**, and then click **Norton AntiVirus 2004**. If you are using the trial version, a dialog box asking you whether or not you would like to purchase the product opens. Click the Try the product for 15 more day(s) option button and click Next. Norton AntiVirus opens.

7. Click the **Scan Now** button. The Norton AntiVirus dialog box opens, showing the progress of the virus scan. Do not click any buttons or press any keys until the scan is finished, which may take several minutes. The amount of time required for the scan depends on the power of the computer's CPU and the number of files on the computer. After the scan is finished, the computer shows a summary of the scan, including the number of files scanned, the number of viruses found, and the number of files repaired, quarantined, deleted, or excluded.

8. Click **Finished**. The Norton AntiVirus summary dialog box closes.

9. Close Norton AntiVirus.

10. To gain an understanding of virus-related terms, you will access the Webopedia Web site. Click **Start**, then click **Internet Explorer**. Internet Explorer opens. In the Address text box, type **www.webopedia.com** and press **Enter**. The Webopedia home page opens.

13

11. In the Enter a word for a definition text box underneath SEARCH, type the term **macro virus** and then click **Go**. Record the definition in your own words.

12. Type the term **worm** into the Enter a word for a definition text box, and then click **Go**. Record the definition of worm (a type of virus) in your own words.

13. Type the term **Trojan horse** into the Enter a word for a definition text box, and then click **Go**. Record the definition of a Trojan horse (which technically is not a virus, but can cause similar damage) in your own words.

14. Log off.

Certification Objectives

Objectives for the Network+ Exam:

➤ Identify the basic capabilities (i.e., client support, interoperability, authentication, file and print services, application support, and security) of the following server operating systems: UNIX/Linux, NetWare, Windows, Macintosh

Review Questions

1. If you receive an infected file as an executable program attached to an e-mail message, which of the following is this program likely to be?

    a. a macro virus

    b. a Trojan horse

    c. a worm

    d. a boot sector virus

2. What is the difference between a Trojan horse and a true virus?

    a. A Trojan horse does not automatically replicate itself, while a true virus does.

    b. A Trojan horse causes harm by simply being on the computer's hard disk, while a true virus file must be executed by the user.

    c. A Trojan horse often can't be detected by a virus scanning program, while a true virus can almost always be detected by such a program.

    d. A Trojan horse will change its binary characteristics to avoid detection, while a true virus's binary characteristics will remain static.

3. Which of the following types of virus checking requires frequent database updates to remain effective?

   a. signature scanning

   b. heuristic scanning

   c. rotation checking

   d. integrity checking

4. If a virus is polymorphic, what is it able to do?

   a. replicate itself over a network connection

   b. change its binary characteristics each time it's transferred to a new system

   c. modify the network properties of a client or server

   d. remain inactive until a particular date

5. What is unique about a time-dependent virus?

   a. It changes its binary characteristics at regularly scheduled intervals.

   b. It can only be eradicated by applying a virus fix at certain times of the day.

   c. It is alternately detectable, then undetectable, by virus scanning software, depending on the date.

   d. It remains dormant until a particular date or time.

6. A macro virus is most apt to affect which of the following programs?

   a. Microsoft Client for Networks

   b. Microsoft Outlook

   c. Microsoft Excel

   d. Microsoft SQL Server

13

Lab 13.2 Uninterruptible Power Supplies (UPSs)

Objectives

A sudden power failure or outage can cause numerous computer problems. If power were interrupted while a computer's files were open, for instance, those files might be corrupted. An uninterruptible power supply (UPS) is a power supply that uses a battery to ensure that any device attached to it will be able to function for some length of time despite a power failure. If the power outage lasts only a few seconds, the UPS will prevent the attached devices from losing power. If the power outage lasts more than a few seconds, the UPS affords you (or a software program) the opportunity to shut down the attached devices gracefully. Alternately, use of a UPS may allow a backup generator time to get up to full operating power.

Depending on the power requirements of your network devices and servers and the amount of power produced by a UPS, you may be able to use one UPS with multiple devices. However, you should check the power requirements of each device against the specifications of the UPS before attempting to do this. You should usually overestimate the power consumption to provide a healthy margin of error. A device's power consumption is commonly measured by its Volt Amp (VA) rating. It may also be measured in amps. The VA rating may be found by multiplying the amps consumed by the device by the incoming voltage. For devices in the United States, this is 120 volts, while for international devices, this is 220 volts. In general, estimating the actual power consumption of a network device is difficult, as an individual device may use more or less power than its manufacturer indicates that it should.

Some servers come with multiple power supplies. If one power supply fails, the other power supply will continue to power the computer. For truly critical servers or network devices, you may find that attaching multiple power supplies to a single UPS is insufficient. If the UPS failed, the device would also fail during a power outage. However, if you plugged each power supply into a separate UPS, the failure of a single UPS would not cause the computer to lose power in case of an overall power failure. Some data centers might also plug each UPS into a different circuit, and each circuit into a different generator. However, these fault-tolerance measures increase costs considerably.

In addition to the smaller UPSs you will investigate in this lab, you can also purchase large models designed to support many devices in large data centers.

After completing this lab, you will be able to:

➤ Perform a cost comparison of UPSs

➤ Discuss the characteristics of UPSs

Materials Required

This lab will require the following:

➤ Pencil

➤ A computer with access to the Internet and online retailers who sell UPSs, such as *www.apcc.com*, *www.tripplite.com*, or *www.liebert.com*

Estimated completion time: **60-90 minutes**

LAB ACTIVITY

ACTIVITY

1. You are the network administrator for Hollisville Manufacturing. Table 13-1 shows the types of devices in your data center, the number of each device, and the VA rating per each device. Calculate and record the total VA rating of the devices in the data center.

Table 13-1 Power consumption of network devices in the Hollisville Manufacturing data center

Device	Number of devices	Volt Amp (VA) rating per device
Router	2	120
Server	8	285
Workstation	20	150
Hub	5	60

2. Choose a model of UPS that exceeds the total power rating for all of the devices in the data center. Record the vendor name.

3. Record the model number.

4. Record the price.

5. Record the amount of time that the UPS will keep a device running after a power failure.

6. Record whether the UPS comes with software that will automatically shut down a computer after a power failure.

7. Repeat Step 2 through Step 6 with two other models of UPS.

Certification Objectives

Objectives for the Network+ Exam:

➤ Identify the purpose and characteristics of fault tolerance

Review Questions

1. What is line conditioning?
    a. the regular testing of the integrity of electrical systems
    b. the periodic application of a large amount of voltage to electrical systems to clean the lines
    c. the continuous filtering of an electrical circuit to protect against noise
    d. the intermittent fluctuation of voltage on a circuit, which over time will cause power flaws for connected devices

13

2. Which of the following devices, when used in conjunction with one or more UPSs, will allow other devices to continue running indefinitely after a power outage?

   a. surge protector

   b. circuit breaker

   c. generator

   d. circuit mirror

3. Which of the following power conditions equates to a power failure?

   a. sag

   b. line noise

   c. surge

   d. blackout

4. Which of the following power conditions would not necessarily cause a power failure, but may adversely affect computer equipment? (Choose all that apply.)

   a. sag

   b. line noise

   c. brownout

   d. blackout

5. What specification is necessary for you to determine the amount of electrical power that your computer devices require?

   a. capacitance

   b. impedance

   c. resistance

   d. wattage

6. What is the difference between a standby UPS and an online UPS?

   a. A standby UPS engages when it detects a power failure, while an online UPS continuously provides power to its connected devices.

   b. A standby UPS requires that the network administrator connect it to key devices when a power failure is detected, while an online UPS can remain connected to devices indefinitely, even when not in use.

   c. A standby UPS continuously provides power to its connected devices, while an online UPS engages when it detects a power failure.

   d. A standby UPS can remain connected to devices indefinitely, even when not in use, while an online UPS requires that the network administrator connect it to the devices when a power failure is detected.

7. Suppose you are working on several documents in Microsoft Word when your Windows XP Professional workstation loses power. Suppose also that you are not relying on a UPS or other alternate power source. Which of the following is a significant risk?

a. The installation of the Word program on your hard disk may become corrupt and require replacement.

b. Your computer's operating system may fail to recognize the Word program in the future.

c. The Word documents you were working on when the power failed may become corrupt.

d. Your computer's power source may become damaged.

LAB 13.3 CONFIGURING RAID

Objectives

If a hard drive on a computer fails, either the computer itself will fail, or the computer will lose data. Redundant Array of Independent Disks, or RAID, allows you to improve disk reliability by combining multiple disks. Depending on how RAID is configured for a computer, it can also help improve disk performance. In this lab you will configure RAID in software. Keep in mind, however, that RAID is also commonly available in hardware. Hardware RAID has several advantages over software RAID, including greater reliability, better performance, and often the ability to swap out hard drives while the computer is still running. Most modern network operating systems, including Windows, Linux, and UNIX, support software RAID. However, Windows server operating systems such as Windows Server 2003 support software RAID, while workstation operating systems such as Windows XP Professional do not.

Each possible RAID configuration involves a different arrangement of disks, and is called a level. RAID Level 0 is called disk striping and requires at least two physical disks (almost always of the same size). Because the computer writes parts of each file onto both physical disks at the same time, RAID Level 0 results in higher performance. As in all levels of RAID, the disadvantage is that less disk space is available to the computer because the computer sees only one logical disk the size of just one of the physical disks. RAID Level 0 does not provide any fault tolerance, and data on both disks will be lost if either of the physical disks fail.

RAID Level 1, which you will configure in this lab, is known as disk mirroring. It requires at least two physical disks, and provides 100% redundancy. Each time the computer writes data to its hard disks, the same data is written to each disk at the same time. If one disk fails, then the computer can continue running normally because the other disk has precisely the same data. As in RAID Level 0, the computer sees only one logical disk that is the size of one of the physical disks. In a variation of disk mirroring known as disk duplexing, the disks also have redundant disk controllers so that the failure of a single controller will not result in the loss of data.

13

RAID Level 5 (commonly known as RAID 5) writes data onto three or more physical disks. It also writes parity data onto each disk. If one of the physical disks fails, the data and parity data written to the other disks can be used to recover any lost data. In RAID Level 5, an amount of disk space equal to the space on one physical disk is unavailable. While disks in a RAID Level 5 configuration take longer to recover from the failure of a disk than disks in a RAID Level 1 configuration, RAID Level 5 allows the computer to have more disk space than RAID Level 1.

To configure a RAID array in software in Windows Server 2003, you must use two or more dynamic disks. The exact number of disks required depends on the level of RAID you wish to use. A dynamic disk may be used in volumes that can be resized as needed withoutre-booting the server, or they may be included in RAID arrays. The disadvantage of using dynamic disks is that other operating systems, including versions of Windows prior to Windows 2000, cannot locally read these disks (although they can read data stored on them if it is shared over a network). In contrast, a basic disk can have primary and extended partitions and logical volumes, which can be read by other operating systems.

After completing this lab, you will be able to:

➤ Configure RAID Level 1 on a Windows Server 2003 computer

Materials Required

This lab will require the following:

➤ A computer running Windows Server 2003 named *SERVER1* with two hard disks installed

➤ No partitions or logical volumes configured on one of the hard disks

➤ Access as the Administrator to the computer

Estimated completion time:	**45 minutes**

LAB ACTIVITY

ACTIVITY

1. On *SERVER1*, press **Ctrl+Alt+Del** to display the Log On to Windows dialog box. Log on as the Administrator. The Windows Server 2003 desktop appears.

2. Click **Start**, point to **Administrative Tools**, and then click **Computer Management**. The Computer Management window appears.

3. In the left pane, click **Disk Management**. Information about the disks installed in the computer appear in the right pane, as shown in Figure 13-2.

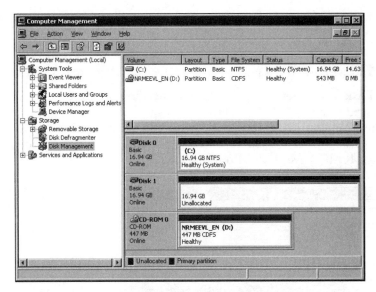

Figure 13-2   Computer Management dialog box

4. At the bottom of the right pane, you see a list of the physical disks on the system. Right-click an area in the grey box around Disk 0, and then click **Convert to Dynamic Disk**. The Convert to Dynamic Disk dialog box opens.

5. Click the **Disk 1** check box so that both the Disk 0 and Disk 1 check boxes are checked. Click **OK**. The Disks to Convert dialog box opens, listing the disks to be converted to dynamic disks.

6. Click **Convert**. The Disk Management dialog box opens, indicating that after conversion you will be unable to start other operating systems installed on those disks.

7. Click **Yes**. The Convert Disk to Dynamic dialog box opens, indicating that any file systems on these disks will need to be unmounted.

8. Click **Yes**. The Confirm dialog box opens, indicating that the computer will be rebooted in order to finish the conversion process.

9. Click **OK**. The computer reboots.

10. After the computer has rebooted, press **Ctrl+Alt+Del** to display the Log On to Windows dialog box. Log on as the Administrator. The Windows Server 2003 desktop appears. The System Settings Change dialog box opens, indicating that you must restart the computer before the changes you have made can take effect.

11. Click **Yes**. The computer reboots again.

12. After the computer has rebooted for a second time, repeat Steps 1 through 3. Both Disk 0 and Disk 1 now appear as dynamic disks.

13. Right-click the rectangle with the yellow bar at the top next to Disk 0, and click **Add Mirror** in the pop-up menu. The Add Mirror dialog box opens.

14. Click **Disk 1** to select it. Click **Add Mirror**. The bar at the top of the rectangles next to both Disk 0 and Disk 1 turns red, and text in each rectangle indicates that each disk is resynching, as shown in Figure 13-3. After a few minutes, each disk is marked C: with a status of healthy. You have successfully created a RAID Level 1 set of disk mirrors.

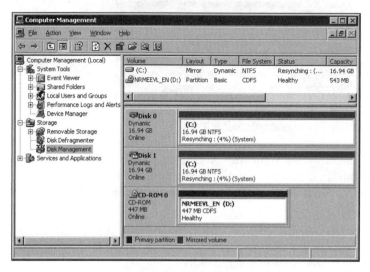

Figure 13-3   Computer Management dialog box while the mirrored drives sync

15. Close the Computer Management window and log off *SERVER1*.

Certification Objectives

Objectives for the Network+ Exam:

➤ Identify the purpose and characteristics of fault tolerance

➤ Identify the basic capabilities (i.e., client support, interoperability, authentication, file and print services, application support, and security) of the following server operating systems: UNIX/Linux, NetWare, Windows, Macintosh

Review Questions

1. Which of the following levels of RAID offers disk mirroring?

    a. 0

    b. 1

    c. 3

    d. 5

2. Why is RAID Level 0 not considered fully fault-tolerant?

    a. If a hard disk fails, its data will be inaccessible.

    b. It cannot stripe files whose size exceeds 64 MB.

    c. It is incompatible with modern NOSs.

    d. It cannot verify whether its fault-tolerance activities are successful.

3. RAID Level 0 achieves performance benefits by simultaneously writing to multiple _____ .

    a. NICs

    b. hard disks

    c. processors

    d. instances of RAID software

4. Which of the following RAID levels provides fault tolerance while also making a large amount of disk space available?

    a. 0

    b. 1

    c. 3

    d. 5

13

5. What is the minimum number of physical hard disks required for disk mirroring?

    a. 1

    b. 2

    c. 4

    d. 5

6. What is one disadvantage of using RAID Level 1 compared to using RAID Level 5?

    a. RAID Level 1 is not fault-tolerant, while RAID Level 5 offers at least some fault tolerance.

    b. RAID Level 5 requires a third-party software program, while RAID Level 1 is provided with every NOS.

    c. RAID Level 1 requires more physical hard disks than RAID Level 5.

    d. RAID Level 1 makes a higher percentage of disk space unavailable when compared to RAID Level 5.

LAB 13.4 BACKING UP A WINDOWS SERVER 2003 COMPUTER

Objectives

In this lab, you will use the Backup utility on a Windows Server 2003 computer to back up files to a floppy drive. Then you will restore the files after you have deleted the original copies. On a real network, you would then back up files either directly to a tape drive or over the network to a tape drive on another machine.

Many companies supply software for backing up data. Examples include Veritas Backup Exec and Tivoli Storage Manager. The capabilities (and the cost) of these programs vary widely. Some software allows you to back up a single machine, while other software allows you to back up an entire data center. Almost all backup software allows you to schedule a backup for a time when activity on the machine is low.

The usefulness of back ups is limited if they are not performed regularly. If you need to restore a user's file and you have not backed that file up in six months, the file will not contain any changes the user has made in the last six months. This may be as unhelpful to the user as no backup at all.

Backups should be stored in a safe, offsite location, because they are useless if the backup media has been destroyed. For instance, if backup media are kept near the servers that store the original data, a fire in the data center could destroy both the server and the backup tapes. For this reason, many organizations regularly rotate copies of their backups to offsite locations so that at least one good copy will be available even after a disaster. Your backup location should also be secure, as your backup tapes will contain any sensitive information on your servers.

After completing this lab, you will be able to:

➤ Back up data

➤ Restore data

Materials Required

This lab will require the following:

➤ A computer running Windows Server 2003 named *SERVER1* with a floppy drive

➤ Access as the Administrator to the computer

➤ Two text files named backup1.txt and backup2.txt that contain any text of your choice, but that are small enough to fit easily onto a floppy disk; the files should be stored in a folder named NetPlus located on the C: drive

➤ A blank, formatted floppy disk

Estimated completion time: **30 minutes**

LAB ACTIVITY

ACTIVITY

1. On *SERVER1*, press **Ctrl+Alt+Del** to display the Log On to Windows dialog box. Log on as the Administrator. The Windows Server 2003 desktop appears.

2. Click **Start**, point to **All Programs**, point to **Accessories**, point to **System Tools**, and then click **Backup**. The Backup or Restore Wizard opens.

3. Click **Next**. The wizard asks if you want to restore or back up files.

4. Make sure that the **Back up files and settings** option button is selected, and click **Next**. The wizard asks what you want to back up.

5. Click the **Let me choose what to back up** option button, then click **Next**. The wizard displays folders on the computer.

6. In the tree in the "Items to back up" pane, double-click **My Computer**. The local drive letters expand underneath it. Double-click the **C:** icon. You see a list of folders on the C: drive, including the NetPlus folder containing the two text files.

7. Select the check box to the left of the NetPlus folder. The NetPlus folder in the right pane also becomes selected. Click **Next**. The wizard asks you where you would like to store the backup.

8. Click **Browse**. The Save As dialog box opens.

9. Insert the floppy disk into the floppy drive. Click the **My Computer** icon on the left side of the dialog box. A list of drives on the computer appears in the right pane. Double-click **3½ Floppy (A:)**.

10. In the File name text box, delete the default entry Backup.bkf and enter **netplus**. Click **Save**. The Save As dialog box closes.

11. Click **Next**. The wizard summarizes the options you have chosen, and indicates that you have finished.

12. Click **Finish**. The Backup or Restore Wizard closes, and the Backup Progress dialog box opens. The status box indicates the various backup states that are being completed.

13. After a few seconds the Backup Progress dialog box indicates that the backup is complete. Click **Close**. The Backup Progress dialog box closes.

14. Now you will test the backup by deleting the files you have just backed up. Click **Start**, then click **My Computer**. The My Computer window opens.

15. Double-click **Local Disk (C:)**. A list of folders in the C: drive appears, including the NetPlus folder.

13

16. Right-click the **NetPlus** folder, then click **Delete** in the pop-up menu. The Confirm Folder Delete dialog box opens, asking if you are sure you want to delete the folder.

17. Click **Yes**. The computer deletes the NetPlus folder.

18. Right-click the **Recycle Bin** on the desktop, and click **Empty Recycle Bin** from the pop-up menu. The Confirm File Delete dialog box opens.

19. Click **Yes**. The computer empties the Recycle Bin.

20. Click **Start**, point to **All Programs**, point to **Accessories**, point to **System Tools**, and then click **Backup**. The Backup or Restore Wizard opens.

21. Click **Next**. The wizard asks whether you would like to back up or restore files.

22. Click the **Restore files and settings** option button, then click **Next**. The wizard asks you which files you would like to restore.

23. In the right pane, double-click **netplus.bkf**. An icon for the C: drive on *SERVER1* appears in the right pane, as shown in Figure 13-4.

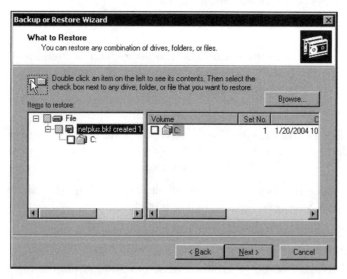

Figure 13-4   Backup or Restore Wizard

24. Click the **C:** check box to select it. Click **Next**. The wizard indicates that you are finished, and summarizes the options you have chosen.

25. Click **Finish**. The Restore Progress dialog box opens. After a few seconds, the Restore Progress dialog box indicates that the restore is complete.

26. Click **Close**. The Restore Progress dialog box closes.

27. Click **Start**, then click **My Computer**. The My Computer window opens.

28. Double-click **Local Disk (C:)**. Double-click the **NetPlus** folder. You see a list of the files you had backed up earlier.

29. Log off *SERVER1*.

Certification Objectives

Objectives for the Network+ Exam:

➤ Identify the purpose and characteristics of fault tolerance

➤ Identify the basic capabilities (i.e., client support, interoperability, authentication, file and print services, application support, and security) of the following server operating systems: UNIX/Linux, NetWare, Windows, Macintosh

➤ Identify the purpose and characteristics of disaster recovery

Review Questions

1. Assume that a company has 50 users (at a single location), a limited budget, and significant security concerns. What method would it most likely use to back up its server data?

   a. online backup

   b. DASD

   c. RAID Level 5

   d. tape backup

2. Which of the following types of backup requires the most attention to the security of data while the backup is taking place?

   a. online backup

   b. DASD

   c. RAID Level 5

   d. tape backup

3. Why do network administrators prefer not to back up every file on their servers every day? (Choose all that apply.)

   a. It would take too much time.

   b. It would be less accurate than periodic backups.

   c. It would be more costly.

   d. It's hard to configure backup software to perform daily backups.

4. Which of the following methods will back up only data that has been changed since the last backup?

   a. full

   b. incremental

13

      c. differential

      d. interval

  5. Which backup method will back up data regardless of whether the data has been changed?

      a. full

      b. incremental

      c. differential

      d. interval

LAB 13.5 BACKING UP A LINUX COMPUTER

Objectives

As with Windows, you can back up a Linux server with either commercial software or built-in commands. The `tar` command, short for "tape archiver," is one of the most common methods for making a backup. In addition to making backups of files on tape, the `tar` command (like the zip program) is also commonly used to package software for distribution. A file created with the `tar` program is often called a tar file. A tar file can be updated incrementally with any files which have changed since the tar file was created.

The `tar` command is commonly used with one of two compression programs, `gzip` and `bzip2`. Each program uses a different algorithm to compress files. The `bzip2` program creates smaller compressed files, but the `gzip` program is faster. A compressed tar file made with the `gzip` program usually ends with the suffix .tar.gz or .tgz, while a compressed tar file made with the `bzip2` program usually ends with the suffix .bz2.

Another useful command for backing up files on a Linux server is the `rsync` command. The name `rsync` is short for "remote synchronization." This command can be used to copy files from one machine to another and to copy files incrementally. An incremental backup copies only the files that have changed since the last backup. In order to copy files remotely, the `rsync` command typically uses the capabilities of another command. In this lab, the `rsync` command will use the `ssh` command to copy files onto the remote server.

After completing this lab, you will be able to:

➤ Back up files on a Linux server with the `tar` command

➤ Back up files on a Linux server with the `rsync` command

➤ Compress files on a Linux server with the `gzip` and `bzip2` commands

Materials Required

This lab will require the following:

➤ A computer running Red Hat Enterprise Linux ES 3.x named *LINUX1.NETPLUSLAB.NET* configured with an IP address of 192.168.54.5 and a subnet mask of 255.255.255.0

➤ A computer running Red Hat Enterprise Linux ES 3.x named *LINUX2.NETPLUSLAB.NET* configured with an IP address of 192.168.54.6 and a subnet mask of 255.255.255.0

➤ Access as the netplus user and as root to both *LINUX1.NETPLUSLAB.NET* and *LINUX2.NETPLUSLAB.NET*

➤ Both computers connected to a hub with straight-through CAT 5 (or better) UTP cables

➤ No firewall software configured on either computer

Estimated completion time: **35 minutes**

13

ACTIVITY

1. At the Welcome to linux1.netpluslab.net screen for LINUX.NETPLUSLAB. NET, enter **netplus** in the Username text box. Press **Enter**. The Password text box appears.

2. In the Password text box, enter the password for the netplus user account. Press **Enter**. The Red Hat desktop appears.

3. Right-click a blank spot on the desktop and then click **New Terminal** in the pop-up menu. A terminal window opens.

4. Type **su –** and press **Enter**. The Password prompt appears.

5. Enter the password for the root account and press **Enter**. The prompt now ends in a pound sign (#), indicating that you are logged on as the root user.

6. Type **echo "Your name" >/usr/local/netplus.txt**, replacing "Your name" with your name, and press **Enter**. The computer creates a text file named netplus.txt containing your name.

7. Type **ls /usr/local** and press **Enter**. The computer displays a list of the files in the /usr/local directory, including the file netplus.txt.

8. In the terminal window, type **tar –zcvf backup.tar.gz /usr/local** and press **Enter**. As shown in Figure 13-5, the computer creates a tar file named backup.tar.gz, backs up all the files in the /usr/local directory, and compresses the files with the gzip program. It displays a list of files as it backs them up. Note that all the files and directories located within the /usr/local directory are included in the archive.

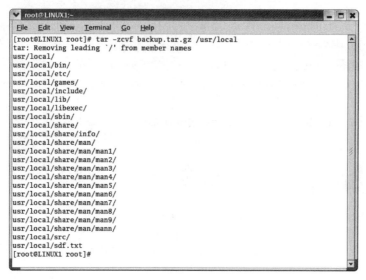

```
root@LINUX1:~                                              _ □ ✕
File  Edit  View  Terminal  Go  Help
[root@LINUX1 root]# tar -zcvf backup.tar.gz /usr/local
tar: Removing leading `/' from member names
usr/local/
usr/local/bin/
usr/local/etc/
usr/local/games/
usr/local/include/
usr/local/lib/
usr/local/libexec/
usr/local/sbin/
usr/local/share/
usr/local/share/info/
usr/local/share/man/
usr/local/share/man/man1/
usr/local/share/man/man2/
usr/local/share/man/man3/
usr/local/share/man/man4/
usr/local/share/man/man5/
usr/local/share/man/man6/
usr/local/share/man/man7/
usr/local/share/man/man8/
usr/local/share/man/man9/
usr/local/share/man/mann/
usr/local/src/
usr/local/sdf.txt
[root@LINUX1 root]#
```

Figure 13-5   Creation of a tar file

9. Type **mv backup.tar.gz /tmp** and press **Enter**. The computer moves the file backup.tar.gz to the /tmp directory.

10. Type **cd /tmp** and press **Enter**. The computer changes your directory to /tmp.

11. Type **tar -zxvf backup.tar.gz** and press **Enter**. The computer unarchives and uncompresses all the files contained in backup.tar.gz.

12. Type **ls /tmp/usr/local** and press **Enter**. The computer displays a list of the files that you have just removed from the tar archive. Note that the tar command has preserved the directory structure of all the files it has archived.

13. Type **cd usr** and press **Enter**. The computer changes your current directory to the /tmp/usr directory.

14. Type **cd local** and press **Enter**. The computer changes your current directory to the /tmp/usr/local directory that was created when backup.tar.gz was untarred. (Do not type cd /local, as that will change your current directory to the /local directory instead.)

15. Type **cat netplus.txt** and press **Enter**. The computer displays the contents of the netplus.txt file.

16. Type **tar -jcvf backup.tar.bz2 /usr/local** and press **Enter**. The computer creates an archive as it did in Step 8, with a name of backup.tar.bz2 and using the bzip2 program.

17. Now you will back up files to a remote machine. Type **rsync -zav -e ssh /usr/local 192.168.54.6:/tmp** and press **Enter**. The -z option tells the rsync command to compress the files like the gzip command, the -a

option tells the rsync command to archive all the files, and the -v option tells it to be verbose, or print detailed messages explaining what the command is doing. The -e option tells the rsync command to use the ssh command. The last two options tell it to copy the /usr/local directory to the /tmp directory on 192.168.54.6. If the "Are you sure you want to continue connecting (yes/no):" prompt appears, type **yes** and press **Enter**. The password prompt appears.

18. Enter the password for the root account and press **Enter**. The rsync command indicates that it is building a list of files to transfer onto the remote computer, lists the files it transfers, and then summarizes the size and speed of the transfer.

19. Type **echo "New file" >/usr/local/newfile.txt** and press **Enter**. The computer creates a text file containing the text "New file."

20. Repeat Steps 17 and 18. The rsync command indicates that it is building a list of files to be copied, and displays the names of the files and directories that have changed. (A directory in Linux changes when the files are added to or removed from it.)

21. On *LINUX2.NETPLUSLAB.NET*, repeat Steps 1 through 5.

22. In the terminal window on *LINUX2.NETPLUSLAB.NET*, type **cd /tmp** and press **Enter**. This is the directory to which the rsync command copied files from *LINUX1.NETPLUSLAB.NET*.

23. Type **cd usr** and press **Enter**. The computer changes the current directory to /tmp/usr.

24. Type **cd local** and press **Enter**. The computer changes the current directory to /tmp/usr/local.

25. Type **ls** and press **Enter**. The computer displays a list of all the files and directories copied over from *LINUX1.NETPLUSLAB.NET*.

26. Type **cat netplus.txt**. The computer displays the contents of the netplus.txt file.

27. Type **cat newfile.txt** and press **Enter**. The computer displays the contents of the newfile.txt file.

28. Log off both computers.

13

Certification Objectives

Objectives for the Network+ Exam:

➤ Identify the basic capabilities (i.e., client support, interoperability, authentication, file and print services, application support, and security) of the following server operating systems: UNIX/Linux, NetWare, Windows, Macintosh

➤ Identify the purpose and characteristics of fault tolerance

Review Questions

1. Which of the following commands could *not* be used in the process of creating backups on a Linux computer?

   a. tar

   b. rsync

   c. bzip2

   d. cat

2. Which of the following commands would create an archive file named march13.tar.gz containing the directory /usr and all of the files and directories within it and compressed by the gzip command?

   a. tar -jzvf march13.tar.gz /usr

   b. tar -zxvf march13.tar.gz /usr

   c. tar -jcvf march13.tar.gz /usr

   d. tar -zcf march13.tar.gz /usr

3. Which programs are likely to have made a file named foo.tar.bz2?

   a. rsync and bz2

   b. ssh and bz2

   c. tar and gzip

   d. tar and bz2

4. Which of the following programs would be used to back up data to a tape drive on a Linux computer?

   a. tar

   b. gzip

   c. rsync

   d. cat

5. You are a network administrator working for Red Rectangle Manufacturing. Red Rectangle has twelve servers, which it would like to back up onto a single server attached to a tape library capable of backing up many computers. How would you go about this using the tools in this lab to accomplish this task?

   a. Use the `tar` command every night to back up each server individually, then transfer the `tar` files onto the backup server with floppies.

   b. Use the `tar` command every night to back up each server individually, then transfer the files using the `ssh` command.

   c. Use the `rsync` command each night to back up each server onto the backup server, then use the `tar` command to create an archive file for each server.

   d. User the `rsync` command each night to back up each server onto the backup server, then use the `tar` command to write each backup onto a separate tape.

13

14

NETWORK SECURITY

Labs included in this chapter

➤ Lab 14.1 Auditing

➤ Lab 14.2 Checking for Vulnerable Software

➤ Lab 14.3 Implementing Password Restrictions in Novell NetWare

➤ Lab 14.4 Implementing Network Address Restrictions on a Linux Server

➤ Lab 14.5 Plain Text Versus Encrypted Protocols

Net+ Exam Objectives	
Objective	**Lab**
Identify the basic capabilities (i.e., client support, interoperability, authentication, file and print services, application support, and security) of the following server operating systems: UNIX/Linux, NetWare, Windows, Macintosh	14.1, 14.2, 14.3, 14.4, 14.5
Identify the basic capabilities (i.e., client connectivity, local security mechanisms, and authentication) of the following clients: UNIX/Linux, Windows, Macintosh	14.1, 14.3, 14.4, 14.5
Given a scenario, predict the impact of a particular security implementation on network functionality (e.g., blocking port numbers, encryption, etc.)	14.1, 14.3, 14.4, 14.5
Given specific parameters, configure a client to connect to the following servers: UNIX/Linux, NetWare, Windows, Macintosh	14.5

LAB **14.1** AUDITING

Objectives

Although preventing security problems should be the first goal of network administrators, security problems cannot always be prevented. Fortunately, auditing can help you identify both security vulnerabilities and potential security breaches.

Auditing is the gathering and analysis of large amounts of network-related information, including data about logons, access attempts, system events, and so on. For instance, auditing can indicate when someone is repeatedly attempting and failing to log on to your domain controller, which could in turn indicate that someone is attempting to compromise your network. Auditing can also help you troubleshoot server problems, such as an unexpected failure.

Auditing is not limited to a network operating system; in most cases, you can configure firewalls, routers, and switches to compile, or log, information (on their own disks or to an external server) as well. Often this information can be useful in determining whether intruders have attempted to access devices on your network.

In Windows Server 2003 (and in most other network operating systems), auditing is not enabled by default because it can affect performance and use a large amount of disk space. Thus, to view the failed logon attempts in a Windows Server 2003 domain, you must first activate auditing for the domain. Then you must activate auditing on the domain controller so that it will capture the logging.

After completing this lab, you will be able to:

➤ Enable auditing in Windows Server 2003

➤ Review information on audited events

Materials Required

This lab will require the following:

➤ A computer running Windows Server 2003 Enterprise Edition named *SERVER1* configured as the domain controller for the netpluslab.net domain with an IP address of 192.168.54.1 and a subnet mask of 255.255.255.0

➤ Access as the Administrator to *SERVER1*

➤ A computer running Windows XP Professional named *WORKSTATION1* configured as a member of the netpluslab.net domain and with an IP address of 192.168.54.3 and a subnet mask of 255.255.255.0

➤ A user account named netplus in the Domain Users group in the netpluslab.net domain

➤ Both computers connected to a hub with straight-through CAT 5 (or better) UTP cables

Estimated completion time: **40 minutes**

LAB ACTIVITY

ACTIVITY

1. On *SERVER1*, press **Ctrl+Alt+Del** to display the Log On to Windows dialog box. Log on as the Administrator. The Windows Server 2003 desktop appears.

2. Click **Start**, point to **Administrative Tools**, and click **Domain Security Policy**. The Default Domain Security Settings window appears.

3. Click **Local Policies** in the left pane. Icons for polices appear in the right pane.

4. In the right pane, double-click **Audit Policy**. Several icons whose names begin with "Audit" appear. As you'll see in the next few steps, you can double-click these icons to define and configure various policies.

5. Double-click **Audit account logon events**. The Audit account logon events Properties dialog box opens. This setting determines whether or not the computer will record every instance of a user logging on or off the domain.

6. If necessary, select the **Define these policy settings**, **Success**, and **Failure** check boxes, and then click **OK**. Figure 14-1 shows the Audit account logon events Properties dialog box. You have now configured the computer to record every attempt by a user to log on, whether successful or unsuccessful.

7. Repeat Steps 5 and 6 for **Audit logon events**. (Note the distinction between "Audit account logon events" and "Audit logon events.") The Audit account logon events settings determine whether or not the domain controller will record every instance of a user logging on or off a computer for which the domain controller performs authentication.

8. In the left pane, right-click **Security Settings** and click **Reload** in the pop-up menu. The computer updates security policy for the domain with the changes that you have made.

9. In order for auditing events to be captured, you must specifically enable logging on the domain controller itself. Otherwise, the domain controller will not know that it is supposed to capture audit events, and will discard them. Click **Start**, point to **Administrative Tools**, and then click **Domain Controller Security Policy**. The Default Domain Controller Security Settings window opens.

14

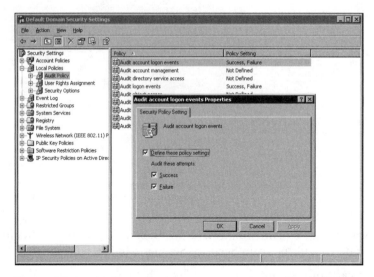

Figure 14-1   Audit account logon events Properties dialog box

10. In the tree in the left pane, click **Local Policies**. A list of icons appears in the right pane. Double-click **Audit Policy**. Policies appear in the right pane.

11. Double-click **Audit account logon events**. The Audit account logon events Properties dialog box appears.

12. Make sure that the **Define these policy settings**, **Success**, and **Failure** check boxes are all checked, and then click **OK**.

13. Repeat Steps 11 and 12 for **Audit logon events**.

14. Right-click **Security Settings**, and then click **Reload**. The computer reloads security policies for the domain controller.

15. On *WORKSTATION1*, press **Ctrl+Alt+Del** to display the Log On to Windows dialog box.

16. Enter **netplus** in the User name text box. Enter an invalid password in the Password text box. Click **OK**. The Logon Message dialog box appears, indicating that the logon attempt failed. Click **OK**.

17. Repeat the previous step.

18. Log on as the netplus user with the correct password. The Windows XP desktop appears.

19. On *SERVER1*, click **Start**, point to **Administrative Tools**, and click **Event Viewer**. The Event Viewer window appears.

20. In the left pane, click **Security**. A list of security events appears in the right pane, including all successful and failed logon attempts.

21. Double-click a **Failure Audit** icon. The Event Properties dialog box opens, as shown in Figure 14-2. The dialog box gives information about a failed logon attempt.

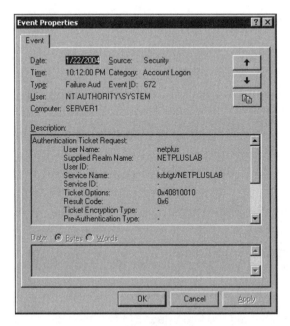

Figure 14-2   Event Properties dialog box showing a failed logon attempt

22. Repeat the previous step with a **Success Audit** icon.

23. Log off both computers.

Certification Objectives

Objectives for the Network+ Exam:

➤ Identify the basic capabilities (i.e., client support, interoperability, authentication, file and print services, application support, and security) of the following server operating systems: UNIX/Linux, NetWare, Windows, Macintosh

➤ Identify the basic capabilities (i.e., client connectivity, local security mechanisms, and authentication) of the following clients: UNIX/Linux, Windows, Macintosh

➤ Given a scenario, predict the impact of a particular security implementation on network functionality (e.g., blocking port numbers, encryption, etc.)

Review Questions

1. Which of the following best describes authentication?

   a. the process of verifying the precise spelling of a user name

   b. the process of accepting and matching a user name with unique account information, such as a password

   c. the process of replicating user logon information from one domain controller to the others on a network

   d. the process of tracking a user's logon habits and collecting that information in an audit log

2. How does knowing about failed logon attempts help a network administrator's security efforts?

   a. The information could help her determine whether stricter password requirements need to be implemented.

   b. The information could help her refine the NOS schema.

   c. The information could help her determine whether an unauthorized user is attempting to log on with that user name.

   d. The information could help her predict the likelihood of future security breaches.

3. Which of the following tools allows you to view security events that have occurred on a Windows Server 2003 computer?

   a. Event Viewer

   b. Authentication Log

   c. Domain Security Policy

   d. Domain Controller Security Policy

4. In the context of Windows networking, why must failed logon attempts be recorded by a domain controller instead of by any random server on the network?

   a. Only a domain controller will have the resources necessary to record and hold the volume of information that auditing requires.

   b. Domain controllers contain a complete set of Windows Server 2003 computer administrative tools, while other servers do not.

   c. Domain controllers typically provide Web and remote access, enabling a network administrator to remotely audit events on a network.

   d. Domain controllers authenticate users.

5. As a network administrator, what should you do if you notice that a user account has experienced multiple failed logon attempts?

    a. revoke the user's logon privileges

    b. change the user's password

    c. contact the user to find out whether she is having trouble logging on

    d. limit the times of day during which that user account may log on

LAB 14.2 CHECKING FOR VULNERABLE SOFTWARE

Objectives

Software patches can reverse potentially dangerous vulnerabilities in a network. However, network administrators commonly compromise their networks' security by running unpatched software. For instance, in 2003 several worms including the MSBlast and Sobig.F worms infected hundreds of thousands of computers even though software patches fixing the vulnerabilities were available. Many administrators simply did not know that they needed to patch their software.

In this lab, you will run a utility that can determine which service packs or hotfixes you need to apply on a Windows Server 2003 computer.

After completing this lab, you will be able to:

➤   Scan a Windows Server 2003 computer to identify whether it is operating with vulnerable software

Materials Required

This lab will require the following:

➤   A computer running Windows Server 2003 Enterprise Edition with Internet access

➤   Microsoft Baseline Security Analyzer 1.2 (currently available from *www.microsoft.com/technet/security/tools/mbsahome.mspx*) installed on the Windows Server 2003 computer

➤   Access as the Administrator to the Windows Server 2003 computer

14

Estimated completion time: **30 minutes**

ACTIVITY

1. On the Windows Server 2003 computer, press **Ctrl+Alt+Del** to display the Log On to Windows dialog box. Log on as the Administrator. The Windows Server 2003 desktop appears.

2. Establish a connection to the Internet.

3. Click **Start**, point to **All Programs**, and click **Microsoft Baseline Security Analyzer 1.2**. The Microsoft Baseline Security Analyzer opens.

4. Click **Pick a computer to scan**. The computer asks you to choose a computer to scan for security vulnerabilities.

5. Click **Start scan**. The computer downloads security information from Microsoft and checks for security vulnerabilities. It then displays the results, as shown in Figure 14-3.

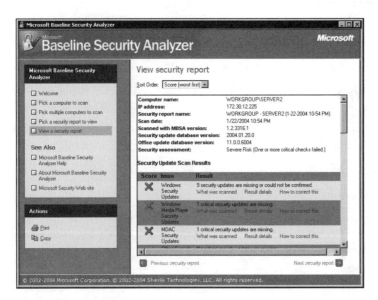

Figure 14-3 Microsoft Baseline Security Analyzer

6. At the top of the report is a summary of the security status of the computer. What is the Security assessment for your computer?

7. Scroll down to the Security Update Scan Results section. A red "X" is displayed for any items that present a serious security risk, a green check mark for any items that do not present a security vulnerability, a blue "i" in a white circle for any informational items, a yellow "X" for any items that should be changed, and a blue star for any items which could be changed. Some types of items may not be present. Which critical security updates, if any, should you install on your computer?

8. Scroll down to the Vulnerabilities section under "Windows Scan Results." What is the status of Automatic Updates on your computer? Do any items represent a serious security risk?

9. Log off the computer.

Certification Objectives

Objectives for the Network+ Exam:

➤ Identify the basic capabilities (i.e., client support, interoperability, authentication, file and print services, application support, and security) of the following server operating systems: UNIX/Linux, NetWare, Windows, Macintosh

Review Questions

1. Which of the following security risks can potentially be addressed by applying a new patch to a software program?
   a. social engineering
   b. insecure data transmissions between a Web client and Web server
   c. IP spoofing
   d. RF emission over a wireless network

2. Which of the following methods of accessing files over the Internet is the most secure?
   a. HTTP
   b. HTTPS
   c. TFTP
   d. FTP

3. Which of the following types of software can be patched to improve their security? (Choose all that apply.)

   a. router OS

   b. Web browser

   c. e-mail client

   d. database program

   e. workstation OS

4. Which of the following types of transmission media is the most secure?

   a. fiber-optic cable

   b. infrared wireless

   c. shielded twisted-pair cable

   d. coaxial cable

5. Which of the following network enhancements can introduce new security risks? (Choose all that apply.)

   a. adding remote access for users who travel

   b. adding time of day restrictions for logons

   c. modifying a tape backup rotation scheme

   d. providing Web access to a server's data files

   e. upgrading the processors on every server

LAB 14.3 IMPLEMENTING PASSWORD RESTRICTIONS IN NOVELL NETWARE

Objectives

Password restrictions are an important part of network security. They should be part of a password policy that prevents users from using passwords that are easily guessed, too short (and hence more easily cracked by an intruder), or kept for a long period of time (for example, longer than 90 days). A sound password policy should also discourage users from writing down their passwords. A password found by an intruder on a sheet of paper could give the intruder access to the network. In this lab, you will set a minimum password length and prevent users from reusing their passwords.

After completing this lab, you will be able to:

➤ Implement password restrictions on a Novell NetWare user account

Materials Required

This lab will require the following:

➤ A computer running Novell NetWare 6.5 named *NETWARE1* configured with an IP address of 192.168.54.6 and a subnet mask of 255.255.255.0

➤ The NetWare 6.5 software installed as a Basic NetWare File Server

➤ Access as the admin user to the Novell server

➤ An eDirectory tree named *NETPLUS*, with *NETWARE1* and the admin account in the administration context

➤ A computer running Windows XP Professional named *WORKSTATION1* with the Novell Client for NT/2000/XP 4.9 software installed and an IP address of 192.168.54.3 and a subnet mask of 255.255.255.0

➤ Console One installed on *WORKSTATION1*, and an icon for ConsoleOne on the desktop

➤ A local Windows account on *WORKSTATION1* named admin whose password is synchronized with the NetWare account named admin

➤ An eDirectory account in the laboratory context named netplus, whose password is synchronized to a local Windows account on *WORKSTATION1* named netplus

➤ Both computers connected to a hub with straight-through CAT 5 (or better) UTP cables

14

Estimated completion time: **35 minutes**

LAB ACTIVITY

ACTIVITY

1. On *WORKSTATION1*, press **Ctrl+Alt+Del** to display the Novell Login dialog box. Log in as the admin user in the administration context. The Windows XP desktop appears.

2. Double-click the **ConsoleOne** icon on the desktop. Novell ConsoleOne opens.

3. Click the **plus sign (+)** next to NETPLUS in the left pane in order to expand the tree underneath it. Click **laboratory** to select it. An icon for the netplus user appears in the right pane.

4. Right-click **netplus** and click **Properties** in the pop-up menu. The Properties of laboratory dialog box opens.

5. Click the **Restrictions** tab. Information about password restrictions is displayed, as is shown in Figure 14-4.

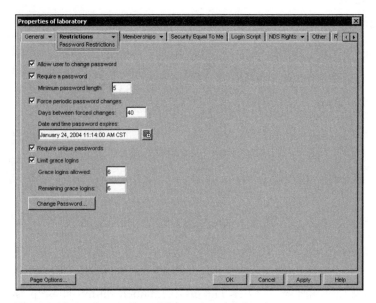

Figure 14-4 Properties of laboratory dialog box

6. Select the **Require a password** check box, the **Force periodic password changes** check box, the **Require unique passwords** check box, and the **Limit grace logins** check box. In the Minimum password length text box, enter **8**. In the Grace logins allowed and Remaining grace logins allowed text boxes, enter **5**. Click **OK**. The Properties of laboratory dialog box closes. You have now configured password restrictions for all users in the laboratory organizational unit.

7. Click **Start**, then click **Log Off**. The Log Off Windows dialog box opens, asking if you are sure you wish to log off.

8. Click **Log Off**. The computer logs you off.

9. Press **Ctrl+Alt+Del** to display the Novell Login dialog box. Log on as the netplus user in the laboratory context. The Confirm dialog box opens. Click **No**. The Windows XP desktop appears.

10. Press **Ctrl+Alt+Del** again. The NetWare Security dialog box opens.

11. Click **Change Password**. The Change Password dialog box opens.

12. In the Old Password text box, enter the current password for the netplus account. Record this password below. (Although recording the password is a poor security practice, performing this lab without writing down the passwords will be confusing.) Do the same for the New Password and Confirm Password text boxes. Click **OK**. The Password Not Changed dialog box opens.

13. Click **OK**. The Password Not Changed dialog box closes.

14. Enter a new password in the New Password and Confirm New Password text boxes. Record the password below. Click **OK**. The Change Password dialog box opens.

15. Click **OK**. The Change Password and NetWare Security dialog boxes close.

16. Repeat Steps 10 and 11 to open the Change Password dialog box again. Enter the password recorded in Step 14 in the Old Password text box, and leave the New Password and Confirm New Password text boxes empty. Click **OK**. The Password Not Changed text box opens, indicating that the password is not long enough.

17. Click **OK**. The Password Not Changed dialog box closes.

18. In the New Password and the Confirm New Password text boxes, enter the original password for the netplus account that you recorded in Step 12. The Password Synchronization Errors dialog box opens, indicating that the new password must be unique.

19. Click **Close**. The Password Synchronization Errors dialog box closes.

20. Enter a new password (not one of the passwords you have recorded in Steps 12 and 14) in the New Password and Confirm New Password text boxes. Click **OK**. The Change Password and NetWare Security dialog boxes close. Record the new password below.

21. Log off the computer.

Certification Objectives

Objectives for the Network+ Exam:

➤ Identify the basic capabilities (i.e., client support, interoperability, authentication, file and print services, application support, and security) of the following server operating systems: UNIX/Linux, NetWare, Windows, Macintosh

➤ Identify the basic capabilities (i.e., client connectivity, local security mechanisms, and authentication) of the following clients: UNIX/Linux, Windows, Macintosh

➤ Given a scenario, predict the impact of a particular security implementation on network functionality (e.g., blocking port numbers, encryption, etc.)

Review Questions

1. Which of the following passwords is the most difficult to guess or crack?

   a. uknowit

   b. sez

    c. 12345678

    d. z2!ffiy8x0

2. What type of encryption is used by PGP?

    a. public key

    b. DES

    c. private key

    d. public and private key

3. Which of the following network services might use RADIUS to authenticate a user?

    a. e-commerce transactions

    b. terminal-to-mainframe sessions

    c. network printing

    d. dial-up networking

4. What does "SSL" stand for?

    a. Single Session Language

    b. Secure Sockets Layer

    c. Strict Security Lease

    d. Shell Sequence Logic

5. Which of the following types of restrictions would help guard against a malicious intruder using a dictionary-based password cracking program to determine a user's password? (Choose all that apply.)

    a. minimum password length

    b. time of day during which a user can log on

    c. use of both numbers and letters in a password

    d. frequency with which a password must be changed

    e. inability to use the same password in a one-year period

---

LAB 14.4 IMPLEMENTING NETWORK ADDRESS RESTRICTIONS ON A LINUX SERVER

Objectives

Most NOSs have some mechanism that ensures that users can only log on from certain Network layer or Data Link layer addresses. The potential advantage to requiring users to log on from only certain machines is that you can prevent them from logging on to the network from any workstation but their own. This can help you keep a closer eye on users, as well as entirely prevent users from accessing certain networks. The disadvantage is that this requires more maintenance. If a user changes machines, then you would have to reconfigure the network address restrictions.

Additionally, some network devices can restrict access by Network layer or Data Link layer addresses. For instance, some switches allow you to configure ports so that only certain MAC addresses can pass traffic through those ports. If a user attempts to plug another machine with another MAC address into the same port, the switch will not allow it to pass traffic and the computer will be unable to use the network.

On a Linux or UNIX server, the most common mechanism for configuring network address restrictions is the use of TCP wrappers. TCP wrappers are used by a variety of programs to determine whether or not they should accept network traffic from a particular address.

A careful intruder can circumvent this sort of protection. For instance, an intruder can manually configure both IP addresses and MAC addresses on a computer, or they can attack a computer with packets containing bogus IP addresses. This is often called spoofing. However, good network security policies should make it difficult or impossible to use bogus addresses from outside a network. In this case, an intruder would need to place a machine physically on the network to circumvent address restrictions.

After completing this lab, you will be able to:

➤ Configure network address restrictions on a Linux server

Materials Required

This lab will require the following:

➤ A computer running Red Hat Enterprise Linux ES 3.x named *LINUX1.NETPLUSLAB.NET* configured with an IP address of 192.168.54.5 and a subnet mask of 255.255.255.0

➤ The firewall software not configured on *LINUX1.NETPLUSLAB.NET*

➤ Access to *LINUX1.NETPLUSLAB.NET* as the root and netplus users

➤ A computer running Windows XP Professional named *WORKSTATION1* configured with an IP address of 192.168.54.3 and a subnet mask of 255.255.255.0

➤ The Cygwin software (available at *www.cygwin.com*) installed on *WORKSTATION1*, with the OpenSSH package installed

➤ Access to *WORKSTATION1* as the Administrator

➤ Both computers connected to a hub with straight-through CAT 5 (or better) UTP cables

Estimated completion time: **35 minutes**

ACTIVITY

1. On *LINUX1.NETPLUSLAB.NET* at the Welcome to linux1.netpluslab.net screen, enter **netplus** in the Username text box. Press **Enter**. The Password text box appears.

2. Enter the password for the netplus account in the Password text box. Press **Enter**. The Red Hat desktop appears.

3. Right-click a blank spot on the desktop, and click **New Terminal** in the pop-up menu. A new terminal window opens.

4. In the terminal window, type **su –** and press **Enter**. The Password prompt appears.

5. Type the root password and press **Enter**. The prompt now ends in a pound sign (#), indicating that you are logged on as the root user.

6. Type **echo "sshd: ALL" >>/etc/hosts.deny** and press **Enter**. The computer appends the text "sshd: ALL" to the file /etc/hosts.deny. This tells TCP wrappers to prohibit computers from any IP address from logging onto *LINUX1.NETPLUSLAB.NET*.

7. Type **cat /var/run/sshd.pid** and press **Enter**. The computer displays the PID for the running sshd daemon. Record this number.

8. Type **kill –HUP** followed by the PID number you recorded in Step 7, and then press **Enter**. The computer restarts the sshd daemon.

9. On *WORKSTATION1*, press **Ctrl+Alt+Del** to display the Log On to Windows dialog box. Log on as the Administrator. The Windows XP desktop appears.

10. Click **Start**, point to **All Programs**, point to **Cygwin**, and click **Cygwin Bash Shell**. A terminal window opens.

11. In the terminal window, type **ssh netplus@192.168.54.5** and press **Enter**. As seen in Figure 14-5, the computer displays the error message "ssh_exchange_identification: Connection closed by remote host."

12. Now you will configure *LINUX1.NETPLUSLAB.NET* to accept SSH connections from *WORKSTATION1*. In the terminal window on *LINUX1.NETPLUSLAB.NET*, type **echo "sshd: 192.168.54.3" >/etc/hosts.allow** and press **Enter**. The computer appends the text "sshd: 192.168.54.3" to the end of the file /etc/hosts.allow.

13. Repeat Steps 7 and 8 to restart the sshd daemon.

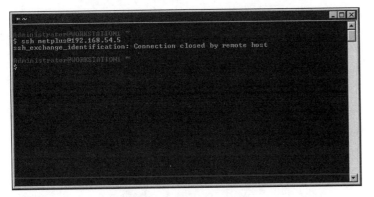

Figure 14-5   An SSH login prevented by TCP wrappers

14. In the terminal window on *WORKSTATION1*, type **ssh netplus@ 192.168.54.5** and press **Enter**. If a message appears indicating that the authenticity of the connection cannot be confirmed, type **Yes** and press **Enter**. The netplus@192.168.54.5's password: prompt appears.

15. Type the password for the netplus account and press **Enter**. The prompt changes, indicating that you have logged onto the remote server.

16. Log off both computers.

Certification Objectives

Objectives for the Network+ Exam:

➤ Identify the basic capabilities (i.e., client support, interoperability, authentication, file and print services, application support, and security) of the following server operating systems: UNIX/Linux, NetWare, Windows, Macintosh

➤ Identify the basic capabilities (i.e., client connectivity, local security mechanisms, and authentication) of the following clients: UNIX/Linux, Windows, Macintosh

➤ Given a scenario, predict the impact of a particular security implementation on network functionality (e.g., blocking port numbers, encryption, etc.)

Review Questions

1. Which of the following is a potential weakness in using restrictions on either Network layer addresses or Data Link layer addresses to control access to a network or server?

   a. For a machine on the same network, both Network and Data Link layer addresses may be configured manually.

   b. For a machine on an external network, both Network and Data Link layer addresses may be configured manually.

   c. Network address restrictions typically require more maintenance.

   d. Network layer addresses may be configured manually, while Data Link layer addresses may not.

2. Which files on a Linux server are used to configure TCP wrappers? (Choose all that apply.)

   a. /etc/hosts

   b. /etc/hosts.allow

   c. /etc/hosts.deny

   d. /etc/tcpwrappers

3. Which of the following network security methods provides the greatest resistance to unauthorized external file access on a server?

   a. a central computer room that is accessible only to authorized personnel through hand–scanning

   b. a NOS that is configured to allow logons only during the hours of 8 a.m. to 5 p.m.

   c. a NOS that requires users' computers to have an address that matches one belonging to their LAN segment in order to log on to the server

   d. a proxy server that disguises transmissions issued from clients on a private LAN

4. What is the best defense against social engineering?

   a. a strong security policy and educating users

   b. employing Kerberos authentication for all users

   c. configuring a firewall to accept transmissions only from certain IP addresses

   d. limiting the ports on a server through which client communication may take place

5. In which of the following situations would it be most beneficial for a network administrator to employ network address restrictions on a TCP/IP-based network (that does not use DHCP) to improve security?

   a. A salesperson accesses a company's network via a dial-up connection to upload sales data every night.

   b. A corporate executive frequently travels to a company's various locations and requires access to confidential information on the server.

   c. A new employee is working on tutorials in temporary quarters until her office can be completely furnished.

   d. A contractor works on a project from a cube specially designated and furnished for use by consultants.

LAB 14.5 PLAIN TEXT VERSUS ENCRYPTED PROTOCOLS

Objectives

Most of the older communications programs still in use, such as Ftp or Telnet, use plain text. Using such a program to administer a server or a network device can make it easy for an intruder to steal account information using a protocol analyzer.

In fact, many network devices are still managed by telnet. This is because some network devices, such as routers and switches, have less powerful processors than servers. Using encrypted protocols (which require more processing power than plain text protocols) rather than telnet would leave less processing power available for routing or switching packets.

The Secure Shell Protocol (SSH) is an alternative to telnet that encrypts text sent over the network, and it is becoming more common among network devices. But as long as they continue to use telnet, network administrators can minimize the security risks by restricting the hosts from which network devices can be accessed. For instance, on many networks one host is specified as the only device from which network devices can be accessed via telnet. (Such a host is called a bastion host.) With a bastion host, even if the telnet password is stolen, compromising those network devices is made more difficult than it would be otherwise because an intruder would also need to compromise the bastion host.

In this lab, you will use a protocol analyzer to examine the dangers of using plain text versus encrypted protocols. It is important to keep in mind that, while a protocol analyzer is an important and valuable tool for network administrators, using a protocol analyzer to obtain the passwords of users or to eavesdrop on their communications without their consent is unethical and illegal. In addition, you should always have clear and specific consent before using a protocol analyzer. This is especially true on a network that is not yours, such as a customer network. On networks that you manage, you should determine whether use of a protocol analyzer is permissible before using one. In some high-security environments, such as a financial or military institution, you may be prohibited from using a protocol analyzer at all. In other environments, you should make sure that you have explicit permission to use a protocol analyzer when necessary.

After completing this lab, you will be able to:

➤ Describe the difference between encrypted and unencrypted network protocols

Materials Required

This lab will require the following:

➤ A computer running Red Hat Enterprise Linux ES 3.x named *LINUX1.NETPLUSLAB.NET* configured with an IP address of 192.168.54.5 and a subnet mask of 255.255.255.0

➤ The telnet server (available on the third installation disk for Red Hat Enterprise Linux ES 3.x) installed on *LINUX1.NETPLUSLAB.NET*

➤ Access to *LINUX1.NETPLUSLAB.NET* as the root and netplus users

➤ A computer running Windows Server 2003 Enterprise Edition named *SERVER1* configured with an IP address of 192.168.54.1 and a subnet mask of 255.255.255.0

➤ The Ethereal protocol analyzer (available from *www.ethereal.com*) installed on *SERVER1*

➤ Access to *SERVER1* as the Administrator

➤ A computer running Windows XP Professional named *WORKSTATION1* configured with an IP address of 192.168.54.3 and a subnet mask of 255.255.255.0

➤ The Cygwin software (available at *www.cygwin.com*) installed on *WORKSTATION1*, with the OpenSSH package installed

➤ The firewall software not configured on *LINUX1.NETPLUSLAB.NET*, and no entries in the /etc/hosts.deny file

➤ Access to the Windows XP computer as an ordinary user

➤ All three computers connected to a hub with straight-through CAT 5 (or better) UTP cables

---

Estimated completion time: **30 minutes**

LAB ACTIVITY

ACTIVITY

1. On *LINUX1.NETPLUSLAB.NET* at the Welcome to linux1.netpluslab.net screen, enter **netplus** in the Username text box. Press **Enter**. The Password text box appears.

2. Enter the password for the netplus account in the Password text box. Press **Enter**. The Red Hat desktop appears.

3. Right-click a blank spot on the desktop and click **New Terminal** in the pop-up menu. A new terminal window opens.

4. In the terminal window, type **su –** and press **Enter**. At the Password prompt, type the root password and press **Enter**. The prompt now ends on a pound sign (#), indicating that you are logged on as the root user.

5. Type **vi /etc/xinetd.d/telnet** and press **Enter**. The vi editor opens the file /etc/xinetd.d/telnet.

6. Use the ↓ key to scroll down to the next-to-last line. Using the → key, scroll over to position the cursor at the beginning of the word "yes."

7. Type **d\$**. The vi editor deletes everything from the cursor to the end of the line.

8. Press **i**. The vi editor enters insert mode.

9. Type **no** and press **Esc**. The vi editor enters normal mode.

10. Type **:wq** and press **Enter**. The computer writes and saves the file.

11. Type **/etc/init.d/xinetd restart** and press **Enter**. The computer restarts the xinetd daemon.

12. On *SERVER1*, press **Ctrl+Alt+Del** to display the Log On to Windows dialog box. Log on as the Administrator. The Windows Server 2003 desktop appears.

13. Click **Start**, point to **All Programs**, point to **Ethereal**, and click **Ethereal**. The Ethereal Network Analyzer window opens.

14. On the menu bar, click **Capture**, then click **Start**. The Ethereal: Capture Options window opens.

15. In the Capture Filter text box, enter **host 192.168.54.5**. This configures Ethereal to capture only packets being sent from or to IP address 192.168.54.5. Click **OK**. The Ethereal: Capture dialog box opens.

16. On *WORKSTATION1*, press **Ctrl+Alt+Del** to display the Log On to Windows dialog box. Log on as the Administrator. The Windows XP desktop appears.

17. Click **Start**, point to **All Programs**, point to **Cygwin**, and click **Cygwin Bash Shell**. A terminal window opens.

18. In the terminal window, type **telnet 192.168.54.5** and press **Enter**. The logon prompt appears.

19. Type **netplus** and press **Enter**. The Password prompt appears. Enter the password for the netplus account and press **Enter**. The computer displays the date and time of your last logon, if any, and a prompt appears, indicating that you have logged on successfully. Figure 14-6 shows a successful Telnet logon.

20. On *SERVER1*, in the Ethereal: Capture dialog box click **STOP**. The Ethereal: Capture dialog box closes, and the packets captured are displayed in the <capture> - Ethereal window.

21. In the Filter text box, type **telnet** and press **Enter**. The computer displays only those packets that have TELNET in the Protocol field.

22. In the top pane, click the first packet. In the middle pane, click the **plus sign (+)** sign next to Telnet. Detailed information about the Telnet portion of the packet appears. (You may need to scroll down in order to see it all.)

23. Using the ↓ key, scroll down through the list of packets. Look for a packet containing the phrase "Red Hat Enterprise Linux." Figure 14-7 shows this packet. Compare the text in this packet to the logon text you saw in Step 19.

14

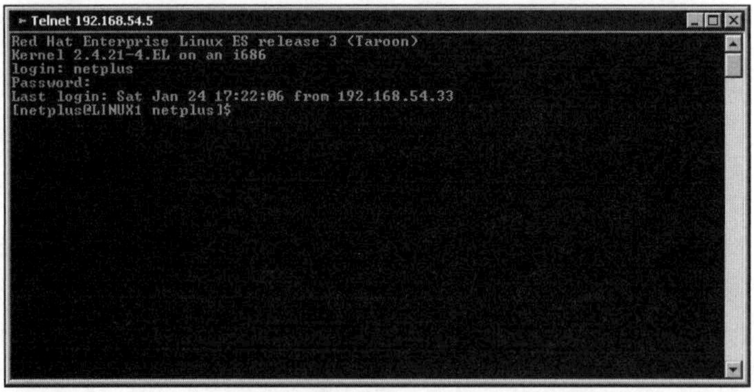

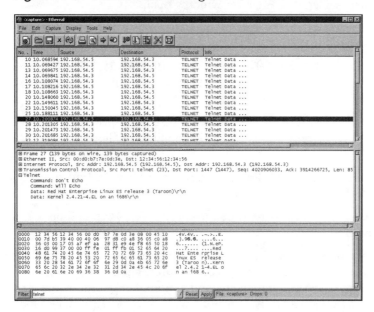

Figure 14-6   Successful Telnet logon

Figure 14-7   Ethereal

24. Scroll down further and look for a packet containing the text "Password." This is the Password prompt you saw in Step 19.

25. Scroll down to the next packet. Record any text in the packet after the word "Data:" below. This will be the first character of your password. The Telnet program sends each character of your password to the remote computer in a single packet immediately after you type it. Repeat until you have recorded your entire password. If you pressed Backspace while entering your password in Step 19, you will see an additional character for the Backspace key too.

26. On *SERVER1*, delete the text "telnet" from the Filter text box. Click **Capture** on the menu bar, then click **Start**. Click **No** when asked to save the capture file. The Ethereal: Capture Options dialog box opens.

27. If the Capture Filter text does not already contain the text **host 192.168.54.5**, add it. Click **OK**. The Ethereal: Capture dialog box opens.

28. In the terminal window on *WORKSTATION1*, type **exit** and press **Enter**. The prompt changes, indicating that you have logged off *LINUX1.NETPLUSLAB.NET*.

29. Type **ssh netplus@192.168.54.5** and press **Enter**. If a message appears indicating that the authenticity of the connection cannot be confirmed, type **Yes** and press **Enter**. The prompt changes to "netplus@192.168.54.5's password:". Enter the password for the netplus account and press **Enter**.

30. Type **df -k** and press **Enter**. The computer prints the disk space available for each mounted file system.

31. On *SERVER1* in the Ethereal: Capture dialog box, click **Stop**. The Ethereal: Capture dialog box closes and the <capture> - Ethereal window displays the captured packets.

32. In the filter text box, type **ssh** and press **Enter**. Ethereal displays only those packets which use the SSH protocol.

33. Click the first packet in the top pane. Click the **plus sign (+)** next to "SSH Protocol" in the middle pane. Click the **plus sign (+)** next to "SSH Version 2" in the middle pane. Use the ↓ key to scroll through the packets until you find a packet with the text "Encrypted response packet" in the Info column. This is data that you sent *LINUX1.NETPLUSLAB.NET* in Step 29 or 30. In the middle pane, the text below SSH Protocol reads "Encrypted Packet:" and is followed by a long string of numbers and letters.

34. Scroll through the remaining packets and look for any information you sent to *LINUX1.NETPLUSLAB.NET* in Steps 28 or 29. Record any that you find.

35. Log off all three computers.

Certification Objectives

Objectives for the Network+ Exam:

➤ Identify the basic capabilities (i.e., client support, interoperability, authentication, file and print services, application support, and security) of the following server operating systems: UNIX/Linux, NetWare, Windows, Macintosh

➤ Identify the basic capabilities (i.e., client connectivity, local security mechanisms, and authentication) of the following clients: UNIX/Linux, Windows, Macintosh

➤ Given a scenario, predict the impact of a particular security implementation on network functionality (e.g., blocking port numbers, encryption, etc.)

➤ Given specific parameters, configure a client to connect to the following servers: UNIX/Linux, NetWare, Windows, Macintosh

Review Questions

1. True or False? Encrypted protocols such as SSH do not send passwords over the network.

2. In which of the following situations would it be most beneficial for a network administrator to restrict the time of day during which the users can log on to the network to improve security?

   a. A salesperson accesses a company's network via a dial-up connection to upload sales data every night.

   b. Groups of customer service representatives access customer financial data during regular business hours.

   c. A corporate executive frequently travels to a company's various locations and requires access to confidential information on the server.

   d. A group of engineers who are establishing an international office in a country several time zones away from the server's location.

3. The practice of falsifying an IP address is known as:

   a. spoofing

   b. faking

   c. impersonating

   d. configuring a secondary IP address

4. Which of the following encryption methods is commonly used to secure transmissions over VPNs?

   a. Kerberos

   b. RAS

   c. PGP

   d. IPSec

5. If someone floods your gateway with so much traffic that it cannot respond to or accept valid traffic, what type of security breach has she accomplished?

   a. IP spoofing

   b. social engineering

   c. denial of service

   d. Trojan horse

IMPLEMENTING AND MANAGING NETWORKS

Net+ Exam Objectives	
Objective	**Lab**
Identify the basic capabilities (i.e., client support, interoperability, authentication, file and print services, application support, and security) of the following server operating systems: UNIX/Linux, NetWare, Windows, Macintosh	15.4
Most of the labs in this chapter do not map directly to objectives on the exam. However, each lab teaches a skill that is valuable to networking professionals.	

LAB 15.1 CREATING A PROJECT PLAN

Objectives

When planning a project—particularly a large, technical project—you must keep track of details pertaining not only to the hardware and software involved, but also to the people responsible for tasks, the time each task might take, and which tasks rely on other tasks. To track all these details, it's helpful to use project planning software.

Microsoft Project 2003 is one of several project planning software packages available. One of the advantages of using project planning software is the ability to create charts and timelines easily. For example, you could create a Gantt chart, that displays the timelines of all project tasks and their relationships.

After completing this lab, you will be able to:

➤ Create a project plan using Microsoft Project 2003

Materials Required

This lab will require the following:

➤ A Windows XP Professional computer with Microsoft Project 2003 installed

➤ Access to the Windows XP computer as an ordinary user

Estimated completion time: **20 minutes**

LAB ACTIVITY

ACTIVITY

1. In this lab, you will use Microsoft Project 2003 to create a Gantt chart. The Gantt chart will provide you with a graphical diagram of a project. Review the task list in Table 15-1.

Table 15-1   Project task list

Number	Task description	Predecessors	Duration
1	Order and ship server hardware	None	7 days
2	Order and ship server software	None	7 days
3	Install server hardware	1	1 day
4	Install server software	2, 3	1 day
5	Add server to LAN	4	1 day

2. On the Windows XP computer, press **Ctrl+Alt+Del** to display the Log On to Windows dialog box. Log on. The Windows XP desktop appears.

3. To open Microsoft Project, click **Start**, point to **All Programs**, point to **Microsoft Office**, and then click **Microsoft Office Project 2003**. (You might find Microsoft Project located elsewhere on your Start menu.)

4. If a new project has not opened, click **File** on the menu bar, then click **New**. The New Project tab is displayed on the left side of the window. Click **Blank Project**. A new project opens.

5. On the left side of the window, look for a column labeled Task Name. You can enter task information in this column. On the right side of the window, look for a chart that marks tasks on the calendar with boxes; this part of the window also shows precedence information. Figure 15-1 shows the window after task information has already been entered. You will enter the same information in the following steps.

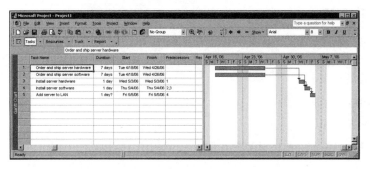

Figure 15-1   Microsoft Project 2003

15

6. In the Task Name column, enter the first task description given in Table 15-1. Microsoft Project automatically fills in the Duration, Start, and Finish columns.

7. Click the cell in the Duration column next to the first entry you've made. Up and down arrows appear in the cell. Click the up arrow until the duration matches the number of days given for that task in Table 15-1.

8. In the Predecessors column, enter the appropriate number or numbers from the Predecessors column in Table 15-1. (Leave the column blank if Table 15-1 indicates that the task has no predecessors.)

9. Right-click the first task and click **Task Information** in the pop-up menu. The Task Information dialog box opens.

10. Click the **Resources** tab. In the top line of the Resources text box, enter your name or the name of your lab partner.

11. Click **OK**. The name you entered in Step 10 appears in the chart in the left pane of the Microsoft Project window.

12. Repeat Steps 6 through 11 with the remaining tasks. When repeating Step 8, be sure to enter the appropriate information in the Predecessors text box.

13. On the menu bar, click **File**, then click **Save As**. The Save As dialog box opens.

14. Enter a unique filename in the File name text box. Click **Save**. The computer saves your project.

15. Close Microsoft Project and log off the computer.

Certification Objectives

Objectives for the Network+ Exam:

This lab does not map directly to an objective on the exam. However, it does teach a skill that is valuable to networking professionals.

Review Questions

1. The task that must be completed before another task is begun is called a:

   a. successor

   b. predecessor

   c. antecedent

   d. dependent

2. In a significant network upgrade project, which of the following tasks takes place first?

   a. Identify which tasks are dependent on other tasks.

   b. Complete a needs assessment survey.

   c. Test the proposed solution on a pilot network.

   d. Assign tasks to the most qualified or appropriate individuals on the project team.

3. Which of the following best describes contingency planning?

   a. obtaining support from high-level project sponsors before committing resources to the project

   b. installing identical software and hardware, on a smaller scale, as the project's proposed solution will require, to test the feasibility of the solution

   c. identifying a team and assigning roles to that team in case of disaster

   d. identifying steps that will minimize the impact of unforeseen obstacles

4. You are a network administrator managing a network backbone upgrade. Your supervisor has scheduled a meeting to discuss the project's status with you. What is the advantage of taking a Gantt chart to the meeting?

   a. A Gantt chart will help the supervisor better understand the project's costs.

   b. A Gantt chart will determine the maximum possible amount of each employee's time to be spent on each task.

   c. A Gantt chart will allow the supervisor to see timelines of each task in addition to the project as a whole.

   d. A Gantt chart will demonstrate why some tasks have taken longer to complete than first anticipated.

5. True or False? One way of predicting how long a task might take is by examining the time taken to complete previous similar tasks.

LAB 15.2 PLANNING AN UPGRADE

Objectives

Even when making relatively minor changes, a project plan can be helpful. The potential benefits include minimizing downtime, creating an efficient implementation, and planning for when something goes wrong. For instance, a project plan for changing the NIC on a server might include contingency plans in case the new NIC is defective, the NIC is accidentally damaged during installation, or the server does not boot after installation. Alternately, a configuration change made on a remote router may cut you off from the router. By having included contingency plans in your project plan, you are better prepared to solve the problem quickly and efficiently.

In environments in which downtime must be minimized at all costs, contingency planning is even more important. Although the odds of a problem occurring may be low, you must be prepared just in case. During a server upgrade, for example, you might have a spare server ready in case the server fails. (Note that you can also use network design to minimize potential downtime. For instance, you might use redundant servers.)

In this lab, you will create a project plan for replacing the NIC in a Windows Server 2003 computer. Your project plan should include a task breakdown, which divides the project into smaller parts, and list of dependencies—that is, a list of tasks that depend on the completion of previous tasks. Your contingency planning should cover situations such as the following: a defective NIC, drivers that are not available for the NIC, a NIC that is damaged during installation, a server that is damaged during installation, and a server that cannot boot after installation of the NIC. Also include a testing plan, in which you outline your plans for determining whether the project or change was successful, and whether the results of the project include any unforeseen side effects. Finally, your plan should contain a timeline, the resources, and the project milestone.

After completing this lab, you will be able to:

➤ Make a project for a network upgrade

➤ Perform a network upgrade

Materials Required

This lab will require the following:

➤ Pencil and paper, or planning software such as Microsoft Project 2003

➤ A computer running Windows Server 2003 Enterprise Edition named *SERVER1* configured as a domain controller for the netpluslab.net domain with an IP address of 192.168.54.1 and a subnet mask of 255.255.255.0

➤ A shared folder on *SERVER1* named NETPLUS

➤ Access as the Administrator to *SERVER1*

➤ An extra NIC (with a driver disk, if necessary)

➤ A computer running Windows XP Professional named *WORKSTATION1* configured as a member of the netpluslab.net domain, and an IP address of 192.168.54.3 and a subnet mask of 255.255.255.0

➤ An ordinary user account in the Domain Users group in the *netpluslab.net* domain

➤ Both computers connected to a hub with straight-through CAT 5 (or better) UTP cables

➤ A toolkit with a Phillips head screwdriver, a ground mat, and a ground strap

Estimated completion time: **60 minutes**

ACTIVITY

1. First, you will verify that the network works properly. On *WORKSTATION1*, press **Ctrl+Alt+Del** to display the Log On to Windows dialog box. Log on with an ordinary user account. The Windows XP desktop appears.

2. Click **Start**, then click **My Computer**. The My Computer window opens.

3. Click **Tools** on the menu bar, then click **Map Network Drive**. The Map Network Drive dialog box appears.

4. If necessary, select **Z:** from the Drive drop-down menu. In the Folder text box, type **\\192.168.54.1\netplus** and click **Finish**. The computer maps the NETPLUS shared folder.

5. Click the up arrow below the menu bar to return to My Computer. The netplus on '192.168.54.1' (Z:) icon now appears underneath Network Drives.

6. Right-click the **netplus on '192.168.54.1' (Z:)** icon and click **Disconnect** in the pop-up menu. The drive mapping disappears as the computer disconnects the network drive.

7. On a separate piece of paper, or in project planning software such as Microsoft Project 2003, write the project plan that will cover the activities in Steps 8-17. Use Steps 2 through 5 as your testing plan.

8. Power down *SERVER1* and remove the power cable. Place the computer on the ground mat.

9. Place the ground strap on your wrist and attach it to the ground mat underneath the computer.

10. Remove any screws from the computer case.

11. Remove the computer case.

12. Unscrew the NIC from its slot in the computer, and carefully remove it.

13. Place the new NIC in the slot.

14. Attach the NIC to the system unit with the Phillips head screwdriver to secure the NIC in place.

15. Replace the computer case and reinsert any screws removed in Step 10. Remove the ground strap and the ground mat.

16. Plug in the computer and turn it on.

17. To verify that the network is working properly, perform the steps in your testing plan.

18. Review your project plan and note anything that did not work according to the plan.

Certification Objectives

Objectives for the Network+ Exam:

This lab does not map directly to an objective on the exam. However, it does teach a skill that is valuable to networking professionals.

15

Review Questions

1. What is the purpose of identifying milestones in a project plan?

   a. They indicate when project staff changes must occur.

   b. They mark significant events of the project's progress.

   c. They offer a quick assessment of how successfully the project is staying within budget.

   d. They help predict the end result of a project.

2. Which of the following are examples of resources related to a project plan that proposes to upgrade the network cards inside each workstation on a network from 100 Mbps to 1000 Mbps? (Choose all that apply.)

   a. NIC device drivers

   b. a team member's time

   c. IP addresses

   d. NICs

   e. switches

3. Which of the following are examples of stakeholders of a project whose purpose is to upgrade an entire network from 100 Mbps to 1000 Mbps? (Choose all that apply.)

   a. network users

   b. network software vendors

   c. high-level managers who approved the project

   d. IT staff who helped implement the change

   e. network cabling vendors

4. Which of the following tools might you use to assess the success of a project whose purpose is to upgrade an entire network from 100 Mbps to 1000 Mbps?

   a. Network Monitor

   b. Sniffer

   c. Microsoft SQL Server

   d. System Monitor

5. Which of the following obstacles could halt or seriously impair the progress of a project whose purpose is to upgrade the NICs in all workstations on a network from 100 Mbps to 1000 Mbps?

 a. the use of two different NIC models

 b. the use of different installation personnel on different shifts

 c. management's requirement that the cost of each NIC remain under $75.00

 d. a group of defective NICs

LAB 15.3 OBSERVING A NETWORK UPGRADE

Objectives

Observing a network upgrade will help you appreciate the complexities that can arise in a real-world situation. Depending on the project, you might be able to observe only a small part of an upgrade at any one time. For larger projects, the networking professional is more likely to have a formal project plan; for smaller projects, the plan might be very informal.

After completing this lab, you will be able to:

➤ Explain how a network upgrade is performed

Materials Required

This lab will require the following:

➤ Pencil and paper

➤ A person (such as a network professional or your instructor) willing to allow you to observe a network upgrade

Estimated completion time: 2 hours

ACTIVITY

1. Visit the site performing a network upgrade.

2. Ask the network engineer who is allowing you to observe the upgrade to discuss any project plans they might use during the upgrade.

3. Ask the network engineer to discuss any contingency planning she or he might have done as part of the upgrade.

4. Record any changes occurring at the site. For example, the upgrade might involve replacing CAT 3 cable with CAT 5 cable. Another change might involve altering the IP addressing scheme.

5. Record the time required for the network upgrade.

6. Send a thank you note to the network engineer who allowed you to observe the upgrade.

Certification Objectives

Objectives for the Network+ Exam:

This lab does not map directly to an objective on the exam. However, it does teach a skill that is valuable to networking professionals.

Review Questions

1. Which of the following best describes project management?

   a. recording and analyzing the time and resources required for each task in a project

   b. assessing network statistics before and after a project is completed

   c. monitoring the needs of users prior to the beginning of a project, then later assessing how the project's completion met their needs

   d. planning for and handling the steps required to accomplish a goal in a systematic way

2. Which of the following projects is most likely to be driven by a company's security needs?

   a. doubling the RAM in a key file server

   b. installing a firewall on a connection to the Internet

   c. upgrading the version of client software on each workstation

   d. changing from the use of static IP addressing to DHCP on an entire network

3. What is one good technique for assessing the feasibility of a suggested project deadline before the project begins?

   a. Begin calculating task timelines from the deadline, working back to the start of a project.

   b. Issue a survey to key staff asking their opinion on the suggested deadline.

   c. Use the Web to research similar projects completed by other companies.

   d. Calculate the ratio of the number of project milestones to the proposed project duration, in months, to check that it does not exceed 2:1.

4. In a very large company (for example, one with over 10,000 employees), which of the following staff is most likely to decide whether a project such as an entire network upgrade will be funded?

     a. network administrator

     b. personnel director

     c. chief information officer

     d. accountant

5. Which of the following situations might necessitate changing all the IP addresses on a company's networked workstations?

     a. The company has moved from one geographical location to another.

     b. The company has hired 50 new employees.

     c. The company has decided to use NAT for all connections to public networks.

     d. The company has decided to establish a Web server with e-commerce capability.

Lab 15.4 Installing and Removing Updates on Windows Server 2003

15

Objectives

Keeping software up-to-date on both servers and network devices is an important part of maintaining and upgrading a network. Usually software updates will consist of patches or other fixes to problems that users and administrators have encountered when using the software. In other cases, a software update might solve a potential security problem, or it might even add a new feature.

Microsoft typically releases its software updates in one of two forms. The first form is a hotfix, which is an update to a specific piece of software, often used to correct a specific problem. For instance, a hot fix might solve a problem with Internet Information Services (IIS), which is the Web server sold by Microsoft. The second form is a service pack, which is a group of numerous software updates. You might install a service pack as part of a server's regular maintenance.

Both forms of updates are accessible through Microsoft's Windows Update service. Additionally, you can automate the installation of hotfixes so that no user intervention is required. Automatic updates can often prevent security problems from occurring, as they can fix a security vulnerability as soon as it is discovered. However, a software update may cause problems. For instance, you might run a certain application on your Windows Server 2003 computers. If this application relies on a piece of software that has been changed in a service pack or hotfix, the application may no longer work after the update has been applied. As a result, you may have to backlevel, or revert to the previous version of the software, after the upgrade. Thus, if at all possible, you should verify that a software upgrade will work in a test environment prior to applying it to production machines. Additionally, you should carefully consider the implications before scheduling automatic updates on important servers. Automatic updates are more safely scheduled for workstations, but it is also possible that an update installed automatically could cause problems on all workstations in your organization. You should carefully weigh the benefits of scheduling automatic updates before you implement them.

After completing this lab, you will be able to:

➤ Install updates to a computer running Windows Server 2003

➤ Remove updates from a computer running Windows Server 2003

Materials Required

This lab will require the following:

➤ A computer running Windows Server 2003 Enterprise Edition with access to the Internet

➤ At least one update or hotfix that needs to be installed on the computer

➤ Administrator access to the computer

➤ Internet Explorer security set to High (the default)

Estimated completion time: **30 minutes**

LAB ACTIVITY

ACTIVITY

1. On the Windows Server 2003 computer, press **Ctrl+Alt+Del** to display the Log On to Windows dialog box. Log on as the Administrator. The Windows Server 2003 desktop appears.

2. Click **Start**, point to **All Programs**, then click **Internet Explorer**. Internet Explorer opens. The Internet Explorer dialog box may open, indicating that the high level of security at which the browser is currently configured may prevent access to network resources. If so, select the **In the future, do not show this message** check box, then click **OK** to close the dialog box.

3. Go to **www.windowsupdate.com**. The Microsoft Windows Update page opens in Internet Explorer. Figure 15-2 shows the Microsoft Windows Update page. If necessary, click **Yes** in the Security Warning dialog box to install and run Windows update.

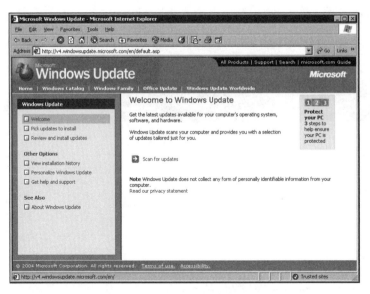

Figure 15-2   Microsoft Windows Update

4. Click **Scan for updates**. The Web page indicates that it is scanning for updates, and then asks you to select and review updates. If necessary, click **Yes** in the **Internet Explorer** dialog box.

5. Click **Critical Updates and Service Packs**. A list of the most important updates, including security updates, appears in the right pane.

6. Click **Review and install updates**. The Web page lists the available updates. If your computer does not have a fast connection to the Internet, you may wish to unselect some of the updates by clicking the **Remove** button before proceeding. Click **Install Now** to install the updates. A window called "Windows Update – Web Page Dialog" appears, indicating that the updates are being installed. Depending on the updates selected, the installation process may vary somewhat from this step. Often not all of the required updates can be installed at the same time. Some of the updates may require other updates to be installed first and the computer rebooted before they can be installed. As a result, you may have to update your computer in stages.

7. If the Microsoft Internet Explorer dialog box opens, indicating that you need to restart the computer to finish installing the updates, click **OK**. After the computer reboots, press **Ctrl+Alt+Del** to display the Log On to Windows dialog box. Log on as the Administrator. The Windows Server 2003 desktop appears.

8. Now you will remove an update added earlier. Click **Start**, point to **Control Panel**, then click **Add or Remove Programs**. The Add or Remove Programs window opens, as shown in Figure 15-3.

15

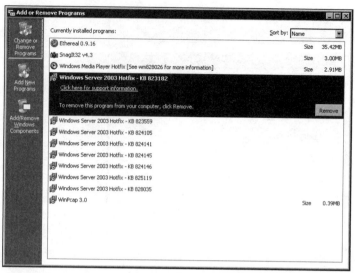

Figure 15-3   Add or Remove Programs window

9. A number of hotfixes are listed, followed by the number of a Microsoft Knowledge Base article describing the problem solved by the hotfix. Click a hotfix chosen by your instructor to select it. A link appears below the name of the hotfix with the text "Click here for support information."

10. Click the link. The Support Info dialog box opens, showing the number of a Knowledge Base (KB) article.

11. Click the link next to "Support Information". If the Internet Explorer dialog box opens, indicating that the content has been prevented from loading by the security settings on Internet Explorer, click **Add**. The Trusted sites dialog box opens. Click **Add** again, then click **Close**. Internet Explorer opens, showing the Microsoft Knowledge Base article describing the flaw solved by the hotfix. What is the number of the KB article, and what problem does it fix?

12. Close Internet Explorer, and click **Close** in the Support Info dialog box. (If the hotfix solves a critical security issue, select another hotfix and repeat Steps 9 through 11.)

13. Click **Remove** for the selected hotfix. The Windows Server 2003 KB*nnnn* Removal Wizard opens, where *nnnn* is the number of the hotfix.

14. Click **Next**. The wizard begins to remove the hotfix. Depending on the hotfix to be removed, additional steps may be required. If a dialog box appears indicating that some programs may not function properly after the removal of the hot fix, click **Yes**. The wizard finishes.

15. Click **Finish**. The wizard closes.

16. Repeat Steps 2 through 7 in order to reapply any necessary hotfixes.

Certification Objectives

Objectives for the Network+ Exam:

➤ Identify the basic capabilities (i.e., client support, interoperability, authentication, file and print services, application support, and security) of the following server operating systems: UNIX/Linux, NetWare, Windows, Macintosh

Review Questions

1. In which of the following situations would it be wise to backlevel?

   a. You have just performed a complete backup of your server's data directories, and you cannot confirm that the backup was successful.

   b. You have just applied a fix to your NOS and have discovered that the fix resulted in a lack of network access for half of your users.

   c. You have just installed a database program on one of your servers and have discovered that you neglected to install an optional component that your users will need.

   d. You have just installed Windows Server 2003 on a new computer and you cannot get the operating system to recognize the NIC.

2. Which two of the following may typically be accomplished by applying a patch to a network operating system?

   a. replacing all the NOS's program files

   b. modifying an existing feature

   c. removing an old feature

   d. fixing a known bug

3. Before installing a major NOS patch, you should:

   a. Remove all protocols installed on the server.

   b. Prevent users from logging on.

   c. Disable Internet services.

   d. Disable network connectivity.

4. In Microsoft terminology, what is a hotfix?

   a. a patch that replaces all or a portion of the NOS

   b. a patch that requires that the server be connected to Microsoft's Web site as it is installed

   c. a patch that updates a specific type of software, often the operating system

   d. a patch that can be installed while users are logged on without causing adverse effects

15

5. What is the primary difference between a software upgrade and a patch?

   a. The software manufacturer issues a patch, whereas an upgrade may be issued by any organization that has the software's source code.

   b. A patch fixes a specific part of a piece of software, whereas an upgrade typically replaces much or all of a software program.

   c. A patch typically does not require that the network administrator test its changes before applying it to a server; an upgrade does.

   d. A patch typically is not supported by the software manufacturer; an upgrade is.

LAB 15.5 RESEARCHING NETWORK SOLUTIONS

Objectives

In this lab, you will research network solutions by examining business case studies on vendor Web sites. By examining these case studies, you can get an idea of how each vendor uses its product line to help customers solve problems or fulfill business needs. It is important to keep in mind, however, that few vendors are objective about their products. When considering a solution, you should look for information from multiple sources. Additionally, you may find it helpful to talk to someone who has attempted to implement a solution such as the one you are considering.

When looking at case studies, you will often find it helpful to look for organizations that are similar to your own. For instance, a large bank with thousands of employees and a high security network environment is likely to have different needs than a small non-profit organization. Seeing how an organization similar to your own has solved certain problems may help you solve similar problems in your own organization.

It is also important to try to anticipate future network trends when researching network solutions. A solution that might help you solve future problems will tend to be more cost effective in the long run than a solution that only addresses an immediate problem. For instance, suppose you are researching software packages that diagnose potential problems in business productivity software on user workstations. If you have noticed a trend towards greater user support of personal digital assistant (PDA) applications, then software packages that also diagnose potential problems in PDA software may prove more useful than ones that do not.

After completing this lab, you will be able to:

➤ Review case studies of networking companies

➤ Identify the needs of the customer in a case study

➤ Identify the solutions provided by the networking companies

Materials Required

This lab will require the following:

➤ Pencil and paper

➤ A computer running Windows XP Professional with Internet access

➤ An ordinary user account on the computer

Estimated completion time: **25 minutes**

ACTIVITY

1. Press **Ctrl+Alt+Del** to display the Log On to Windows dialog box. Log on as an ordinary user. The Windows XP desktop opens.

2. Perform whatever steps are necessary for the computer to access the Internet.

3. Start Internet Explorer.

4. Go to **www.novell.com/success/**. You see a list of case studies that demonstrate how Novell products have helped Novell customers. Click **View all** to see a list of all case studies. (If the Web page has changed since this writing, click **SEARCH** at the top of the page and search for the text "case study." Case studies will appear in the search results.)

5. Review a case study of your choice. Record the name of the customer and type of business in the case study.

6. Record background information on the company in the case study. This information might include the type of business, the size, and the networking hardware or software it used.

7. Record the business need or challenge for the company that was the customer in the case study.

8. Record the Novell solution. Be sure to identify the software or hardware solution that was implemented.

9. Record the results of the solution.

10. Go to **www.microsoft.com**.

11. In the "Search Microsoft.com for" text box, type **case study**, and then press **Enter**. A list of links for this search term displays.

15

12. Select a case study from the search results by clicking the case study's title. The case study's page appears. Scroll through the page and read the details of the study. Record the name of the customer and the type of business you reviewed.

13. Record background information on the company in the case study. This information might include the type of business, the size, and the networking hardware or software used.

14. Record the business need or challenge for the company that was the customer in the case study.

15. Record the Microsoft solution. Be sure to identify the software or hardware solution used.

16. Record the results of the solution.

17. Close your Web browser.

Certification Objectives

Objectives for the Network+ Exam:

This lab does not map directly to an objective on the exam. However, it does teach a skill that is valuable to networking professionals.

Review Questions

1. You are trying to decide whether or not to purchase a software package from a vendor. Who among the following is most likely to provide objective information about the software package?

    a. the vendor's sales staff

    b. a business partner of the vendor

    c. a current customer of the vendor

    d. a vendor who makes a competing product

2. You are researching a new Internet access router for your company's network. You have also noticed a trend towards greater use of your company's network resources from home. Given this, which of the following features would you expect to be most valuable in a new Internet access router?

    a. support for additional routing protocols

    b. support for virtual private networks

    c. support for additional security features

    d. support for multiple protocols

3. When implementing a network solution, why is it important to anticipate future trends to the extent that it is possible? (Choose all that apply.)

    a. so that the solutions you implement meet the future needs of your users

    b. so that the solutions you implement meet the current needs of your users

    c. so that the solutions you implement are more scalable

    d. so that you can justify the purchase of the solution to management

4. You work for the Best Roast Coffee Company, which has 100 employees in nine retail stores. You are looking at case studies for a product you are researching. Which of the following case studies is most likely to be helpful?

    a. a case study for an automobile manufacturer with hundreds of thousands of employees

    b. a candy maker with 200 employees that sells candy in 13 malls across the country

    c. an insurance company with thousands of employees in three locations, plus hundreds of agents all over the country

    d. a small school district with 300 employees and 10,000 students

5. When investigating a network solution, which two of the following should you do?

    a. Get information about possible solutions from only one source

    b. Get information about possible solutions from multiple sources

    c. Look at the product lines from only one vendor

    d. Talk to someone who has implemented a similar solution

15